D1717770

Marxism, Intellectuals and Politics

Marxism, Intellectuals and Politics

Edited by

David Bates   2007

cf. Science & Society

First published in 2007 by
PALGRAVE MACMILLAN
Houndmills, Basingstoke, Hampshire RG21 6XS and
175 Fifth Avenue, New York, N.Y. 10010
Companies and representatives throughout the world

PALGRAVE MACMILLAN is the global academic imprint of the Palgrave
Macmillan division of St. Martin's Press, LLC and of Palgrave Macmillan Ltd.
Macmillan® is a registered trademark in the United States, United Kingdom
and other countries. Palgrave is a registered trademark in the European
Union and other countries.

ISBN-13: 978–1–4039–4998–1 (Cloth)
ISBN-10: 1–4039–4998–0 (Cloth)

This book is printed on paper suitable for recycling and made from fully
managed and sustained forest sources.

A catalogue record for this book is available from the British Library.

Library of Congress Cataloging-in-Publication Data

Marxism, intellectuals, and politics/ edited by David Bates.
    p. cm.
Includes bibliographical references and index.
ISBN-13: 978–1–4039–4998–1 (Cloth)
ISBN-10: 1–4039–4998–0 (Cloth)
    1. Communism and intellectuals. 2. Intellectuals – political
activity – History – 20th century. I. Bates, David, 1972–

HX528.M375 2007
320.53'2—dc22   2006049482

10 9 8 7 6 5 4 3 2 1
16 15 14 13 12 11 10 09 08 07

Printed and bound in Great Britain by
Antony Rowe Ltd, Chippenham and Eastbourne

Contents

List of Contributors   vii

Acknowledgements   x

Introduction: Marxism, Intellectuals and Politics   1
David Bates

Part I

1   Marx and Intellectuals   21
    Paul Blackledge

2   Lenin, Trotsky and the Role of the Socialist
    Intellectual in Politics   43
    Ian D. Thatcher

3   Gramsci and the Intellectuals: Modern Prince versus Passive
    Revolution   68
    Peter Thomas

4   'Unhappy Consciousness': Reflexivity and
    Contradiction in Jean-Paul Sartre's Changing
    Conception of the Role of the Intellectual   86
    Leon Culbertson

5   Althusser: Intellectuals and the Conjuncture   107
    Warren Montag

6   T. W. Adorno as a Critical Intellectual in the
    Public Sphere: Between Marxism and Modernism   119
    Gerard Delanty

Part II

7   Analytical Marxism and the Academy   137
    Jason Edwards

8   Philosophy and Ideology: Marxism and the
    Role of Religion in Contemporary Politics   152
    Sean Sayers

9   Intellectual Labour and Social Class   169
    David Bates

10 Critical Intellectuals and the Academic Labour Process   186
    Frank Worthington

11 Mediated Intellectuals: Negotiating Social Relations
    in Media   205
    Lee Salter

12 Enduring Echoes: Feminism, Marxism and the Reflexive
    Intellectual   221
    Jayne Raisborough and Dawn S. Jones

Index   238

List of Contributors

David Bates is Senior Lecturer in Social Science at Canterbury Christ Church University, and Programme Director in Politics. His research explores contemporary and classical Marxism, the sociology of class, the sociology of knowledge and the political economy of intellectual labour.

Paul Blackledge is Senior Lecturer in Politics at Leeds Metropolitan University. He is author of *Reflections on the Marxist Theory of History* (Manchester University Press, 2006) and *Perry Anderson, Marxism and the New Left* (Merlin Press, 2004). He is the co-editor of *Historical Materialism and Social Evolution* (Palgrave, 2002) and *Alisdair MacIntyre's Engagement with Marxism: Essays and Articles 1953–1974* (Leiden, 2007). He serves on the editorial boards of *Historical Materialism* and *International Socialism*.

Leon Culbertson is Senior Lecturer in the Philosophy of Sport at Edge Hill College. He studied at the University of Brighton, writing his doctoral thesis on Jean-Paul Sartre's dialectical conception of the historical event. His major interests are in the philosophy of Sartre, phenomenology, the philosophy of mind, the philosophy of Wittgenstein and the philosophy of sport. His publications include articles on Sartre's progressive-regressive method, bad faith and moral responsibility in self-deception.

Gerard Delanty is Professor of Sociology at the University of Liverpool. He is editor of the *Handbook of Contemporary European Social Theory* (Routledge, 2006), *T.W. Adorno*, 4 Volumes, Masters of Modern Thought Series (Sage, 2004), author of *Rethinking Europe: Social Theory and the Implications of Globalisation* (Routledge, 2005) and co-author (with Chris Rumsford) of *Community* (Routledge, 2003).

Jason Edwards is Lecturer in Politics at Birkbeck College, London. His Ph.D thesis was on analytical Marxism. He is completing a book, *The Radical Attitude and the Modern State*. His current research interests focus on the concepts of the state and politics in early modern political theory.

Dawn S. Jones is Senior Lecturer in Sociology at Liverpool Hope University. Her research focuses on the relationship between discourse, perception, and reality. Her recent publications have explored the relation between expert knowledge and risk perception. She is currently researching women's perception of risk in pregnancy, with findings published in I. Wilkinson and S. A. *Peterson's Risk, Health and Vulderability* (2006) and J. Raisborough and J. Scott (eds.) *Risk, Identity and the Everyday* (forthcoming).

Warren Montag is Professor of English and Comparative Literary Studies at Occidental College, Los Angeles. His areas of research include the Restoration and eighteenth-century British Literature, the Enlightenment, and twentieth-century French philosophy. He has published numerous books on philosophy and literature, including *Louis Althusser* (Palgrave, 2003).

Jayne Raisborough is Senior Lecturer in the School of Applied Social Sciences at the University of Brighton. Her research interests gravitate around the discursive and material conditions of identity construction. Her recent work has focussed on serious leisure, auto/biography, feminist debates around cosmetic surgery and ethical consumption. She is currently working on an edited collection entitled *Risk, Identity and the Everyday*, with Julie Scott of Manchester Metropolitan University.

Lee Salter is Lecturer in Journalism and Media Studies, in the School of Cultural Studies at the University of the West of England. He writes on issues of media, the information age and politics.

Sean Sayers is Professor in Philosophy at the University of Kent. A member of the editorial board of the journal *Radical Philosophy*, he has written extensively on Marx and Hegel. His published work includes *Marxism and Human Nature* (Routledge, 1999), *Plato's Republic: An Introduction* (Edinburgh University Press, 1998), *Socialism and Democracy* (co-edited with David McLellan) (Macmillan, 1991), *Reality and Reason: Dialectic and the Theory of Knowledge* (Basil Blackwell, 1985), and *Marx, Hegel and Dialectic* (with Richard Norman) (The Harvester Press, 1980).

Ian D. Thatcher is Reader in Modern European History at Brunel University. His latest books are *Trotsky* (2003) and *Late Imperial Russia: Problems and Prospects* (2005). He has also published in numerous international journals, including: *History, the Historical Journal, Historical Research* and *English Historical Review*.

Peter Thomas studied at the University of Queensland, Australia, Freie Universitäet, Berlin, and Università Federico II in Naples. He is a member of the editorial board of *Historical Materialism*, the author of articles on Gramsci, Althusser, Spinoza, Young Marx and critical realism, and the translator of numerous articles on political theory. His book *The Gramscian Moment* is due out in the *Historical Materialism* book series in 2007.

Frank Worthington is a Lecturer in Management at the University of Liverpool Management School. He has a specialist interest in labour process studies, critical management theory and the politics of work organisation. He has conducted research into the politics of change management in large-scale manufacturing organisations in the United Kingdom and the United States, and is currently conducting research into the politics of organisational 'culture change' in public sector organisations, including the NHS.

Acknowledgements

This project has its origins in a conference on Marxism, Intellectuals and Politics, held at Canterbury Christ Church University in 2003. I would like to thank all those who attended this conference for their stimulating discussion. I would also like to thank all the contributors to this book for their remarkable patience, and my colleagues at Christ Church for their support in what has been a challenging period. The last word of thanks goes to June Scott, for if it had not been for her, this project would not have been completed.

Introduction: Marxism, Intellectuals and Politics

David Bates

Contemporary social theory is replete with attempts to understand and theorise the location of intellectuals. There are studies of academic intellectuals, public intellectuals, media intellectuals, Marxist intellectuals and postmodern intellectuals to name but a few. In part, the expansion of the literature on intellectuals is a result of the contradictory times in which we live. Technological innovations such as those in the realm of new media have opened up spaces of political intervention in which intellectuals can bring their knowledge to bear. On the other hand, it seems that intellectual labour is increasingly deskilled and, some have insisted, proletarianised. The ideal of the radical intellectual so typified by thinkers such as Sartre often seems a distant memory. This has led one writer on the topic to ask 'where have all the intellectuals gone?' (Furedi 2004).

In this book, the focus will be to address these and related concerns as they pertain to the Marxist tradition in particular. There are after all few political traditions which, for better or for worse, have been concerned more with attempting to come to grips with the role of the intellectual in society. This is perhaps because the role of the intellectual has brought with it more difficulties and tensions for Marxism than any other tradition. In the introduction which follows, however, an attempt will also be made to situate these debates, and thus to make comparisons with the wider literature on intellectuals, from the Dreyfus affair to 'postmodernity'.

What is an intellectual?

There are many possible ways in which we might answer this question; nevertheless perhaps the two main ones can be characterised following

Jennings and Kemp-Welch (1997) as the political definition and the sociological definition. Whereas the latter considers intellectuals primarily in relation to a specific location in the division of labour, the former definition identifies as intellectuals those people of 'intellect' who bring their knowledge to bear through visible intervention in the public political arena. In this introduction, I aim to elucidate some of the strengths and weaknesses of both these approaches.

Those who use such a public political definition of intellectuals often at some point return to questions of origin (see, for example, Feuer 1976; Said 1993; Jennings and Kemp-Welch 1997). When, they ask, did the term intellectual first take on this particular usage as a noun? And there are a range of such points of origin to which we might refer. Raymond Williams, for example, has cited Byron who, in 1813, remarked 'I wish I may be well enough to listen to these intellectuals'. In Byron's remark, as Williams has noted, we see a view of the intellectual which implies 'coldness, abstraction and, significantly, ineffectiveness' (Williams 1976: 141). That is, this early definition of the intellectual contains within it a normative critique of intellectuals as a social group. Yet the point at which most studies begin is with the Dreyfus affair of 1898. In the Dreyfus affair, figures such as Proust and Zola aimed to speak out against the unjust treatment of Captain Alfred Dreyfus (see Arendt 1951; Feuer 1976; Said 1993; Jennings and Kemp-Welch 1997). This intervention was condemned by the conservative writer Brunetière (in a fashion not unlike more contemporary right wing writings on intellectuals by figures such as Hayek 1998). For Brunetière, the idea of those who may only have a specialised form of scholarly expertise claiming authority to speak out on public political manners was at best derisory. Now whilst it is the case that the negative component has been evident throughout many discussions of intellectuals since this point (a fact which is true of tracts of both the left and the right), it is also true that the use of the noun began to broaden out after this affair. Feuer, for example, has noted how from the Dreyfus affair: 'A new definition of the intellectual began to emerge: the intellectuals were that section of the educated class which had aspirations to political power either directly by seeking to be society's political rulers or indirectly by directing its conscience and decisions' (Feuer 1976: 49).

Although there is much importance in this return to origins, such an approach might also be considered to present certain difficulties. For to identify the word intellectuals strictly with the contextual origins of its first use as a noun, it becomes difficult to make meaningful associations between different groups prior to (and indeed after) this context, groups which it would seem to be of scholarly interest to make connections between. Thus such – admittedly – diverse figures as Socrates, John Locke, John Stuart Mill and indeed (of particular concern in relation to this book) Karl Marx would have to seemingly be considered outside of the sphere of our discussion, as would certain groups such as *les philosophes*. Brief comment can be made at this juncture – though in no way should this be seen to prejudice the discussion in the chapters in this collection. Jennings and Kemp-Welch write

> the meaning of the word … is itself parasitic upon the broader socio-logical definition that refers to those who by profession and occupa-tion are engaged in 'intellectual' as opposed to 'manual' labour … the intellectual's emergence in the limited political sense was not only contingent upon a dramatic extension of the opportunities for intel-lectual labour in the nineteenth century, but also upon a pattern of development characterised by a progressive extension over a period of at least three centuries of their independence from such established institutions as the Church and State. (Jennings and Kemp-Welch 1997: 7)

Two points might be noted here. First, if the conditions of possibility for the emergence of 'intellectuals' (defined here in the public political sense) existed prior – and we might say significantly prior – to the utter-ance of the noun, then is it not perhaps a mistake to say that we can speak of intellectuals only after this utterance? There must have existed before this moment a significant contextual web that allowed this noun to come into being. Second, as an aside, it could be maintained that the division of labour which may initially have comprised the conditions of possibility for the existence of the type of public political intellectual which they identify, may have come to represent something of an obsta-cle to their existence. Arblaster has noted how a significant feature of the twentieth century (though we can trace such developments to the end of the nineteenth century) has been the 'institutionalisation of intellectual life' (Arblaster 1973). And Small has pointed out that, given such changes 'many have doubted whether the academic can plausibly be an intellectual, especially when the institution providing him or her with financial support seeks in some measure to define the kinds of work undertaken' (Small 2002: 2). Indeed, it could be claimed that the specific ideal of intellectuals such as John Stuart Mill, for example, comes to be replaced with the reality of often politically disengaged uni-versity academics, concerned more with their career aspirations, than with any ideal of collective solidarity or (political) engagement with the wider community.[1]

To return to the public political definition of the intellectual – this definition need not retain such a strong focus on origins. There is nothing inconsistent about maintaining that the role of the intellectual is political in the above sense, whilst at the same time not focusing excessively on a particular moment where 'the intellectual' came in to being. A possible way of doing this may be through a stress on the epistemological grounding of intellectual activity. For example, we could adopt a definition of the intellectual such as 'those men and women of intellect who engage in the public realm so as to speak the truth in the face of injustice'. With this definition, truthfulness need not in itself be considered as inherently political; rather, truthfulness only has a political character when asserted in a particular context (primarily against those who hold power).[2] Montefiore, on the other hand, has provided a somewhat different epistemological characterisation. Thus he writes: 'By "an intellectual" I mean here to refer to anyone who takes a committed interest in the validity and truth of ideas for their own sake, i.e., for the sake of their truth and validity rather than that of their causal relationships to whatever other ends' (Montefiore 1990: 201). And he continues, crucially, to insist that:

> Truthfulness is, among many other things, a political virtue. It is political in as much as the nature and degree of truthfulness within a community is a major determinant of the nature of the public or political space in which the community conducts or contests its affairs. And it is a virtue of especial significance to whoever may be regarded as an intellectual. (Montefiore 1990: 228)

Whatever their relative merits, both of these characterisations enable one to provide a wider understanding of the intellectual than that allowed by the limited contextual emphasis. Indeed a more focused attention is given to the particular basis of authority from which such intellectuals claim to speak – that is the basis in 'truth'. For intellectuals (so this argument goes), engrossed as they are in the realm of ideas, are better fitted to 'speak the truth' than other less enlightened members of society; indeed, they are sometimes considered as possessing final authority on such matters. Thus we reach beyond the Dreyfus affair and speak instead of the Enlightenment intellectual and the modern intellectual, and perhaps indeed of the ancient intellectual.

But what about the type of intellectual with which we are interested in this book – the Marxist intellectual? Such intellectuals have strong political commitments clearly; however, the epistemological basis to their commitment is not quite the same as with those just mentioned. Marxist intellectuals are paradigmatically concerned not with the above somewhat abstract form of political engagement, but with the further-ance of the cause of a particular social group. It is therefore important that we do not exclude such intellectuals from the bounds of our definition. Nevertheless, it could be argued that there is an element of commonality here. For both views of the intellectual are seemingly products of the project of modernity, and therefore share something of that project's epistemological aspirations, not least the aspiration of explaining and criticising the social world using the tools of reason and social science. Both can (though there are perhaps a number of important exceptions to this case) therefore be included under the heading of the intellectual as 'legislator', to use Bauman's (1987) terminology.

Indeed, the use of Bauman's terminology perhaps allows us to iden-tify a further limitation with our definition. Bauman has suggested that postmodernity has necessitated a new understanding of the intellec-tual. The explicit commitment of postmodernism is to the view that truth claims are contextual and local. The postmodern intellectual is the intellectual as 'interpreter'. Here the intellectual does not speak the truth, conceived in relation to an appeal to higher authority; rather she or he has a primarily hermeneutical role – as translator rather than arbiter – a role which can nevertheless be viewed as 'political', though obviously in quite a different fashion to how we have tended to use the term above.[3] Now, setting aside the relative merits of this particular argument, what is important to note is that to limit our definition to those with a strong commitment to 'the truth' may lead one to exclude unnecessarily a wide range of figures from this category. Figures such as Foucault, Derrida, Laclau and Mouffe, and indeed Bauman, have all articulated their own strong political commitments, but are neverthe-less critical of the epistemological foundations from which past – particularly Marxist – intellectuals have attempted to speak. In short their family resemblance is such that it would seem quite difficult to locate such thinkers outside of the category which comprises the object of our investigation.

Thus, it would appear again that there is a need to widen out further this characterisation of the intellectual. Of course, this presents a further difficulty. For in the end, presumably, we are forced to define the intellectual along the lines of any man or women of intellect who brings their knowledge (however this is formulated) to bear in the realm of politics (however conceived). And this is a wide definition indeed, a definition which in the terminology of the sociologist, it may be rather difficult to 'operationalise'.

With these points sketched out, let us now return to the sociological definition, and particularly the difficulties therein. Importantly, the prime focus of those who use such a sociological definition is neither with contextual or indeed epistemological issues; rather they are concerned with a specific division of labour. Intellectuals may thus be understood as those who are located on the mental (and hence intellectual) side of the mental/manual division of labour. Put bluntly, intellectuals are intellectuals because they engage in intellectual work, by which we mean work of the mind. One advantage with such an approach is that it allows one to draw comparisons between occupations such as sociologists, philosophers, Shakespeare experts, physicists and mathematicians, all of whom are considered together without reference to their activity or indeed non-activity within the public political sphere. Of course, those who characterise the intellectual in a political fashion – whether or not they appeal to a specific point of origin – would state that to include these groups under the heading of intellectuals is to stretch the use of the term too far.

The potential difficulty of the non-manual characterisation of course is that it stretches the use of the term even more widely. For this characterisation would potentially include such disparate groups as accountants, company clerks and simple administrators. Few thinkers would want to go so far. For potentially, in making this move it could be argued that the term 'intellectual' loses all analytical purchase. If this is to be considered as a difficulty to be addressed, then it would seem that we must return to questions of content; that is, we must return presumably to the particular work which people do. There are no doubt many different ways in which we could do this. We could, for example, give attention to issues of formality (function) and complexity. Take the issue of formality. All groups in society contribute to the development of knowledge structures, in that they have a conception of the world which is elaborated and disseminated in their (spontaneous) day-to-day activity; but it could be noted that not all groups do this as an essential feature of their job. Intellectuals – because of their specific location in the division of labour – are formally employed to think, to document and communicate their thoughts, and to contribute to the totality of human knowledge.

Second, we might give attention to the notion of complexity. In order that the term 'intellectual' sustains its necessary purchase, this knowledge must have a depth which takes it beyond the level of simple technique. It is not enough that a specific group produces in a non-material fashion; that which they produce – from a course on Derrida, to a paper solving an age-old mathematical problem – must be a genuinely innovatory and sophisticated attempt to engage with that which is the object of its investigation.[4] And some may wish to go even further and make a stronger epistemological claim. That is, they might wish to insist that the ideas which intellectuals produce must at least purport to be true. For, does not the pursuit of truth represent a certain standard against which the intellectual endeavour ought to be judged?

There are a number of difficulties here. First, if we make the epistemological caveats too strong, we are likely to be presented with the very same difficulties mentioned in relation to the political definition of the intellectual. How can we speak of the postmodern intellectual? Indeed, more generally, it would seem impossible to speak of artist intellectuals or literary intellectuals. For their contribution to knowledge is usually not assessed in terms of its 'truthfulness', though of course it may well be. Second, whether or not we stress an epistemological caveat, for all this, it might be protested that we are still not really discussing intellectuals; we are rather, Sartre might insist, concerned only with 'technicians of practical knowledge'.[5] Third, but related to this point, this stress on the characteristics we have identified, when combined with what we have termed, following Arblaster, the 'institutionalisation of intellectual life', may lead one to take the noun 'intellectual' to be almost synonymous with that of 'academic'. Nevertheless, this need not be the case. For, although it is difficult to argue against the view that the institutionalisation of intellectual life is a tendency of modern societies, it is not necessarily the case that 'academics' and 'intellectuals' as categories are to be considered here as one and the same. Though a significant proportion of intellectuals will also be professional academics, this will not be so with all. In accordance with this viewpoint, there may be intellectuals who are employed as journalists, as novelists, as movie directors and as playwrights. There may be independently wealthy critics and 'men of letters', and even inquisitive amateurs. All of these people might be thought of as intellectuals in the sense that they contribute to the production and advancement of human knowledge in totality, but they would not necessarily be academics in the typical sense of that term.

But in relation to the overarching themes of this book, the above characterisation brings a further difficulty which is not necessarily evident with the public political view of intellectuals. Perhaps, it could be insisted, such an approach places too great an emphasis on the scholarly and theoretical dimension of intellectual work, an account which could therefore potentially under stress a substantial aspect of what preoccupied many of the great intellectuals explored in this book. For, though Lenin and Trotsky, for example, can be thought of, without much controversy, as building on the intellectual tradition of Marxism specifically, and political philosophy more generally, their contribution – put somewhat simplistically – is located at the intersection between theory and practice; the task of theoretical understanding is to provide the knowledge necessary to make emancipatory agency a possibility. This of course potentially moves us back to the public political characterisation of the intellectual with which we have just identified some difficulties. However, this need not be a problem; for we could argue that to be an intellectual is the function of a specific location in a division of labour, whilst at the same time insisting that there is not one type of intellectual; as Shils (1972) implies, the 'political intellectual' is just one form of intellectual among many.

There is also a final, but no less important, point. This pertains to the problematical distinction between the 'political' and the 'non-political' on which our discussion has often relied. When referring to the political definition of the intellectual, I have deliberately prefaced this with the word 'public'. The notion of the political therefore comes to be equated with a type of representative activity and visible engagement. Now as I stated earlier – particularly when discussing the work of Bauman – postmodernism has been highly critical of such a limited conception of 'the political'. And feminism has drawn our attention to the 'personal as political'. Indeed, there is rarely a field of human activity from which political considerations are excluded. As Aristotle put it, human beings are political animals. Therefore in one sense, all intellectuals are political intellectuals by virtue of the fact that they are humans. Now while this fact is of little use for purposes of definition, there is an important way in which a broader understanding of the political is important for the discussion of sociological accounts of the intellectual. For, in stressing intellectual activity in terms of a specific site in the division of labour, we are also – at least those of us with a broadly Marxist orientation – compelled to explore the relations of power, exploitation and subordination endemic to this division of labour. As such, whilst we may without contradiction maintain here that not all intellectuals take on public political roles, there is a precise (as well as general) way in which all intellectuals are political.

Mapping a problem

Marxism has since its birth contained a tension. On the one hand the tradition has placed a stress on proletarian self-emancipation as a necessary condition of successful socialist revolution; on the other hand, social scientific theory has been regarded as an indispensable element in the struggle for a new society, theory which has not typically been produced by members of the working class. Marx and Engels, in the often-cited 'Circular Letter' to members of the International maintained that 'When the International was formed we expressly formulated the battle-cry: The emancipation of the working classes must be conquered by the working classes themselves' (Marx and Engels 2000: 622). Yet Marx also considered the understanding of capitalist social relations provided in his own works – in particular *Capital* – to be a necessary tool for emancipatory socialist struggle. G. A. Cohen hits the nail on the head, when – characterising Marx's position – he writes 'Capitalism is obscure. Only science can illuminate it' (Cohen 2000: 338). It is only once emancipation has been achieved, that such social scientific knowledge ceases to be necessary.

Some such as Gouldner (1979; 1985) and Harding (1997) have insisted that this apparent tension masks a deeper underlying elitism in Marx's thought. In doing so, they echo a criticism which goes back at least as far as the writings of the Russian anarchist Bakunin. Thus, Bakunin maintained that: 'It [socialist society] will be the reign of scientific intelligence ... There will be a new class, a new hierarchy of real and pretend scientists and scholars, and the world will be divided into a minority ruling in the name of knowledge and the immense ignorant majority. And then, woe betide the mass of ignorant ones!' (Bakunin 1990: 38). Marx, Harding (1997) maintains, performed an 'audacious conjuring trick', whereby the very subject which he claimed to hope for the (self-) emancipation of would be judged as adequate to this task only to the extent that it lived up to the theoretical (political) role ascribed to it by Marx, a petty bourgeois intellectual. Such arguments it has been insisted contain deep flaws, flaws which Paul Blackledge does much to uncover in Chapter 1 in this book.

Perhaps the most well-known 'resolution' to this tension can be found in the writings of Lenin (1947a; 1947b), though the conditions with which Lenin was concerned were substantially different to those faced by Marx in the nineteenth century. For Lenin, the workers left to their own devices could never reach beyond the level of trade union consciousness, that is, beyond the economic struggle. Political consciousness could only be brought to the workers from 'without', by revolutionary intellectuals. Lenin's view was at the heart of his conflict with Trotsky, and the reason for the Bolshevik–Menshevik split in 1903, though as Ian Thatcher makes clear, the critical relationship of Lenin and Trotsky was more complex than is sometimes acknowledged. This

debate ought not only to be considered in the context of Russian conditions. It was after all Kautsky on which Lenin drew when developing the
arguments in *What is to be Done?* Moreover, the debate sent ripples
beyond Russian Marxism. One of the earliest and most profound critics
of Lenin was Rosa Luxemburg. For Luxemburg, Lenin's theory of organisation was representative of a form of extreme centralism, a centralism
which threatened to deliver 'the still unclear proletarian movement ... up to a handful of intellectuals (Luxemburg 1971: 301)'.

Luxemburg's argument was in many ways a case for a return to Marx's
principles as set out in the 'Circular Letter'. As such, it might be viewed
as something of a negative critique. A substantially less negative engagement with Lenin's arguments can be found in the context of Italy, in the
work of perhaps the most influential Marxist writer on intellectuals –
Gramsci. Indeed, it is possibly not too much of an exaggeration to view
Gramsci's work as an assertion of Lenin's arguments against Marx; for
the Russian Revolution was argued by Gramsci (1994) to be a great 'revolution against *Capital*', a revolution which reasserted the role of the
political will against the abstract determinism of 'objective' economic
forces. The organic intellectuals of which Gramsci wrote in the *Prison
Notebooks* were not only his bridge between theory and the masses; they
were integral to – in that they emerged organically from – the very classes
which they functioned to represent. Thus, with Gramsci, the tension
between self-emancipation and the necessity of the vision provided by
theory is, at least explicitly, overcome.

Despite Gramsci's important theoretical advance, the tension generated by the role of traditional intellectuals in the revolutionary movement remained. Take post-Second World War France as an example.
When we think of intellectuals in this context we are usually referring
not to the proletarian organic intellectuals which feature so strongly in
Gramsci's thought, but rather to the politically engaged academic intellectuals perhaps best exemplified by Sartre; intellectuals who came for
various reasons to adopt a revolutionary stance, and to therefore align
themselves (from without) with the cause of proletarian revolution.

Sartre's existentialism fits oddly with the Marxist tradition, such that he
can perhaps only tangentially be regarded as a Marxist. Sartre was in
many ways a very traditional philosopher who was to (attempt to)
become a revolutionary, in what was a very specific set of historical conditions. The fact that Sartre was something of an outsider (despite a period
of involvement with the PCF which came to an end in 1956)[6] to Marxism
might raise the somewhat obvious question of why consider him in relation to what we have identified as a problem for Marxism. There are (at

least) two possible responses here. First, there are few other philosophers who conjure in people's minds a vision of a revolutionary intellectual, at least in terms of those who have some kind of perception of the events of 1968. But this is not reason enough. Second therefore is the fact that Sartre, perhaps more so than any other public political intellectual, might be regarded as embodying the difficulties faced by (traditional) intellectuals wishing to bring their knowledge to bear in political struggles which engage primarily social classes external to their own; indeed, as Culbertson makes clear in Chapter 4, as Sartre's political (as opposed to philosophical) understanding developed his view of his own role as intellectual specifically, and the role of the intellectual in politics more generally, underwent a process of significant transformation; indeed, it could be maintained that a true awareness of the requirements of self-emancipation only became apparent for Sartre when he came to recognise, in the latter stages of his career, that the role of the 'revolutionary intellectual' was not a role which he himself could perform. (The very high point of Sartre's writings on the intellectual is thus perhaps the recognition of the difficulties – no less important – with which we are concerned here, not a resolution of them.)

Comparable tensions persist in the work of Althusser, the topic of Warren Montag in Chapter 5. Althusser's philosophy is more firmly routed in the Marxist tradition than Sartre's existentialism. Moreover, Althusser's engagement with Marxism should not be viewed as that of an autonomous academic (outsider), who aimed to bring his wisdom to the revolutionary movement from without (an impression one often gets of Sartre). Rather, in Althusser's work, we see the activity of a critical intellectual who, whilst his structural location placed him outside of the working class – nevertheless considered of fundamental importance party discipline and organisation, discipline and organisation which he clearly thought would establish his connection with the proletarian movement. Majumdar (1995) writes of Althusser's position as follows:

> One may consider Althusser as an intellectual, determined to maintain his intellectual integrity (like Sartre for instance), but as part of a revolutionary movement, not outside it. This view would see him as neither slavish hack of the PCF nor a 'free' intellectual. His membership of the party would, in one sense fulfil the requirements of practice essential for any Marxist trying to develop Marxist theory. It could be seen as a way of maintaining contact with the experience of the working class at little real cost to the intellectual. (Majumdar 1995: ix)

But there is perhaps something a little misleading about the final sentence of this quotation. Though revolutionary intellectuals may be shielded from the often violent costs of revolutionary engagement, as Marx long before Lenin insisted, those petty bourgeois intellectuals who come to the revolutionary movement must pay the very real costs of a renunciation. For, Althusser maintains that the ideological predispositions of the petty bourgeois intellectuals – such as himself – could only be overcome as a result of 'a long, painful and difficult re-education. An endless external and internal struggle' (Althusser 1971: 16). The continual process of self-criticism in which Althusser engaged throughout the period of his activity as revolutionary philosopher/intellectual can perhaps best be viewed as the result of a willingness to subject himself to such discipline, such 're-education', and a desire to purge himself – and his philosophy – of 'petty bourgeois' ideological contaminants (i.e. to subject himself as theorist to the demands of the proletarian movement?). And whilst this in no way removes the emancipatory tension with which we are concerned, it does soften its effect substantially; for in subjecting her/himself to the proletarian movement, the intellectual must give up any claim to an exalted position. The intellectual becomes an auxiliary to the proletarian movement, and not its leader.

If in these two authors we see intellectuals drawn to Marxism in the process of political engagement, in other quarters of Marxism we observe something of a retreat into the academy. Take for example one of the founders of the approach which we have come now to refer to as critical theory – Adorno. Adorno challenges not only the possibility of proletarian self-emancipation specifically, but the possibility of socialist society more generally. In Adorno's work, the relationship between the intellectuals and the masses comes to be reconceptualised, and the role of the intellectual prioritised. Capitalism – and mass popular culture – had so eradicated the critical potential of the masses that even the idea of bringing revolutionary consciousness to them from without ceases to be a possibility. Such an idea of emancipatory critique comes to be replaced by a notion of immanent critique, in which as Delanty notes, 'The role of the critical intellectual ... was not to create or recover meaning, but to demonstrate the limitations of existing ways of thinking.' This 'public' political role is very much a role which stands out against the attempts by figures such as Gramsci to democratise intellectuality. For, given mass culture's pacifying role, it was to high culture that Adorno turned when searching for the resources of such critical potentiality. Indeed, in Adorno's work specifically – and with critical theory more generally – we start to observe what some have referred to as a 'crisis of Marxism'. Though becoming particularly apparent in the 1970s, the origin of this crisis has been located by some substantially earlier. In the late 1970s, for example, Eric Hobsbawm wrote:

> The forward march of labour and the labour movement, which Marx predicted, appears to have come to a halt in this century about twenty five to thirty years ago. Both the working class and the labour movement since then have been passing through a period of crisis, or, if you prefer to be mealy-mouthed about it, of adaptation to a new situation. (Hobsbawm 1978: 1)

There were many roads travelled out of this 'crisis' by intellectuals. Some turned their back on the labour movement and made a shift to the right. But the move made by others was less easy to characterise. Take 'post-Marxism' as an example. Laclau and Mouffe write: 'There is no logical and necessary relation between socialist objectives and the position of social agents in the relations of production ... The era of "privileged subjects" – in the ontological, not practical sense – of the anti-capitalist struggle has been definitively superseded' (Laclau and Mouffe 1985: 86–87). (Though quite different in philosophical orientation to Adorno, there are similarities here which are telling.) Not only is the internal connection between the working class and the socialist project eroded, but the very idea of socialism ceases to be a possibility. Indeed, socialism itself comes to be replaced with 'radical democracy'. Moreover, this specific political 'anti-essentialism' is combined by the authors with a more general philosophical anti-essentialism; this is an anti-essentialism in which truth as correspondence comes to be ruled out as naïve and outdated. The 'truth' of a philosophical proposition is to be established not in relation to how far it reflects an 'essential reality' 'out there'; rather 'human beings socially construct their world, and through this construction – always precarious and incomplete – they give to a thing its being' (Laclau and Mouffe 1990: 104). For Laclau and Mouffe, their argument generates highly democratic conclusions; anti-essentialism brings with it a radical decentring. Indeed, it is not only the working class who lose their ontological privilege, so too must the role of the intellectual as social scientist be set aside.

Yet, other authors who locate themselves more firmly within the Marxist tradition have argued differently (see Geras 1990a; 1990b; Wood 1998). It has been insisted, for example, that Laclau and Mouffe's anti-essentialism may ultimately lead them to privilege intellectuals over and above other members of society. For who is better situated to bring hegemonic order to this radically decentred world than intellectuals? Wood provocatively makes such a point when she writes: 'In the final analysis, everything depends on intellectuals in conducting a "complex of discursive hegemonic operations." And so we have it: In the beginning (and the end) was the Word, and the Word was with God, and the Word was God, the ultimate Subject made incarnate in ... Laclau and Mouffe?' (Wood 1998: 74).

One of the sites of struggle which Laclau and Mouffe mention in their 'decentred' political landscape is that of feminism – which forms the topic of Raisborough and Jones in Chapter 12. Now if there has been a 'crisis' in Marxism, so too feminism has undergone a parallel 'crisis', a crisis which has been amongst other things of an epistemological character. Therefore, in relation to feminism it is worth making what may appear to be something of a detour at this juncture. Despite often strong democratic aspirations, it has been suggested that feminism has in the past tended to consider the political role of the intellectual in somewhat elitist terms; that is, 'the intellectual' is a political agent involved primarily in the process of 'consciousness raising'. At the basis of this notion is a view that there exists an essential female identity and corresponding set of interests 'out there', which it is the task of the intellectual to render perspicuous. Post-structuralists (and post-feminists) have insisted that gender identity is a discursive product, and that therefore there are no such interests. Nevertheless, as with post-Marxism, some critics have detected elitist undercurrents here. For example, it has been suggested that so-called post-feminism, though claiming to be a democratic repost to more traditional feminism, in actuality involves a retreat into the academy, and accordingly a move away from the real concerns of women. Moreover, the emphasis on discursive construction, it could be argued, has generated in post-feminism the kind of difficulty which Wood identified with Laclau and Mouffe; that is, a prioritisation of the intellectual by the back door.

Now Marxism as a political project can learn much from the various responses of feminist intellectuals in these debates. It is difficult to doubt, for example, that the post-structuralist critique forced most feminist intellectuals to be critical of their assumptions, and re-evaluate their claims to know. Indeed, more than this. Perhaps the most significant lesson in relation to our concerns may be the form of reflexive shift which Raisbourough and Jones do so much to explore. This is perhaps best summed up in their argument for an increased awareness of a 'need ... to recognise that we [Marxist and feminist intellectuals alike] are as much a part of the object of our analysis as those we are attempting to "intellectualise" about'.

If the importance of an un-blinkered Marxism is demonstrated by the productivity of a meaningful encounter with feminism, we must nevertheless avoid the conclusion that only through engagement with resources outside of the Marxist tradition can Marxists say something of use in relation to the questions with which we are occupied here. Marxism, put perhaps rather crudely, can learn much from its own theoretical resources.

Some therefore have also argued for the importance of a return to Marx. And the precise character of this 'return' has important implications for our concerns. In many ways the most profound restatement of a certain form of Marxian orthodoxy can be found in G. A. Cohen's *Karl Marx's Theory of History: A Defence*, perhaps the founding text of 'Analytical Marxism'. In this text Cohen has attempted to provide a systematic reconstruction of historical materialism, a reconstruction which expunges Marx's work of its dialectical residues. In this reconstruction, as we have seen, Cohen stresses the importance, for Marx, of social scientific theory in rendering perspicuous capitalist social relations. At the same time, however, there is little discussion in this reconstruction of Marx of the working class and their political role specifically, nor indeed much about politics more generally. For in Cohen's work, the relations of production are considered as an effect of specific levels of development of productive forces (a view characterised by Cohen as the 'primacy thesis'). Thus in reality, the combination of the (implicit) downgrading of class struggle and a very particular stress on conceptual rigour, might be considered again, as Edwards argues in Chapter 7, ideologically in relation to a retreat of Marxist intellectuals into the academy, and therefore perhaps as an exacerbating affect, rather than effective way out of, this 'crisis'.

Others have returned to the themes of Marxism, at least as they relate to our concerns here, in perhaps a more direct fashion. Thus they have argued for a need not necessarily for a reconstruction of historical materialism, but in many ways for a stress on the conceptual tools developed by Marx and subsequent Marxists. Such a 'return', they have insisted, might enable one to think again about the possibilities of working class self-emancipation in the light of new realities. Here there is perceived to be a need for a reflexive return, a return in which Marxists apply their own theoretical tools in order to understand both their social location as well as the social location of the working class more traditionally conceived. These Marxists focus, primarily in a sociological fashion, on the specific sites in which 'intellectual labour' is carried out. And these sites, as we have noted earlier, are multiple. Salter in Chapter 11, for example, has argued in relation to 'media intellectuals', that these intellectuals are 'workers ... situated in an institutional complex which itself is part of the industrial complex of production, consumption and exchange ...' And I have stressed in my chapter the view that the site of intellectual labour is paradigmatically a proletarian one, one in which labour is increasingly exploited in a capitalist fashion.[7] This approach potentially removes one problem, but replaces it with another. For on the one hand it ceases to make much sense to view significant proportions of academic labour as external to the working class. But on the other hand, these intellectual proletarians would seem to come to be subjected to the forces of ideology which constrain the working class more generally, forces which Sayers explores in Chapter 8. The challenge to this viewpoint is therefore to seek out points of emancipatory tension within these various sites of intellectual labour, a challenging task indeed, though for Salter at least, by no means an impossible one.

The contributions which comprise this book are ordered into two parts. Part I contains chapters on Marx, Lenin and Trotsky, Gramsci, Sartre, Althusser and Adorno. The focus here is on how these authors have understood the social location of the intellectual, particularly as this pertains to the emancipatory political project of Marxism. Part II is primarily – though not exclusively – thematic in orientation. Here there are chapters on analytical Marxism and the academy, ideology and religious criticism, the class location of the contemporary intellectual, Marxist and feminist attempts to theorise the role of the critical intellectual, and intellectuals and the media.

Notes

1. For some interesting reflections on the impact which such 'institutionalisation' has had on – specifically analytical – Marxism, see Chapter 7 in Part II of this book.
2. I set aside the very important issue of how to characterise those who claim to speak in favour of existing power relations.
3. See also Foucault's (1977) distinction between the 'universal' and the 'specific' intellectual.
4. In an interesting article, Edward Shils (1990) has maintained that such an approach is the cornerstone of intellectual work and at the very heart of the notion of intellectual responsibility.
5. Culbertson gives a great deal of attention to these issues in Chapter 4.
6. See Elliot (1994).
7. Note that the stress on exploitation in understanding academic labour is not peculiar to typically Marxist approaches. Worthington, for example, in Chapter 10, has used the broader resources of labour process theory to understand.
8. The site of academic labour and what he terms 'peer exploitation'.

References

Althusser, L. (1971) *Lenin and Philosophy*, London: New Left Books.

Arblaster, A. (1973) 'Ideology and Intellectuals', in R. Benewick *et al.* (eds), *Knowledge and Belief in Politics – The Problem of Ideology*, London: George Allen and Unwin, 115–129.

Arendt, H. (1951) *The Origins of Totalitarianism*, New York: Harcourt.

Bakunin, M. (1990) *Marxism, Freedom and the State*, London: Freedom Press.

Bauman, Z. (1987) *Legislators and Interpreters*, Cambridge: Polity.

Cohen, G. A. (2000) *Karl Marx's Theory of History: A Defence*, Oxford: Oxford University Press.

Elliot, G. (1994) 'Contentious Commitments: French Intellectuals and Politics', *New Left Review*, 206, 110–114.

Feuer, L. (1976) 'What is an Intellectual?, in A. Gella (ed.), *The Intelligentsia and the Intellectuals*, London: Sage, 47–57.

Foucault, M. (1977) 'The Political Function of the Intellectual', C. Gordon (trans.), *Radical Philosophy*, 17 (Summer), 12–15.

Furedi, F. (2004) *Where Have All the Intellectuals Gone?*, London: Continuum.

Geras, N. (1990a) 'Post-Marxism?', in N. Geras, *Discourses of Extremity – Radical Ethics and Post Marxist Extravagances*, London: Verso, 61–126.

Geras, N. (1990b) 'Ex-Marxism Without Substance: A Rejoinder', in N. Geras, *Discourses of Extremity – Radical Ethics and Post Marxist Extravagances*, London: Verso, 127–168.

Gouldner, A. W. (1979) *The Future of the Intellectuals and the New Class*, London: Macmillan.

Gouldner, A. W. (1985) *Against Fragmentation*, Oxford: Oxford University Press.

Gramsci, A. (1971) *Selections From Prison Notebooks*, London: Lawrence and Wishart.

Gramsci, A. (1994) *Pre-Prison Writings*, Cambridge: Cambridge University Press.

Harding, N. (1997) 'Intellectuals and Socialism: Making and Breaking the Proletariat', in J. Jennings and A. Kemp-Welch (eds), *Intellectuals in Politics: From the Dreyfus Affair to Salman Rushdie*, London: Routledge, 195–224.

Hayek, F. A. (1998) *The Intellectuals and Socialism*, London: IAE.

Hobsbawm, E. (1978) *The Forward March of Labour Halted*, London: Pluto.

Jennings, J. and Kemp-Welch, A. (1997) 'The Century of the Intellectual: From the Dreyfus Affair to Salman Rushdie', in J. Jennings and A. Kemp-Welch (eds), *Intellectuals in Politics: From the Dreyfus Affair to Salman Rushdie*, London: Routledge, 1–21.

Laclau, E. and Mouffe, C. (1985) *Hegemony and Socialist Strategy*, London: Verso.

Laclau, E. and Mouffe, C. (1990) 'Post-Marxism Without Apologies', in E. Laclau (ed.), *New Reflections on the Revolution of Our Times*, London: Verso, 97–132.

Lenin, V. I. (1947a) *One Step Forward, Two Steps Back*, Moscow: Progress Publishers.

Lenin, V. I. (1947b) *What is to be Done?*, Moscow: Progress Publishers.

Luxemburg, R. (1971) 'Organizational Questions of Russian Social Democracy', in D. Howard (ed.), *Selected Political Writings of Rosa Luxemburg*, New York: Monthly Review Press, 283–306.

Majumadar, M. A. (1995) *Althusser and the End of Leninism*, London: Pluto Press.

Marx, K. and Engels, F. (2000) 'Circular Letter', in D. McLellan (ed.), *Karl Marx: Selected Writings*, Oxford: Oxford University Press, 620–622.

Montefiore, A. (1990) 'The Political Responsibility of the Intellectuals', in I. Maclean, A. Montefiore and P. Winch (eds), *The Political Responsibility of the Intellectuals*, Cambridge: Cambridge University Press, 201–228.

Said, E. (1993) *Representations of the Intellectual*, London: Vantage.

Shils, E. (1972) *The Intellectuals and the Powers and Other Essays*, Chicago, IL: Chicago University Press.

Small, H. (2002) 'Introduction', in H. Small (ed.), *The Public Intellectual*, London: Blackwell, 1–18.

Williams, R. (1976) *Key Words*, London: Fontana.

Wood, E. M. (1998) *The Retreat From Class* (Second Edition), London: Verso.

Part I

1

Marx and Intellectuals

Paul Blackledge

Marx did not write a systematic treatise on intellectuals, and when he did comment on members of the intelligentsia he tended to use the phrase 'educated people', or, if in a more scornful mood, 'literati' to describe them (Draper 1978: 481, 516). In a sense this is a surprising lacuna in his thought, for Marx and Engels were themselves, as Lenin pointed out, obviously intellectuals cut from the most traditional cloth (Miliband 1977: 36); and in failing to provide a detailed analysis of intellectual radicalism they, in effect, obscured their own position within the socialist movement. Alvin Gouldner has argued that Marx's reticence when it came to commenting on the role of the intelligentsia in the socialist revolution is symptomatic of a deeper problem with his political theory: beneath its self-image as a model of proletarian socialism, in practice Marxism functions as an ideology of a new class of revolutionary intellectuals whose goal is the rational reconstruction of society in its own image (Gouldner 1985: 25, 48).

There is obviously some power to Gouldner's arguments; revolutions in China, Cuba and elsewhere in the twentieth century have been led by intellectuals, and are evidence that the proletariat is not inevitably a revolutionary class in even the most revolutionary of situations. Nevertheless, the force of Gouldner's critique of Marx's political theory is undermined by his deployment of a crude caricature of Marx's theory of revolution, according to which, for instance, Marx's own class background negates his claim to have articulated a theory of proletarian socialism (Gouldner 1985: 6). Fortunately for Marxists, this will not do as a critique of the origins of historical materialism, for Marx did not construct a crude model of historical development according to which individuals are forever trapped in a specific consciousness determined

21

by their location within the class structure. Moreover, he did not believe that intellectuals had nothing to contribute to the socialist movement. Indeed, the obvious venom with which he criticised intellectual 'hired prize-fighters' of the bourgeoisie implied an ethical commitment to the search for truth which, nominally at least, most intellectuals would claim to share (Marx 1873: 97). However, Marx was circumspect about the revolutionary potential of the intelligentsia, and believed that intellectuals should be welcomed into the socialist movement on the condition that they resolutely broke with the elitist culture which afforded them a sense of identity.

Marx arrived at this conclusion through his political and intellectual break with the Young Hegelian circles in Germany in the 1840s. Central to this rupture was his 'discovery' of the proletariat as an active agent rather than a passive victim of history. Contrary to popular belief,[1] Marx did not think that the proletariat would automatically and unproblematically realise this potential: he was well aware of the dehumanising and fragmenting consequences that the division of labour had on the working class. Yet, he argued that the proletariat's location within the division of labour, whilst alienating, simultaneously created the possibility that it might come to perceive the capitalist system in a new light, as a totality which it created and which it could therefore recreate. Conversely, he believed that the location of intellectuals within the division of labour mediated against their embrace of this worldview.

Despite this suggestion, Marx was well aware that individual intellectuals could contribute to the workers' movement in various ways; for instance as 'ideological innovators', or in more general roles within the movement which required a degree of educational training; such as editors, etc. Further, he argued that intellectuals could act as technical experts in the service of post-revolutionary regimes (Draper 1978: 539–545). Marx also recognised that certain sections of the intelligentsia were themselves experiencing the pressures of proletarianisation such that an *a priori* rejection of their role in the struggle for socialism would be absurd. Nonetheless, Marx was aware that the layer which Gramsci would later label traditional intellectuals was formed within a specific location in the division of labour which afforded it a very different perspective on the world to that experienced by workers. He thus insisted that intellectuals could make a positive contribution to the workers' movement only if they came to see the world from the perspective of revolutionary workers (Lukács 1971: 21, 149–209).

Human nature, alienation and the division of labour

At its core Marxism is a democratic theory of working-class self-emancipation: Marx believed that ordinary workers were capable of developing the intellectual skills needed to run a modern complex society. Marx's political theory thus stands in marked opposition to the assumption, generally accepted since at least the time of Plato, that a natural hierarchy of intelligence exists which underpins social stratification. Nevertheless, Marx recognised that most workers in 'normal' conditions tended not to exhibit the talents associated with leadership; in fact they were socialised from birth to be led rather than to lead. Accordingly, he envisaged socialism as a system within which this division between leaders and led, or as Marx would have it, between mental and material labour, is overcome (Ratanssi 1982: 56).

It does not require a vivid imagination to realise that this perspective challenges much that is sacrosanct to most intellectuals, including their self-identity as members of an inherently intellectually superior social layer. This conflict between Marxism and intellectual common sense in turn produces an interesting dynamic. For, as we shall see below, while Marxism predicts that sections of the intelligentsia will be predisposed towards a form of radicalisation in response to the market's tendency to reduce their status towards that of the proletariat, many intellectuals will simultaneously be repulsed by Marxism's apparent embrace of the logic of this process. One consequence of this contradiction is that intellectual radicalisation may well evolve as an elitist rejection of working-class politics. Moreover, even amongst those intellectuals whose radicalism leads them into the socialist movement, their intellectual background will lend itself to a particularly philanthropic, and elitist, interpretation of their role within the movement.

Marx's response to the elitist tendencies exhibited even by socialist intellectuals was twofold. Theoretically, he challenged the notion that the historical division between mental and material labour was an essential character of all human societies, whilst politically he guarded against the malign consequences of the actions of well-meaning intellectuals within the labour movement. To make sense of these theoretical and political strands to Marx's analysis of intellectuals it is useful to locate them within his broader analysis of the division of labour.

At the centre of Marx's anthropology is the concept of social production, understood as conscious and purposeful activity (Braverman 1974: 46). According to this model, humans socially produce with the conscious aim of transforming the world to meet their changing needs. However, whilst production in pre-class societies was a unified process of conception and execution, Marx believed that the emergence of a social division between mental and material labour paved the way for the rise of class societies within which this purposeful process came to be increasingly fragmented, as one class rose to direct production in its own interests, while a second actually did the work of producing (Marx and Engels 1845: 51; Engels 1877: 341).[2] Beyond this basic process, Marx argued that once class societies had been established, the separation between conception and execution within the production process developed to its highest form under capitalism (Braverman 1974: 114).

In *The German Ideology* the concept of the division between mental and material labour was primarily deployed as a synonym for the division between social classes – whereas mental labourers directed the production process, material labourers did the concrete work of producing. However, Marx was well aware that the division between mental and material labour was much more complex than this simple diptych would suggest. In addition to this primary denotation, Marx pointed out that there existed a secondary division between those sections of the ruling class who were directly involved in the production process and those intellectuals who acted to ideologically justify this process. Traditional intellectuals, according to this model, operated at the level of society's ideological superstructure, at some distance removed from the more basic role of those who directed production (Marx and Engels 1845: 65; Lukács 1972: 13; Lowy 1979: 15). Moreover, this division of labour within the ruling class was not negligible, but could 'develop into a certain opposition and hostility between the two parts' (Marx and Engels 1845: 65).

Nevertheless, while Marx and Engels were aware of the importance of this division, they insisted that so long as it remained a division within the ruling class it was a secondary social cleavage, such that in periods of crisis 'when the class itself is endangered', the great bulk of the individuals on the two sides of the division would unify against common enemies (Marx and Engels 1845: 65). So, whatever the verbal radicalism of traditional intellectuals, Marx and Engels were careful to insist that workers should beware of the radical intelligentsia's backsliding tendencies. In this sense, the location of the bulk of traditional intellectuals within the ruling class, although at some distance removed from the production process, meant that in the final analysis they would rather accommodate with the old order than fight for its revolutionary overthrow. Bourgeois intellectuals, according to this model, like the rest of the bourgeoisie, while just as alienated from the product of their labour as are proletarians, feel at home in this alienation: only the proletariat, Marx and Engels argued, experience their alienation as an imperative to revolt against the system (Marx and Engels 1844: 36).

Unfortunately, while proletarians were therefore impelled to revolt against the capitalist division of labour, the division of labour itself tended to make them unfit for rule (Marx and Engels 1845: 51–57, 95).[3] Indeed, Engels pointed out that 'in the division of labour, man is also divided. All other physical and mental faculties are sacrificed to the development of one single activity. This stunting of man grows in the same measure as the division of labour, which attains its highest development in manufacture' (Engels 1877: 355; cf. Braverman 1974: 73; cf. Draper 1978: 483). So, while Engels insisted that the development of society's productive forces created the conditions whereby the division of labour might be 'swept away', and Marx argued that increases in the productivity of labour associated with the growth of capitalism ensured that 'the technical reason for the lifelong attachment of the worker to a partial function is swept away', Marx also added that, simultaneously, 'the barriers placed in the way of the domination of capital by this same regulating principle now also fall' (Marx 1867: 491; Engels 1877: 342). Marx therefore argued that while the increases in the productivity of labour associated with the deepening of the division of labour under capitalism had created the objective potential for socialism, he also saw that the existence of the division of labour acted as a fundamental barrier to the realisation of this potential. In this sense he re-engaged with a problem that had troubled Adam Smith.

In *The Wealth of Nations*, Smith had famously argued that the tendency towards the division of labour was a basic facet of human nature: the division of labour 'is the necessary, though very slow and gradual consequence of a certain propensity in human nature which has in view no such extensive utility; the propensity to truck, barter and exchange one thing for another'. Moreover, the division of labour gave rise to great increases in the productivity of labour, a consequence of which was an increase in 'that universal opulence which extends to the lowest ranks of the people'. However, Smith recognised that in addition to this positive consequence of the division of labour, there existed a negative corollary: those who worked on the most menial tasks became intellectually debased by the deskilled nature of their work. Indeed, Smith argued that philosophers and manual workers differed less in natural abilities than did a spaniel from a sheep dog, and that it was the division of labour experienced from childhood that gave rise to the differential educational capacities of the two groups in later life (Smith 1776: 117, 115, 120).

Furthermore, Smith went so far as to suggest that 'the man whose whole life is spent performing a few simple operations ... has no occasion to exert his understanding ... He generally becomes as stupid and ignorant as it is possible for a human creature to become' (Smith quoted in Marx 1867: 483).

Thus stated, there are a number of obvious problems with Smith's defence of the division of labour. First, his universalisation of the propensity to truck, barter and exchange, acts to obscure the novelty of the capitalist mode of production (Brenner 1989: 272). Second, given that by his own admission the division of labour tends to reduce the bulk of humanity to a greater or lesser state of idiocy, it is not at all obvious why we should follow him in accepting that this division is in the universal interest. Smith recognised this latter problem and, as Marx pointed out, attempted to mediate against the negative consequences of the division of labour by proselytising a universal system of education through which the tendency to narrow proletarian intellectual horizons would be mediated. However, Marx realised that the arguments of Smith's bourgeois critics, who suggested that by educating workers the state would act to undermine the division of labour itself, could not adequately be countered without overcoming the division of labour itself; for educated people would be repelled by the mind-numbing work carried out in the new factories of his day (Marx 1867: 484).

As an antidote to the stupefying consequences of the division of labour, Marx seemed to agree with Hegel that an educated person is one that 'can do what others do' (Hegel quoted in Marx 1867: 485). But one can do what others do if there is no division of labour, and if there is no division of labour then, according to Smith, humanity will revert back to a primitive state. This may be a desirable condition, but it is scarcely a practicable one, and it is certainly not Marx's mature vision of the socialist future.[4] How then did Marx square his critique of the division of labour with the view that socialism required a relatively high level of economic development? The answer to this question lies, primarily, in the differentiation he made between two distinct aspects – the social and the manufacturing[5] – of the division of labour; and secondarily, in his analysis of the dynamic process through which capital accumulation tended to overcome the practical need for a division between mental and manual labour.

In relation to the first of these suggestions, Marx, in his mature work, insisted that while social or occupational divisions within the production process are a universal feature of human history, the most dehumanising element of the modern division of labour – the manufacturing or technical division of labour – is a product of modern capitalist production. Thus Marx differentiated between the social division of people into various specialist occupations and the technical division of individual jobs, and thereby the people who worked them, into increasingly simple component parts.

In the *Economic Manuscripts of 1861–1863*, Marx argued that Smith 'constantly confuses these very different senses of the division of labour, which admittedly complement each other, but are also in certain respects mutually opposed' (Marx 1861–1863: 266). It was as a consequence of this confusion that Smith 'did not grasp the division of labour as something peculiar to the capitalist mode of production'. As he argued in *Theories of Surplus Value*, whereas occupational specialisation was a relatively universal feature of human history, the subdivision of jobs into their relatively unskilled component parts, whilst built upon this earlier division, was a peculiar product of capitalist manufacture (Marx 1861: 268). Moreover, where Smith equated the manufacturing division of labour with both the social division of labour and the tendency towards increased productivity, Marx argued that the development of the manufacturing division of labour is better understood as that process through which the subsumption of labour to capital moved from its formal to its real phase. Consequently, Marx insisted, the manufacturing division of labour was not instituted primarily as a means of increasing labour productivity, but was rather used as a means of enforcing a capitalist discipline on the labour force by deskilling the labour process (Braverman 1974: 119; Thompson 1989: 75). Indeed, whereas the social division of labour facilitated increases in the productivity of labour by occupational specialisation, the technical division involves the subdivision of jobs such that individual workers perform increasingly simple tasks for which they require only a minimum of training (Ratanssi 1982: 150). For where capitalism had emerged, in part at least, out of pre-capitalist modes of production by enforcing the discipline of the market upon existing labour processes – the formal subsumption of labour to capital; with the development of factory production the nature of the labour process was itself transformed such that labour was deskilled and becomes really 'subsumed under capital' (Marx 1861–1863: 271, 279; cf. Marx 1867: 1019–1024). In this new situation, Marx argued, 'the division of labour within the workshop implies the undisputed authority of the capitalist over men' (Marx 1867: 477).

Accordingly, for Marx, the social and the manufacturing divisions of labour could be differentiated thus: the former allowed increases in labour productivity, while the latter was primarily designed to increase capital's control over the labour process. Marx suggested that whilst the former process was an inevitable precondition of economic and social advance, the tendency immanent in it towards 'crippling of the body and mind' by occupational specialisation was taken to an extreme in the factory for reasons that had little to do with increasing the 'universal opulence'. Rather, the manufacturing system emerged to ensure capital's control over the labour process and was an 'entirely specific creation of the capitalist mode of production' (Marx 1867: 484, 480).

If the technical or manufacturing division of labour therefore tended to dehumanise manual workers by robbing them of the chance of partaking in meaningful productive activity, its malign consequences also reached up to the division between mental and manual labour. Indeed, Braverman insisted that in the twentieth century the bulk of the once privileged clerical labour undertaken in most offices had, as a consequence of capital's quest to control the labour process by increasing the polarisation between those who conceive and those execute the labour process, become just as 'manual' as the material labour carried out on the factory floor (Braverman 1974: 316).

In opposition to this conceptualisation of recent social developments, Nicos Poulantzas argued that 'the mental/manual labour division characterises the new petty bourgeoisie as a whole, which in contrast to the working class is located on the 'side', or in the 'camp', of mental labour, either directly or indirectly' (Poulantzas 1978: 251–252). According to this model, all those, including intellectuals, who are involved in 'unproductive' activity are best characterised as members of a new petty bourgeoisie. In contrast, Ellen Wood and Erik Olin Wright have argued that this claim relies upon an unpersuasive suggestion that mental and manual divisions within the labour force constitute a class division rather than a simple division within the working class, and implying an absurdly narrow definition of the working class (Wright 1978: 53; Wood 1986: 39). Similarly, Callinicos has argued that 'unproductive' labour is best understood as a necessary constituent part of what Marx called the 'collective worker' (Callinicos 1987: 19). Nevertheless, even if we accept Callinicos' broad conceptualisation of the proletariat, and agree that the intelligentsia has experienced a remarkable expansion in size and proletarianisation since Marx's day, divisions between intellectuals and workers remain.

Nigel Harris has suggested that in the twentieth century, even more than in the nineteenth, the term intelligentsia 'cuts across class analysis', while Erik Olin Wright has persuasively argued that within modern capitalist relations of production, intellectuals should best be understood not as part of the working class, despite their need to sell their labour power, nor as a wholly distinct social class – either bourgeois or petty bourgeois. Rather, intellectuals exist as part of a social stratum that occupies a 'contradictory class location between the working class and the petty bourgeoisie at the economic level, but between the working class and the bourgeoisie at the ideological level' (Wright 1979: 204; Harris 1991: 98). So, despite selling their labour power modern intellectual producers, economically, experience a degree of autonomy at work that is closer to that felt by the petty bourgeoisie than it is to that of most workers, whilst, ideologically, they are expected to articulate and disseminate bourgeois ideology.

The key point here is that the intelligentsia is not a class but a stratum, and that different intellectuals operate at very different points on the economic and ideological continua between the proletariat and the petty bourgeoisie. Thus, the tendencies towards economic proletarianisation and ideological autonomy are experienced very differently across the intelligentsia. Nevertheless, as Marx and Engels argued, even in the nineteenth century the malign effects of the spread of the market tended to debase *all* forms of social activity, such that the process of capital accumulation tends to break down the division between intellectuals and the mass of workers by the proletarianisation of the former: 'The bourgeoisie has stripped of its halo every occupation hitherto honoured and looked up to with reverent awe. It has converted the physician, the lawyer, the priest, the poet, the man of science, into its paid wage labourers' (Marx 1848: 70). And while this process would tend to produce a radical response amongst all the groups thus affected, because intellectuals are not a homogeneous group, their response to these pressures would be complex and mediated.

Revolution

The logic of Marx's discussion of the division of labour appears to suggest that the condition of the proletariat is both too fragmented and too intellectually narrow for it to act as a realistic agency of its own emancipation. Nevertheless, as Braverman pointed out, while the aim of the technical division of labour is to reduce workers to the position of cogs in a machine, the intelligence of those performing even the most menial tasks is never completely suppressed (Braverman 1974: 325). Similarly, Marshall Berman has pointed out that *Capital* contains the voices of many workers who, when interviewed by factory inspectors, while showing no signs of revolutionary militancy exhibited a 'stoical endurance' and 'austere intelligence' in the face of the overbearing pressures of manual labour in nineteenth-century England (Berman 1999: 83). Indeed, it was Marx's contention, based upon his experience in socialist workers' circles in the mid-1840s, that it was the intelligence and the humanity of these workers, which could not be expunged from the machine, which acted as the mainspring of the struggle for freedom, and that through their struggle for freedom workers could break the sociological binds that alienated them from each other and the rest of society. In fact, Marx distinguished himself from other socialists of his day through the link he drew between socialism and the democratic struggle from below (Draper 1977: 59). In throwing himself into the radical campaign for democracy in Germany in the 1840s, he found that the working class acted as the most resolute arm of the democratic movement, and in so doing added a social depth to the demands of the movement. Indeed, his experience of workers' struggles in Germany and France acted as a catalyst which pushed him to the conclusion that Hegel's critique of proletarianisation was one-sided: where Hegel had argued that this process merely created a fragmented rabble (Taylor 1975: 407 and 436), Marx suggested that workers could move, through their engagement in combined struggles for a better life, from being an atomised and dehumanised group, towards becoming a potential collective agency of universal social and political emancipation. So, Marx differentiated himself from the utopian socialists in conceptualising workers not merely as victims of the system but also as agents of its possible overthrow: 'they see in poverty nothing but poverty, without seeing in it the revolutionary, subversive side' (Marx 1847: 120–121).

The revolutionary nature of workers' struggles was crucial to Marx's political theory because it was only through such struggles that workers could overcome the intellectually and morally debilitating consequences of the division of labour. Indeed, Marx and Engels argued that a revolution was necessary to overthrow capitalism not simply because the ruling class could not be removed in any other way, but more importantly because it was only through the tumultuous struggles associated with a revolution from below that the proletariat could rid 'itself of all the muck of ages and become fitted to found society anew' (Marx and Engels 1845: 95). So, it was only through the act of making a revolution that working people, socialised by their class location to assume subservient social roles, could become masters of their own destiny. In fact, the class analysis of the coming revolution so informed Marx and Engels' social theory that, rather than use the abstract word socialism to

of the role of intellectuals in the French revolutionary struggles of 1848, Marx mocked the gap between the care with which the 'experts' wrote constitutional treatise, and their lack of concerns with the need of the real movement on the ground. As August Nimtz points out, while the liberal intelligentsia penned magnificent constitutions, they were 'unwilling to take the political step that would have been necessary to guarantee the constitution itself'. Conversely, in their contemporary writings Marx and Engels argued that it was the mobilization of the masses, not the writing of fine constitutions, that was the priority of the day (Nimtz 2000: 114).

To move from writing constitutions to leading mass movements, traditional intellectuals had to unlearn many of the skills which provided them with a sense of self-worth in the first place. Engels praised the young Kautsky as an atypical intellectual precisely because he struggled to break from the hair-splitting pedantry imbued in him by his university education (Draper 1978: 531). Conversely, Marx was savage in his critique of the German academic Adolph Wagner, in part, because when Wagner wrote of universal 'man' in his treatise on political economy he actually gave an unwitting concrete form to this abstract idea. And, like all those who imagine that they stand above such matters, the concrete form of human nature assumed by Wagner was filled with his own narrow prejudices. Thus, the professor imagined the universal characteristics of human nature to be the very singular characteristics of the academic: 'Everything that the professor is unable to do himself, he makes "man" do; but this man is himself nothing more than the *professorial man* who claims to have understood the world once he has arranged it under abstract heading' (Marx 1879–1880: 193). So, behind the grand façade of Wagners' theorizing lay a set of ill thought through and indefensible assumptions about human nature which were uncritically drawn from Wagners' own narrow experiences as a bourgeois intellectual.

Generally, Marx found that the intellectual slovenliness expressed in Wagners' work was common amongst intellectuals. Indeed, when the Berlin academic Eugen Dühring produced a crude interpretation of human history, Marx and Engels felt compelled to counter his arguments – Engels was delegated to write *Anti-Dühring* – not because of the strengths of these arguments, but because the naivety of his approach appealed to a layer of intellectuals who had joined the German Social Democratic Party. Nimtz comments that Dühring's attraction to this layer of intellectuals could be found in the way that he, unlike Marx and Engels, was willing to make 'ready-made answers' to complex questions (Nimtz 2000: 255).

Beyond their tendency to lazy thinking, many intellectuals who were drawn to the nineteenth-century German socialist movement proved to be bad teachers within the movement. Engels complained that the bulk of the German party's intellectuals translated their elitism into a form of 'schoolmarmish supercilious snobbery' which did nothing for their relations with ordinary workers (Draper 1978: 523). As a result, the elitism of intellectuals proved to be a significant barrier to their involvement in a proletarian movement. In this sense, socialist intellectuals tended to betray their cultural background. For their elitism was, in effect, a variant of the disdain shown by traditional intellectuals to manual workers throughout the history of class society (cf. Kiernan 1969: 58).

Nevertheless, Marx believed that intellectuals could experience radicalising influences which might lead them to serve the workers' movement by breaking with the intelligentsia's typical elitism. He and Engels, as we have noted, outlined a material basis for the emergence of a form of intellectual radicalism in the *Communist Manifesto*, where they argued that the very dynamism of capitalism tended to break down those traditional hierarchies which had previously guaranteed the status of intellectuals. One consequence of this marketisation of the world was that intellectual labour, in addition to material labour, increasingly came to be directed towards production for the market. Further, as some intellectuals became winners in the marketplace, others lost and experienced the gravitational attraction of the process of proletarianisation. Moreover, Marx and Engels insisted that it was not simply intellectuals but 'entire sections of the ruling class are, by the advance of industry, precipitated into the proletariat, or are at least threatened in their conditions of existence'. Whilst the prospect of this process might terrify average members of the bourgeoisie and petty bourgeoisie, intellectual or not, it did open the possibility, as Marx and Engels continued, that this layer might 'supply the proletariat with fresh elements of enlightenment and progress' (Marx and Engels 1848: 77). Consequently, the proletarianisation of intellectuals might begin, *de facto*, to overcome the separation between mental and manual labour.

Beyond this process, Marx also believed that in the democratic struggles against the feudal and absolutist regimes, bourgeois revolutionaries would be compelled to appeal to the proletariat for support against the old order. However, in so doing they would begin to engage the proletariat in a discourse of rights and justice which workers could subsequently hold up against bourgeois society: 'In all these battles, [the bourgeoisie] sees itself compelled to appeal to the proletariat, to ask for help, and thus, to drag it into the political arena. The bourgeoisie itself, therefore, supplies the proletariat with its own elements of political and general education, in other words, it furnishes the proletariat with weapons for fighting the bourgeoisie' (Marx and Engels 1848: 76). Hence, the very radicalism through which the bourgeoisie was compelled to fight for its liberty against feudal society would introduce the mass of producers into political society from which they had previously been so securely excluded.

However, as Engels pointed out in his study of the sixteenth-century peasant wars in Germany, once the genie of lower class radicalism had been let out of the lamp by bourgeois radicals, these radicals were want to divide between a minority – such as those led by Thomas Munzer in Engels' narrative – who were prepared to take the struggle to communist conclusion, and a majority – such as those led by Martin Luther – who did everything in their power to suppress the popular movement from below (Engels 1850: 62–68). Therefore, while intellectual radicalism might open the door to proletarian radicalism, only those intellectuals such as Munzer who 'resolutely broke' with their class background could become true leaders of the popular struggles from below (Engels 1850: 70).

If Engels gave a concrete example of intellectual radicalism in his *The Peasant War in Germany* (1850), he and Marx had begun to theorise such a model in the *Communist Manifesto*. In this pamphlet they argued that individual members of the ruling class could, under pressure of economic and political crises, break with their social situation, and become class traitors by joining forces with the proletariat:

> Finally, in times when the class struggle nears the decisive hour, the progress of dissolution going on within the ruling class, in fact within the whole range of old society, assumes such a violent, glaring character, that a small section of the ruling class cuts itself adrift, and joins the revolutionary class, the class that holds the future in its hands. Just as, therefore, at an earlier period, a section of the nobility went over to the bourgeoisie, so now a portion of the bourgeoisie goes over to the proletariat, and in particular, a portion of the bourgeois ideologists, who have raised themselves to the level of comprehending theoretically the historical movement as a whole. (Marx and Engels 1848: 77)

However, if Marx insisted that the act of perceiving the world in such a way could not be attained through abstract contemplation, then neither could it be achieved merely by looking at the world from the perspective of the working class; for the division of labour ensured that when workers were not engaged in class struggles their viewpoint was fragmented. Rather, it was only from the perspective of workers in the highest level of struggle that a truly scientific socialism could be articulated (Rees 1998: 236).

In *The Poverty of Philosophy*, Marx had predicated this perspective on the proletariat's position in the division of labour:

> What characterizes the division of labour in the automatic workshop is that labour has there completely lost its specialized character. But the moment every special development stops, the need for universality, the tendency towards an integral development of the individual begins to be felt. The automatic workshop wipes out specialists and craft-idiocy. (Marx 1847: 138)

Commenting on these lines, and some similar in Marx's *A Contribution to the Critique of Political Economy* (Marx 1857: 104; Marx 1859: 210), Gerry Cohen has argued that, beside the tendency to deskill and impose capitalist control of the production process, Marx saw in the division of labour 'a liberating aspect' which facilitated in the proletariat, precisely because they had been reduced to general labourers, an ability to perceive the totality of the productive system in a way that had been precluded by the narrow parochialism associated with their craft specialist ancestors (Cohen 1988: 195).[8]

Nevertheless, as István Mészáros has forcefully argued, the division of labour also leads not only to the fragmentation of the working class, but also to the fragmentation of workers' struggles. Indeed, he insists that 'under normal circumstances, internally divided and fragmented labour is at the mercy not only of the ruling class and its state, but also of the objective requirements of the prevailing social division of labour' (Mészáros 1995: 930). Nonetheless, Mészáros' claim that the political consequences of this problem has been 'greatly underestimated' by Marxists, need not be accepted (Mészáros 1995: 924). For it was precisely as an answer to these problems that Marx engaged in the project of building a vanguard party.

This project did not, contra Gouldner, Harding and Avineri, involve Marx smuggling the concept of an intellectual elite into his formally democratic theory, but neither, contra-Holloway did Marx dismiss the concept of leadership (Holloway 2002: 128). Rather, it is evidence that Marx was aware of the powerful tendencies mediating against the development of a socialist class consciousness within the proletariat, which if they were to be overcome had to be met by organised socialist activity.

The party, in this conception, aimed both at overcoming the division between mental and manual workers within its own ranks, and at overcoming the tendencies towards the fragmentation of the workers' movement more broadly (Lowy 2003: 134, 146). It is in this sense that the famous lines from the *Communist Manifesto* are best understood:

> The Communists are distinguished from the other working-class parties by this only: 1. In the national struggles of the proletarians of the different countries, they point out and bring to the front the common interests of the entire proletariat, independently of all nationality. 2. In the various stages of development which the struggle of the working class against the bourgeoisie has to pass through, they always and everywhere represent the interests of the movement as a whole. (Marx and Engels 1848: 79)

The socialist party, thus conceived, acts essentially within the tension created by the division of labour: for, on the one hand, the division of labour creates the possibility that the proletariat might perceive the system as a totality which can be consciously reshaped; while, on the other hand, the division of labour also acts to fragment workers and reinforce the power of the bourgeoisie. These contradictory but equally economic aspects of the proletariat's existence mediate against the view that Marx held to a crude economic model of proletarian radicalisation. Moreover, they help explain Marx's political practice both in the 1840s and in the period of the First International. For, in both of these periods, Marx was concerned, centrally, with the need to foster the struggles of the working class as a class, whilst simultaneously challenging those forces, for instance anti-Irish racism in England, which grew out of and acted to reinforce and extend divisions within the proletariat (Collins and Abramsky 1965: 39, 45; Gilbert 1981; Harris 1990: 44–45).

In this situation, intellectual elitism, however well meant, served only to reinforce the subservient position of workers. Thus, in 1890, Engels fumed at those intellectuals who believed that their 'academic education' provided them 'with an officer's commission and a claim to a corresponding post in the party'. Indeed, he insisted that all party members 'must serve in the ranks', and that the intellectuals 'have far more to learn from the workers, all in all, than the latter have to learn from them' (Draper 1978: 515; Nimtz 2000: 268). Moreover, in as far as intellectuals perceived their role in philanthropic terms, and correspondingly conceived the workers as mere victims of the system, then they tended towards political reformism: they would fight as an elite for the workers, rather than with the workers for their liberation. Indeed, this tendency towards reformism was reinforced when intellectuals took seats in the Reichstag as the German Social Democratic Party began to experience some parliamentary success in the nineteenth century (cf. Hobsbawm 1973: 259; Draper 1978: 517; Barker 1987: 194, 263; Nimtz 2000: 267).

Conclusion

Marshall Berman has expanded on Marx's discussion of the radicalising tendencies experienced by intellectuals under capitalism. He suggests that because intellectuals pour their souls into their work they feel the fluctuations of the market 'in a far deeper way' than do most workers who merely give their time but not their heart to their employer. However, because capitalism is such a revolutionary system, it can frustrate the radicalism of even the most disaffected intellectuals by generating markets for their radical ideas. Moreover, even when intellectuals attempt to turn their back on capitalism, as they have done for instance by attempting to sanctifying themselves as an avant-garde, they remain doomed to be incorporated within the capitalist system. Indeed, Berman argues that this is just as true of the activists organised in revolutionary parties as it is of the projects for 'pure science' of 'art for arts sake'. Thus, Berman argues, we confront a system that it is hard to imagine anyone transcending (Berman 1983: 115–120).

Fortunately, Berman's 'pessimism of the intellect' need not be contagious. As we have seen, Marx's conception of a vanguard party, and Lenin's too once we move away from the crude caricatures (Cliff 1975–1979; Harding 1977–1981; Le Blanc 1990; Liebman 1975; cf. Blackledge 2005), operates at the fault-line generated by the division of labour between revolutionary movements of the proletariat against alienation, and fragmented struggles of individual groups of workers within the system. Marx believed that these moments of the struggle both within and against capital were neither mutually exclusive nor did they automatically flow into each other. Rather, he realised that the tension which existed between the two elements of the struggle called for a revolutionary party to act as the organised political voice of the more advanced sections of the workers' movement. In this framework, intellectuals could contribute to the socialist movement only if they broke with their inherited elitist frame of reference, and looked at society from the standpoint of the most advanced sections of the working class. If, however, intellectuals attempted to smuggle elitist attitudes into the workers' party, then, as Marx and Engels wrote in a circular letter sent to a number of leading members of the German Social Democratic Party on

17–18 September 1879, the party should not be afraid to break with them: 'if these gentlemen form themselves into a Social-Democratic Petty-Bourgeois Party they have a perfect right to do so; one could then negotiate with them, form a bloc according to circumstances, etc. But in a workers' party they are an adulterating element'. Consequently, while Marx was keen to realise the positive contribution that intellectuals could make to the workers' movement, he was also aware that intellectuals had a tendency to distort the movement in their own image. It was on account of this tendency that Marx's attitude to those intellectuals who sought to join workers' parties was, as Hal Draper has argued, one of 'mistrust tempered by hope, or apprehension sweetened by expectation' (Draper 1978: 511).

Notes

Thanks to David Bates, Kristyn Gorton, Paul Reynolds and Peter Thomas for their comments on this essay in draft, and to Dom Lowe for an inspirational conversation.

1. See for instance Carol Johnson's argument that 'Marx tends to depict proletarian revolutionary consciousness as something that develops automatically and inevitably as the proletariat and the contradictions of capitalism develop' (Johnson 1980: 73, 93).
2. For a discussion of Marx's developing understanding of the division of labour in general and his increasingly sophisticated articulation of its relationship to the emergence of social classes see Ratanssi (1982: 79).
3. It was through the concept of the division of labour that Marx gave a materialist depth to his concept of alienation (Beamish 1992: 8).
4. I am aware that Marx's views on the division of labour and the parameters of its possible suppression developed from a utopianism that is evident in his earlier work towards a more realistic analysis in his mature work. Unfortunately, considerations of space preclude a discussion of this intellectual evolution (cf. Ratanssi 1982; Beamish 1992).
5. Later commentators have tended to rename the manufacturing division of labour, the technical division of labour.
6. For a comprehensive rebuttal of Avineri's arguments see Draper (1978: 636–643).
7. The word *erziehung* is usually translated as upbringing in this sentence; thanks to Peter Thomas for pointing out that the more common translation as education is also better in this context.
8. See also the discussion, in the *Grundrisse*, of the emergence of a 'general intellect' (Marx 1857: 706).

References

Avineri, S. 1967 (1990) 'Marx and Intellectuals', in B. Jessop and C. Malcolm-Brown (eds), *Karl Marx's Social and Political Thought: Critical Assessments*, Vol. II, London: Routledge, 401–411.

Barker, C. (1987) 'Poland 1980–81: The Self Limiting Revolution', in C. Barker (ed.), *Revolutionary Rehearsals*, London: Bookmarks, 169–216.

Beamish, R. (1992) *Marx, Method, and the Division of Labour*, Chicago, IL: University of Illinois Press.

Berman, M. (1983) *All That is Solid Melts into Air*, London: Verso.

Berman, M. (1999) *Adventures in Marxism*, London: Verso.

Blackledge, P. (2005)' "Anti-Leninist" Anti-Capitalism: A Critique', *Contemporary Politics*, Vol. 11, No. 2/3 June–Sept 2005, 99–116.

Braverman, H. (1974) *Labour and Monopoly Capitalism*, New York: Monthly Review.

Brenner, R. (1989) 'Bourgeois Revolution and the Transition to Capitalism', in A. L. Brier *et al.* (eds), *The First Modern Society*, Cambridge: Cambridge University Press, 271–304.

Callinicos, A. (1987) 'The "New Middle Class" and Socialist Politics' in A. Callinicos and C. Harman (eds), *The Changing Working Class: Essays on Class Structure Today*, London: Bookmarks, 13–51.

Cliff, T. (1975–1979) *Lenin*, 4 Vols, London: Pluto Press.

Cohen, G. A. (1988) *History, Labour and Freedom*, Oxford: Clarendon.

Collins, H. and Abramsky, C. (1965) *Karl Marx and the British Labour Movement*, London: Macmillan.

Draper, H. (1977) *Karl Marx's Theory of Revolution*, Vol. I, New York: Monthly Review.

Draper, H. (1978) *Karl Marx's Theory of Revolution*, Vol. II, New York: Monthly Review.

Engels, F. 1850 (1956) *The Peasant War in Germany*, Moscow: Progress Publishers.

Engels, F. 1877 (1947) *Anti-Dühring*, Moscow: Progress Publishers.

Gilbert, A. (1981) *Marx's Politics*, Oxford: Martin Robertson.

Gouldner, A. (1985) *Against Fragmentation*, Oxford: Oxford University Press.

Harding, N. (1977–1981) *Lenin's Political Thought*, 2 Vols, London: Macmillan.

Harding, N. (1996) *Leninism*, London: Macmillan.

Harris, N. (1990) *National Liberation*, London: I.B. Taurus.

Harris, N. (1991) 'On the Petty Bourgeoisie – Marx and the Twentieth Century', in N. Harris, *City, Class and Trade*, London: I.B. Taurus, 95–123.

Hobsbawm, E. (1973) *Revolutionaries*, London: Phoenix.

Holloway, J. (2002) *Change the World Without Taking Power*, London: Pluto Press.

Johnson, C. (1980) 'The Problem of Reformism and Marx's Theory of Fetishism', *New Left Review*, 119 Jan/Feb, 70–96.

Kiernan, V. (1969) 'Notes on the Intelligentsia', in R. Miliband and J. Saville, (eds), *The Socialist Register*, London: Merlin, 55–84.

Le Blanc, P. (1990) *Lenin and the Revolutionary Party*, New Jersey: Humanities Press.

Liebman, M. (1975) *Leninism Under Lenin*, London: Jonathan Cape.

Lowy, M. (1979) *Georg Lukács: From Romanticism to Bolshevism*, London: Verso.

Lowy, M. (2003) *The Theory of Revolution in the Young Marx*, Leiden: Brill.

Lukács, G. (1972) *The Question of Parliamentarianism and Other Essays*, London: New Left Books.

Lukács, G. (1971) *History and Class Consciousness*, London: Merlin.

Marx, K. 1843 (1975) 'Introduction to A Contribution to the Critique of Hegel's Philosophy of Right', in Karl Marx, *Early Writings*, London: Penguin, 243–257.

Marx, K. 1844 (1975) 'Economic and Philosophic Manuscripts', in Karl Marx, *Early Writings*, London: Penguin, 279–400.

Marx, K. 1845 (1974) 'Theses on Feuerbach', in Karl Marx, *The German Ideology*, London: Lawrence and Wishart, 121–123.

Marx, K. 1847 (1978) *The Poverty of Philosophy*, Peking: Foreign Language Press.

Marx, K. 1851 (1973) 'The Eighteenth Brumaire of Louis Bonaparte', in Karl Marx *Surveys from Exile*, London: Penguin, 143–249.

Marx, K. 1857 (1973) *Grundrisse*, London: Penguin.

Marx, K. 1859 (1970) *A Contribution to the Critique of Political Economy*, London: Lawrence and Wishart.

Marx, K. 1861 (1973) *Theories Of Surplus Value*, Part III, London: Lawrence and Wishart.

Marx, K. 1861–1863 (1988) 'Economic Manuscripts of 1861–63', in Karl Marx and Frederick Engels, *Collected Works*, Vol. 30, London: Lawrence and Wishart.

Marx, K. 1867 (1976) *Capital*, Vol. I, London: Penguin.

Marx, K. 1873 (1976) 'Postface to Second Edition' of *Capital*, Vol. I, London: Penguin, 94–103.

Marx, K. 1875 (1972) *Critique of The Gotha Programme*, Peking: Foreign Languages Press.

Marx, K. 1879–1880 (1975) 'Notes on Adolph Wagner' in T. Carver (ed.), *Karl Marx: Texts on Method*, Oxford: Blackwell, 179–219.

Marx, K. and Engels, F. 1844 (1975) 'The Holy Family', in Karl Marx and Frederick Engels, *Collected Works*, Vol. 4, London: Lawrence and Wishart, 3–211.

Marx, K. and Engels, F. 1845 (1974) *The German Ideology*, London: Lawrence and Wishart.

Marx, K. and Engels, F. 1848 (1973) 'The Communist Manifesto', in D. Fernbach, *The Revolutions of 1848*, London: Penguin, 62–98.

Mészáros, I. (1975) *Marx's Theory of Alienation*, London: Merlin.

Mészáros, I. (1995) *Beyond Capital*, London: Merlin.

Miliband, R. and Saville, J. (eds) (1969) *The Socialist Register*, London: Merlin.

Miliband, R. (1977) *Marxism and Politics*, Oxford: Oxford University Press.

Nimtz, A. (2000) *Marx and Engels: Their Contribution to the Democratic Breakthrough*, New York: Suny.

Ollman, B. (1976) *Alienation*, Cambridge: Cambridge University Press.

Poulantzas, N. (1978) *Classes in Contemporary Capitalism*, London: Verso.

Ratanssi, A. (1982) *Marx and the Division of Labour*, London: Macmillan.

Rees, J. (1998) *The Algebra of Revolution*, London: Routledge.

Smith, A. 1776 (1974) *The Wealth of Nations*, London: Penguin.

Taylor, C. (1975) *Hegel*, Cambridge: Cambridge University Press.

Therborn, G. (1976) *Science, Class and Society*, London: New Left Books.

Thompson, P. (1989) *The Nature of Work*, London: Macmillan.

Wood, Ellen M. (1986) *The Retreat from Class*, London: Verso.

Wright, E. O. (1978) *Class, Crisis and the State*, London: Verso.

Wright, E. O. (1979) 'Intellectuals and the Class Structure of Capitalist Society', in P. Walker (ed.), *Between Labour and* Capital, Hassocks: Harvester Press, 191–211.

2
Lenin, Trotsky and the Role of the Socialist Intellectual in Politics

Ian D. Thatcher

It is often assumed that without socialist intellectuals of the Bolshevik mould, Russia would not have experienced a revolution of the type represented by October 1917 (Pipes 1990). After all, Russia was clearly unripe, economically, culturally and socially for a socialist takeover. Prior to 1914 the economy had undergone impressive growth, but modernisation was highly uneven, and a modern proletariat was a small minority of a population overwhelmingly peasant in composition. Indeed, it was a mater of dispute how far capitalist class relations had replaced a feudal-type estate order. Russia's economic and social backwardness was matched by a low cultural level, evident in poor literacy rates and no tradition of respect for basic human rights, including freedom of expression and association. In 1917, Lenin and Trotsky were equally guilty of the worst type of political adventurism. They promised an ignorant but desperate people, suffering from the ravages of defeat in war, a golden future. When the people realised that they had been sold false promises and turned against the Bolsheviks, the Bolsheviks responded with brutal repression. Lenin and Trotsky had established a dictatorship of socialist intellectuals, albeit in the name of the proletariat. Such a view of the Russian revolution and of the anti-democratic nature of Lenin and Trotsky's politics has been highly influential (Read 1996).

Equally influential, however, is the view that in 1917 Trotsky performed a unique and unexpected *volte-face* (Deutscher 1954: 290–291; Knei-Paz 1978: 230). After all, he joined the Bolsheviks, a faction of Russian social democracy that he had until that point criticised as an undemocratic and dictatorial trend. The dispute between Lenin and Trotsky about the nature of the party and its relationship to the working class began at the Second Congress of the Russian Social Democratic and Labour Party (RSDLP) in 1903. Here, and subsequently, Trotsky opposed what he saw as Lenin's attempt to substitute the independent action of the workers by leadership of a vanguard clique of socialist intellectuals.

This chapter will argue that both views outlined above represent only a partial account of Lenin and Trotsky's position about the role of the intellectual in the socialist movement. There were differences in the pre-1917 period, but these differences were never as great as some commentators claim. Ultimately both Lenin and Trotsky prioritised the vanguard position of intellectuals in leading the working class to socialism and communism. This consensus guided socialist politics in the Soviet Union and in many left-opposition groups that battled against the Stalin and post-Stalin leadership in the USSR.

Lenin and the role of the intellectual, 1894–1902

Lenin became a radical opponent of tsarism not as a worker, but as an intellectual. He became familiar with the key questions of socialism through study circles, organised largely by students at the universities. Lenin was known mainly as the brother of Alexander Ulyanov, who had been executed for his part in an attempt in 1887 to assassinate Tsar Alexander III. Alexander Ulyanov's fate had an influence upon the future tactical considerations of radical opposition circles. Individual acts of terror may bring high-profile publicity but at an extreme price: speedy arrest and punishment and the decimation of fragile organisations. When Lenin joined the circles previously occupied by his brother, the movement had already resolved to pursue propaganda work among the workers over conspiratorial attacks on leading government figures (White 2001).

The first pamphlets penned by Lenin in 1890s St. Petersburg attempted to pursue workers' immediate demands and link dire conditions at the factory with the more general oppression of the capitalist order. At this time Lenin thought that the workers would gravitate naturally towards socialism through conflicts over working conditions at the factories. Intellectuals such as he could aid the workers in a supporting role, chiefly by discussing tactics during specific strikes and in encouraging the workers to see their individual disputes in terms of a broader national and international class conflict. In this way the socialist movement would grow and prosper.[1]

There were however several problems with these tactics. The workers could be suspicious of the intellectuals' wider aims. Workers were interested in intellectuals to the extent that they served vital functions. The workers would depend upon intellectuals to draw up lists of demands and publish them in leaflet form. Intellectuals were also useful as teachers in the absence of formal educational opportunities for workers. Here the workers wanted knowledge in order to pursue social mobility. They could be annoyed by the intellectuals' political aims. To workers, intellectual outsiders seemed overly preoccupied with theoretical concerns. Intellectuals and workers thus had different aims and expectations of the workers' study circles. The workers could be quite impervious to the intellectuals' tactics. Another problem with the decision to opt for propaganda work was that it did not overcome the problem of arrests. The tsarist secret police, the okhrana, was quite successful at identifying and arresting radicals. Indeed, the workers could be frustrated that they could fall foul of the police because of the intellectuals' political opposition to tsarism. An opportunity for education became an unnecessary threat of arrest. Studies of worker attitudes to radical intellectuals stress the ambivalent nature of the relationship, and of ultimate worker suspicion of the intellectuals (Pipes 1963).[2]

The unsatisfactory relationship between workers and intellectuals, and the difficulties of the growth of a socialist movement in inhospitable Russian conditions, produced a tense debate between Russian socialists. Taking the experience of the strike of textile workers of 1896 into account, some socialists argued that the workers were quite capable of leading the movement. After all, the leadership of Russia's largest strikes to date, which had successfully led to the reduction of the working day to 11.5 hours, had fallen to the workers. It was quite natural that the workers' liberation should be the primary concern of the workers themselves. Intellectual revolutionaries had a role to play, but as auxiliaries. Intellectuals could not lead workers in a direction not produced by the workers' own experiences. The workers would become conscious of their economic and political interests out of the conditions of their lives, applying their own knowledge and initiative. Only when the workers expressed an interest in particular issues and called upon intellectuals for further elucidation could intellectuals make a genuine contribution. It was even argued that the intellectuals should refrain from raising some concerns with workers, for example political agitation, until the workers voiced political issues on their own initiative. The socialists who thought that the workers should predominate over intellectuals argued their case in a host of publications, most notably in

K. M. Takhtarev's *Our Reality* (1899), E. D. Kuskova's *Credo* (1899) and in the newspaper *Rabochaya mysl* (Workers' Thought) (Harding and Taylor 1983; Pipes 1963).

It was in response to a growing tendency amongst younger social democratic activists to limit their activity to the immediate economic demands of the workers that Lenin produced a vigorous defence of the primacy of politics and of the role of the intellectual, professional revolutionary in the socialist movement. Lenin set out his case in a series of statements issued between 1899 and 1901. Lenin did not wish to minimise the importance of economic demands but stressed that they were only one aspect of social democracy. Social democrats knew that the workers could only achieve substantial progress if the political order was radically transformed from an autocracy to a democracy. The important rights of freedom of association and expression would be won via a political struggle, in which the power of the state was wrested from the tsar and given to the people. Social democrats had thus set themselves the task of creating a revolutionary party of social democracy in Russia. This party would represent the interests of the workers in the country's political life, as well as supporting the workers in their current economic disputes. For Lenin the essence of Marxism was precisely that it joined economic with political struggle. Furthermore it was the role of full-time party professional revolutionaries, organised around specific tasks directed by a controlling centre, to direct the workers to their ultimate goal of socialism:

> Divorced from social democracy, the workers' movement degenerates and inevitably becomes bourgeois: in carrying on the purely economic struggle, the working class loses its political independence, becomes an appendage of other parties and betrays the great principle that 'the emancipation of the workers should be a matter of the workers themselves.' (Harding and Taylor 1983: 260)

For Lenin the revolutionary vanguard was the method by which the workers could be saved from opportunism and falling under the leadership of hostile class forces. A strictly organised band of professional revolutionaries could turn isolated strikes and disputes into a general attack on tsarism and a victorious revolution. A major question for Lenin's tactics was how would this vision progress in a country devoid of political rights? Lenin's first answer was the production of a daily newspaper on an all-Russian scale. This would itself demand an organisation of agents across the Russian Empire.

Lenin drew the thoughts and conclusions from separate publications and presented them in a systematic and rounded fashion in the pamphlet *What is to be Done?* (1902). This is largely a polemical tract directed against 'Economism', defined by Lenin as the belief that socialism is best pursued by the current workers' struggle for economic betterment. Lenin emphasised that this was impossible. The natural means for this struggle is trades unions. Lenin did not dismiss trades unions; he considered them a vital element of the socialist movement. However, trades unions were not a revolutionary social democratic party. Only the latter could provide the vital political leadership to direct a workers' assault on tsarism. Here Lenin drew a distinction between higher 'social-democratic' and lower 'trade union' forms of consciousness. A 'social-democratic' consciousness can analyse contemporary society and world history from a revolutionary-Marxist perspective. It includes knowledge of each and every form of oppression – religious, national, social, political, economic – and how to overcome these. A 'social-democratic' consciousness is thus sufficiently informed to pronounce upon a broad range of issues, understanding each in its national and international context and how it relates to the current state of the class struggle. A 'trade union' consciousness is quite narrow, focusing upon particular economic demands in a specified trade or occupation. A 'trade union' consciousness is also, on Lenin's terms, a bourgeois consciousness, for it seeks not the overthrow of capitalism, but its reform in the workers' favour.

Left to their own devices, the workers would, according to Lenin, be able to reach only a 'trades union' consciousness. The means of information and communication are so dominated by the bourgeoisie that the workers, despite an innate yearning for socialism, would fall naturally under the sway of bourgeois ideology. It was the socialist intellectuals who had mastered revolutionary Marxism that had to bring a 'social-democratic' consciousness to the workers 'from outside'. Lenin considered this claim to be rather obvious and uncontroversial. Just as the founders of modern socialism, Marx and Engels, belonged to the 'bourgeois intelligentsia', so social democracy in Russia arose not out of the 'spontaneous growth of the working class movement', but out of the 'development of thought among the revolutionary socialist intelligentsia' (Lenin 1977: 114). Even an advanced workers' movement in a democracy, as in contemporary Germany, continued to rely upon socialist intellectuals as the permanent leadership. This fact, for Lenin, brought tremendous opportunities and grave responsibilities to the social-democratic intellectual.

On the one hand, the successful social-democratic intellectual could make a genuine contribution to the forward march of history. History had given contemporary society two competing ideologies, capitalism and socialism; there was no other alternative. Without the socialist intellectual, socialism would not be victorious over capitalism; for it was precisely the socialist intellectual who guided the workers to the correct consciousness. For Lenin, 'without revolutionary theory there can be no revolutionary practice' (Lenin 1977: 109). It was also the socialist intellectual who would lead a political revolution:

> Marxism ... gives a gigantic impetus to the initiative and energy of the Social-Democrat, opens up for him the widest perspectives, and ... places at his disposal the mighty force of many millions of workers 'spontaneously' rising for the struggle ... I [have] in mind an organisation of revolutionaries as an essential factor in 'bringing about' the political revolution. (Lenin 1977: 128 and 177)

On the other hand, social democrats had to accept blame if the workers were not being won over to a higher consciousness. Incorrect leadership was a great threat and could render an otherwise healthy movement ineffective. Such was the case, according to Lenin, in contemporary Russian socialism. This was in crisis precisely because there was a 'lag of the leaders behind the spontaneous upsurge of the masses' (Lenin 1977: 172).

The key task for Lenin was the creation of a centrally organised, secret, narrow party of professional revolutionaries. For Lenin, the very notion of a professional revolutionary was too undervalued. There would be strict membership requirements. First of all, the professional revolutionaries should be ideologically pure. There was no room in Lenin's party for opportunists or opportunism. It was best he thought to split from and expel all ideological deviations from revolutionary Marxism. The professional revolutionaries would also be professional. There would be a strict division of labour according to speciality, so that each and every task would be carried out to maximum efficiency. Any trace of amateurism should be purged:

> Our task is not to champion the degrading of the revolutionary to the level of an amateur, but to *raise* the amateurs to the level of revolutionaries. (Lenin 1977: 190)

The professional revolutionaries would be experts, for example, in the workings of the secret police and know best how to avoid detection and arrest. This was vital if the movement was to have the firm and consistent leadership it so desperately required. Although the professional revolutionaries would be recruited from intellectuals, Lenin emphasised that it was important to promote the 'most promising' workers to professional revolutionaries. These 'worker professional revolutionaries' would be taken onto the party payroll and assigned a range of tasks to widen their outlook and experience (Lenin 1977: 194–195).

The professional revolutionaries would be organised in the first instance primarily through the production of an all-Russian revolutionary newspaper. The organisation of a newspaper on such a scale would itself generate an all-Russian social-democratic political organisation. Lenin also thought a newspaper was the main medium for influence over the minds of Russian workers. The workers would be brought out of their parochialism and economism by a social-democratic press that brought national and international outlooks to their attention. The combination of professional revolutionaries and an all-Russian newspaper would, for Lenin, guarantee leadership capable of guiding the workers in their immediate concerns and of preparing them for an eventual, timely assault on tsarism. A victory here would raise the Russian workers to a position of leadership in international social democracy.

Lenin, Trotsky and the role of the intellectual, 1902–1905

Lenin took the convictions outlined in *What is to be Done?* to the Second Congress of the RSDLP held in the summer of 1903. It had been five years since the first congress, during which time no real progress had been made in establishing a RSDLP. This was Lenin's chance to imprint his vision of a centralised organisation of professional revolutionaries upon an infant RSDLP. This explains why the debate around the definition of a party member generated such heat. Lenin's draft differed from his old comrade Martov's in one regard only. Lenin insisted that a party member should render 'personal participation in one of the party's organisations'; Martov thought 'regular assistance under the direction of one of the party organisations' was sufficient. Lenin opposed Martov's formulation precisely because it would turn 'all and sundry into party members'. This could only help infect the party with wavering and opportunistic members when the party had to guard its integrity and purity. How could the party's highest body, the Central Committee, for example, be held responsible for and direct a mass membership? Lenin emphasised his view of the RSDLP as an elite, vanguard organisation intended for leadership:

> The party should be only the vanguard, the leader of the vast mass of
> the working class, the whole (or nearly the whole) of which works
> 'under the control and direction' of party organisations, but the
> whole of which is not, and should not be, a part of the party ... It is
> our task to safeguard the firmness, consistency and purity of our
> party. We must try to raise the vocation and significance of the party
> member high, higher and higher still. (Harding and Taylor 1983:
> 285–286)

Lenin's vision of how a RSDLP should be organised and what its key
tasks should be aroused much controversy. Leon Trotsky was one of
Lenin's opponents. Trotsky was considered to be a youngster, although
one of the RSDLP's rising stars. Indeed, Lenin and Trotsky had enjoyed a
warm relationship. Lenin was impressed by Trotsky's journalism and
had promoted his candidature amongst the party elders. At the Second
Congress, however, Trotsky was perplexed by Lenin's organisational
plans for a pure, narrow, party of professional revolutionaries. Trotsky
doubted that opportunism could be 'exorcised by rules'. Trotsky also
thought that individual intellectuals rather than actual workers would
find it easier to abide by Lenin's definition of a party member. If Lenin's
plans should prevail then, Trotsky warned, the RSDLP would become a
party of 'student associations and young ladies', when the field of the
party's activities should be 'the proletariat' (Harding and Taylor 1983:
282–283).

Trotsky expounded upon the case against Lenin in a report to the
Siberian Union, which he had represented at the Second Congress. This
claimed that Lenin had played the most disruptive role out of all the delegates. Lenin had been fixated on a 'metaphysical' problem of rooting
out opportunism, but had actually lost sight of how a real party organisation actually works. Lenin demanded strict centralisation with power
residing in a Central Committee. In reality, however, central bodies and
local cells served and advised one another as complex practical issues
were confronted. There was no simple line of authority; this varied from
central to local bodies depending upon circumstances. Indeed, warned
Trotsky, Lenin's centralism would produce not only Lenin's personal dictatorship over the party but a party that would become so far removed from
the everyday concerns of workers that it would lose all significance for the
workers. Lenin had hoped that a band of professional revolutionaries
would offer wise leadership to an ever more entranced proletariat.

Trotsky recalled the experience of the French Revolution to show why Lenin's model of the party, although intended to defeat opportunism, would reap only destruction. Casting Lenin in the role of Maximilien Robespierre, Trotsky argued that

> [t]oo many hopes are placed on a party 'government' ... a regime that begins by expelling some of the best party workers promises too many executions and too little good. It inevitably leads to disappointments that could prove disastrous not only for Robespierre and the helots of centralism, but also for the idea of a unitary fighting party organisation. Then the masters of the situation will be the social democratic opportunistic 'Thermodorians' and the doors of the party will be thrown wide open. (Trotsky 1997: 118–119)

The differences in Lenin and Trotsky's conceptions of the role of the intellectual in the socialist movement were sharpened and deepened in the polemics surrounding Lenin's defence of his position and actions at the Second Congress.

In the lengthy brochure *One Step Forward, Two Steps Back*, written over the first half of 1904, Lenin argued that the RSDLP had split into two wings at the Second Congress. One group, the revolutionary social-democratic, had remained loyal to the concept of a centralised organised vanguard of professional revolutionaries as the essential organisational basis for the RSDLP. The other group, the opportunist social-democratic, had opposed the revolutionary social-democratic during several resolutions, most notably over the definition of a party member (discussed above). The opportunists had preferred an organisation of decentralised local bodies, which could only result in confusion and amateurism. Lenin reiterated that a centralised, organised revolutionary vanguard was the most effective way of leading the proletariat in all of its struggles. Only a revolutionary vanguard could elevate the workers to a social-democratic consciousness; only a revolutionary vanguard could organise a political victory. A truly efficient vanguard would involve far more workers in the class struggle than could otherwise be the case. It was also true that the vanguard, while leading the proletariat and to some extent taking appropriate recruits from the working class, had to remain separate from the workers

> [t]he stronger our Party organisations, consisting of *real* Social Democrats, the less wavering and instability there is *within* the Party, the broader, more varied, richer, and more fruitful will be the Party's

influence on the elements of the working-class *masses* surrounding it and guided by it ... precisely because there are differences in degree of consciousness and degree of activity, a distinction must be made in degree of proximity to the Party. We are the Party of a class, and therefore *almost the entire class* (and in times of war, in a period of civil war, the entire class) should act under the leadership of our Party ... it would be ... 'tail-ism' to think that the entire class, or almost the entire class, can ever rise, under capitalism, to the level and consciousness of its vanguard, of its Social-Democratic Party ... To forget the distinction between the vanguard and the whole of the masses gravitating towards it, to forget the vanguard's constant duty of *raising* ever wider sections to its own advanced level, means simply to deceive oneself, to shut one's eyes to the immensity of our tasks, and to narrow down these tasks. (Lenin 1977: 286–287)

In one respect, however, Lenin did concede that the proletariat's every-day experience gave the workers an advantage over the social-democratic opportunists. Large-scale factory production had taught the workers to value discipline and the subordination of the individual to the collective. An isolated worker was weak and vulnerable. The workers united into one fighting body were strong and threatening. In rejecting a hierarchical organisational structure of vanguard professional revolutionaries, Lenin claimed that the social-democratic opportunists were displaying the characteristics of a bourgeois intellectual. It was precisely the bourgeois intellectual who valued his individual freedom above anything else. The bourgeois intellectual could not succumb to proletarian discipline and was rightly mistrusted by the workers. The bourgeois intellectual was noted for his wavering and doubts, for a 'wishy-washiness', for preferring an anarchist form of organisation for it gives free reign to the views of each individual over a disciplined collective.

Lenin's focus upon the organisation of the RSDLP was quite natural. For Lenin, the organisation was the proletariat's only weapon in its struggle for power. It was no accident, therefore, that the split in the RSDLP between real revolutionaries and opportunists had taken place around organisational issues. Henceforth there were two wings of the party: a 'proletarian trend ... expressed by orthodox Social-Democracy' and a 'trend of the democratic intelligentsia ... expressed by opportunist Social-Democracy' (Lenin 1977: 384–385).

Trotsky wrote an impassioned critique of Lenin's latest exposition of his organisational plans in the pamphlet *Our Political Tasks* (1904). Here Trotsky accused Lenin of 'substitutionism'. This was true, Trotsky claimed, in several senses. Above all, Lenin had prioritised an organisational vision of the RSDLP over the autonomous self-activity of the working class. Trotsky worried that Lenin's emphasis upon the production of an all-Russian newspaper, for example, would substitute for actual contact with genuine workers. Lenin may be able to produce a newspaper on his methods, but this would not mean that a worker would actually read it or be guided by it. Such, after all, had been the previous experience of similar exercises in 'propaganda politics'.

For Trotsky, the main task of the social-democratic intellectual was to work as an auxiliary to the workers. The workers' own experience of capitalism would lead them into conflict at the workplace. In this sense the workers' movement would arise as a spontaneous by-product of a capitalist economy. The workers would also become more convinced of the need for socialism and more confident in their tactics as they learnt hard lessons from the political school of struggles and defeats. In this process the social-democratic intellectual would agitate to rouse the masses to involvement by a variety of services. He would spread the workers' slogans through the spoken and written word, offer political leadership in negotiations with other political forces, everywhere pursuing the workers' goals. However, the leader would not run ahead of the workers. The intellectual should ensure that he was expressing ideas advanced and supported by the workers themselves.

The ultimate aim of socialist politics, argued Trotsky, was that the autonomous workers would undertake their own politics by the time of the final assault for socialism. Trotsky thus implicitly disagreed with Lenin's assertion that the workers could not be ahead of their vanguard before a socialist revolution. Indeed, Trotsky's tactics aimed at guaranteeing the workers control of the socialist movement in advance of the revolution. Trotsky's goal is to promote 'the self-activity of the proletariat', for 'the proletarian theory of political development cannot substitute for a politically developed proletariat' (Trotsky, n.d.: 36). He therefore contrasts his version of a RSDLP, one that 'educates and mobilises' the proletariat to think for itself, with Lenin's RSDLP, one that 'thinks for the proletariat, which substitutes itself politically for it' (Trotsky n.d.: 72). Trotsky ridiculed Lenin's apparent disregard for the workers on the one hand, but on the other, turned to the workers to save the party from the pitfalls of 'bourgeois intellectual individualism':

the very proletariat who you were told yesterday 'spontaneously tends towards trade unionism', is today invited to give lessons in *political* discipline! And to whom? To the same intelligentsia which in yesterday's plan was given the role of bringing proletarian political consciousness to the proletariat from the outside! Yesterday the proletariat was crawling in the dust; today it is raised to unimagined heights! Yesterday too the intelligentsia was the bearer of socialist consciousness; today it is required to go through the process of factory discipline! (Trotsky n.d.: 104)

The second sense in which Trotsky accused Lenin of substitutionism was in the internal politics of the RSDLP. If Lenin was substituting the party for the proletariat, he was also guilty, Trotsky thought, of substituting the leadership for the party. Lenin was concerned, for example, that an ideologically pure Central Committee should safeguard the RSDLP from 'opportunism', partly by directing a core of dedicated revolutionaries in specialised tasks and partly by expelling 'opportunists'. This was no way, Trotsky argued, to build a party of creative and energetic comrades. Lenin had not, for instance, raised the very serious problem of how each 'professional revolutionary' would ever be linked to the general tasks of the party. Lenin was interested only in a series of robots carrying out orders. But this was precisely the aspect of the factory regime, Trotsky argued, that workers and social democrats most hated. Just as socialism would be firmer the more the workers could take control of their own politics, so the RSDLP would be stronger the more its individual members were capable of independent thought. In turn a democratic and lively RSDLP would be better able to link up with an autonomous and self-active proletariat:

The barracks regime could never be the regime of our Party, no more than the factory could be its model ... The guarantee of the Party's stability must be sought in its base, in the actively, autonomously-acting proletariat. (Trotsky n.d.: 95, 104)

Trotsky combined the different aspects of Lenin's 'substitutionism' into one sentence that has been taken as a prophetic warning of the fate of the Bolshevik Party post-1917:

In the internal politics of the Party [Lenin's] methods lead to the Party organisation 'substituting' itself for the Party, the Central Committee substituting itself for the Party organisation, and finally the dictator substituting himself for the Central Committee. (Trotsky n.d.: 77)

Lenin, Trotsky, intellectuals and the workers' movement, 1905–1917

The theoretical disputes between Lenin and Trotsky about the relationship between intellectuals and the party and between the party and the workers were given a practical test in the Russian Revolution of 1905. Although this point was not made at the time, Trotsky may well have felt that his ideas stood the test of experience better than Lenin's. After all, it was in 1905 that Trotsky argued that the Russian workers founded the most advanced form of democratic socialist politics to date in the Soviets.

Soviets, or councils, were formed in several of the major cities, principally St. Petersburg and Moscow. They were composed of delegates elected by factories and workplaces, for example, on the principle of one delegate per 500 electors. Elections were continuous. There was no fixed membership, which was in a constant state of flux. The Soviets had their executive bodies, but the principle of control and leadership by the worker delegates was fiercely guarded. At the peak of its membership the St. Petersburg Soviet, for example, had some 562 delegates that represented 147 factories, 34 workshops and 16 trade unions. It was overwhelmingly male in composition (only six of its delegates were women), with the largest proportion of deputies coming from the capital's metal workshops and factories. At its second meeting of 14 October 1905 the St. Petersburg Soviet elected a deputy from the Union of Print Workers, Georgiy Khrustalev-Nosar, as chairman. He subsequently outlined the various campaigns that the Soviet led and the tasks it undertook under his chairmanship:

> The Soviet of Workers' Deputies led three strikes (October, November, and the post-telegraph); ... it issued up to 500,000 proclamations and news-sheets to the workers, soldiers, and other groups; ... it declared freedom of the press and implemented this during October in St. Petersburg; ... it attempted to introduce the 8-hour working day; ... it formed self-defence units and armed the workers; ... it organised help for the unemployed; ... it united all St. Petersburg workers; ... it tried to unite the whole working class of Russia in local Soviets and an All-Russian Congress; ... it joined forces with all fighting organisations for joint efforts; ... it aided the coming together of the revolutionary proletariat with the revolutionary army. (Khrustalev-Nosar 1906: 148)

It was at the Soviet's fourth meeting that the role of social-democratic revolutionary intellectuals was outlined. Here an Executive Committee of the Soviet was formed. It consisted of 31 worker delegates, 22 worker deputies from the Soviet and 9 party representatives (3 Bolshevik, 3 Menshevik and 3 Socialist-Revolutionaries). It was as a Menshevik that Trotsky was co-opted onto the Executive Committee. He, like the other 'politicals', had a consultative voice only. This was in keeping with the Soviet's determination to be a non-party body elected by, for, and answerable to the workers. Indeed, although Trotsky worked energetically for the Soviet, winning towards the end of its existence the brief honour of being one of three Co-Chairmen, he subsequently made clear that the main driving force in the Soviet came from the workers themselves:

> On all important questions – strikes, the struggle for the 8-hour working day, the arming of the workers – the initiative came not from the Soviet, but from the more advanced factories. Meetings of worker-electors passed resolutions that were then taken by deputies to the Soviet. In this way the organisation of the Soviet was, factually and formally, an organisation of the overwhelming majority of St. Petersburg's workers ... representatives of the party did not enjoy neither in the Soviet nor in the Executive Committee a deciding vote; they participated in debates but not in the voting. The Soviet was organised by the principle of representation of workers according to factory and profession, not according to party groups. Party representatives could serve the Soviet by their political experience and knowledge, but they could not have a deciding vote breaking the principle of workers' self-representation. (Trotskii 1906: 312–313, 317)

The attempt at workers' self-government in the capital ended in failure when the tsarist police arrested the Soviet delegates and closed the institution. However, Trotsky could take pride in the fact that the model of RSDLP intellectuals aiding and serving autonomous workers in political and economic battles seemed to have worked in the 1905 Revolution.

Trotsky was arrested in 1905 as a delegate to the Soviet. He was subsequently tried and sentenced to internal exile. He escaped and fled abroad. Like Lenin he was to return to Russia following the collapse of tsarism in February 1917. Although sharing the émigré experience, obviously removed from Russian workers by distance and lifestyle, there is some evidence that Lenin and Trotsky continued to differ in their evaluations of the role of the intellectual in the socialist movement. Lenin is often presented as concerned above all with control of the RSDLP. He continued to be obsessed with 'organisational issues', seeing the organisation of the vanguard and its purification from 'opportunism' as the key sign of the movement's health. Trotsky, on the other hand, tried to communicate with workers in a shared language, trying to root his politics in the self-activity of the workers.

Several studies of workers and revolutionaries in St. Petersburg between 1907 and 1917 argue that, to the extent that it existed, workers dominated the socialist movement. These worker-leaders were chiefly skilled, literate male employees of the Russian capital's heavy industries. They were proud to consider themselves the vanguard of the working class and were defensive of their status, prestige and independence. In one of the most detailed accounts of workers and revolutionaries in St. Petersburg of this period, R. B. McKean claims that workers were suspicious of revolutionary-intellectuals. The workers were keen to maintain control of their own demands and would reject advice from revolutionaries. Indeed, McKean's findings support Trotsky's view that the workers would gravitate towards socialism not because of a vanguard of professional revolutionaries but out of their actual work conditions:

> The radicalisation of a minority of skilled male hands (both artisanal and factory) in the two and a half years before the First World War owed far more to the their acquaintance with urban and industrial life than to their peasant roots, their 'youth', the sway of Social Democratic intellectuals or the indoctrination of Bolshevik cadres ... Working-class militants, desirous of self-organisation, opposed the intellectuals' striving to control workers. (McKean 1990: 189, 485)

For McKean, Lenin exerted minimal influence on the workers, partly because he did not share their interest in trades unions and insurance funds. It is also true that Lenin did not succeed in publishing a regular newspaper; the plan of action outlined in *What is to be Done?* remained a 'mirage' (McKean 1990: 71, 77–78, 86, 145, 157–158, 172–173, 179–181, 188–189, 266, 306, 396, 475, 485). Lenin's 'splitting' tactics in organisational affairs perplexed workers who preferred social democrats of whatever label to unite in a common cause. McKean is not impressed by claims that Lenin's tactics did pay dividends from 1912 onwards when 'Bolsheviks' gained control of key trades unions. Such trades unions, McKean argues, were often paper institutions only. The authorities were quite effective at repressing trades unions. Furthermore, local Bolsheviks were not rubberstamps for Lenin's views but displayed independence, often despairing at Lenin's émigré factionalism. McKean does concede, however, that the socialist intellectual who had some support amongst the workers was Leon Trotsky. In 1909 Trotsky began publication of the newspaper, *Truth*. This was produced in Vienna but distribution did reach St. Petersburg. It managed to have some appeal to the workers precisely because it avoided polemical articles of Lenin's style, and was written in an accessible language concerned with the workers' own issues. Indeed, Trotsky sought to make the newspaper the mouthpiece of working-class militants inside Russia (McKean 1990: 51, 59).

Geoffrey Swain is similarly impressed with Trotsky's model of the intellectual in politics over Lenin's. In a study of the St. Petersburg labour movement between 1906 and 1914, Swain claims that conscious workers rejected Lenin's model of vanguard leadership by party committees. A body of largely male, skilled workers showed themselves capable of leading the socialist movement without falling victim to 'revisionism'. Indeed, the conscious workers favoured by Trotsky successfully promoted social-democratic principles in a democratic party organisation. It is for this reason that Swain identifies Trotsky as the 'hero' of his study, claiming that the 'party of 1914 was far more [Trotsky's] creation than Lenin's'. Swain regrets that in the summer of 1917 Trotsky 'declared that his ideas on party organisation were wrong and Lenin was right, and the "mezhraionka" merged ignominiously with Lenin's party' (Swain 1983: 184, 192).

Leninism and Trotskyism, 1907–1940

While it is clear that there were serious differences of opinion on the role of the socialist intellectual in politics between Lenin and Trotsky prior to 1917, it may not be the case that their alliance of that year was a 'bolt from the blue'. After all, in the pre-1917 period there were also strong elements of agreement. Lenin and Trotsky were, after all, self-confessed professional revolutionaries. Both appealed to the workers and tried to influence the workers' actions through the written and spoken word. Both saw themselves as a judge on the current state of the workers' consciousness. Their main occupation was as theorists and writers, with various publication projects as their chief means of communication with the workers. That Lenin and Trotsky had an equal concern with the correct theoretical and tactical response to current issues is clear, for example, in their respective responses to the outbreak of the First World War in August 1914. Lenin and Trotsky agreed that the socialist parties that supported the war effort had struck an irredeemable blow to the Second International. They dubbed the socialist outlook that declared 'peace' with national governments for the duration of hostilities as 'social-patriotism'. Both Lenin and Trotsky launched an ideological crusade against 'social-patriotic' influence over the workers. It is true that Lenin and Trotsky promoted alternative responses to a 'correct' revolutionary socialist response to the war. Lenin favoured turning the imperialist war into a civil war, while Trotsky called for peace as a first step towards an all-European revolution. Nevertheless Lenin and Trotsky acted in similar ways to guide the proletariat to a 'proper' politics.

Furthermore, Trotsky had for long accepted the leadership role of the socialist party over the masses. He may have placed more emphasis upon the party training workers to take up positions of leadership. Indeed in a pamphlet of 1910 directed at the Austrian Marxist Max Adler, Trotsky argued that the intelligentsia was not interested in socialist politics, partly because the workers were successfully producing leaders from within their own ranks. Here, however, Trotsky makes an overly optimistic assumption that the 'most intelligent individuals, groups and strata' from the proletariat to join social democracy would retain a sense of unity with their non-party brethren. In this context, Trotsky distinguishes between the individualistic intellectual and the disciplined worker in terms not dissimilar to the Lenin of *One Step Forwards, Two Steps Back*:

> A worker comes to socialism as a part of a whole, along with his class, from which he has no hope of escaping. He is even pleased with his feeling of moral unity with the mass, which makes him more confident and stronger. The intellectual, however, comes to socialism, breaking his class umbilical cord as an individual, as a personality, and inevitably seeks to exert influence as an individual. (Trotsky 1974a: 8)

Trotsky did not consider that workers promoted to positions of leadership within the socialist movement would lose a sense of unity and association with their less advanced colleagues, becoming a vanguard that substituted itself for the class. Studies of the pre-revolutionary working class, for example, emphasise how workers distinguished amongst themselves by, amongst other factors, dress, language, reading and cultural pursuits. 'Advanced' workers would all too often look down on 'backward' workers (Thatcher 2005). Trotsky did not address the issue of vanguardism arising within the working class, of the likely domination of the socialist movement by a proletarian elite, that his conception of politics also contained the danger of 'substitutionism'. Nor did he raise the issue of what should happen if the 'conscious' workers were unable or unwilling to carry out their assigned tasks. In these circumstances would it be acceptable for an 'intellectual elite' to guide the workers to a revolution? Overall, 'substitutionism' was not a developed and well thought out concept in Trotsky's writings.

In any event, while Trotsky rejected what he took to be Lenin's super-centralism and vanguardism, even Trotsky accepted that the Russian party had to act as a vanguard organisation. This is clear, for example, in discussions of 1907 when some comrades thought that the RSDLP could be re-established as an open, mass party of a West European type, with perhaps as many as one million members. For Trotsky, such a broad-based organisation would 'hinder the real formation of the Social-Democratic Party by consolidating, in terms of programme and organisation, the political primitiveness of the broad masses' (Trotsky 1994: 108). It was precisely the proletariat's low political culture that necessitated, for Trotsky, the vanguard leadership of the social-democratic party. In the context of British politics Trotsky made distinctions that sound remarkably 'Leninist'. Trotsky urged British social democrats not to merge with trades unions and the British Labour Party for they displayed 'bourgeois prejudices' (Trotsky 1994: 119). British, like Russian social democrats, should be an 'independent vanguard, conscious and vigilant'. Only in this way could social democrats fulfil their various 'vanguard' tasks

> [t]o bring consciousness and organisation into the masses who are drawn into the political maelstrom ... to arouse the slumbering class consciousness of the masses, to introduce cells of organisation into its chaotic midst, to train worker-leaders in every factory and workshop, to link the scattered parts of the great whole ... that is the work of our Party. (Trotsky 1994: 66, 145)

In this context Trotsky spoke of being proud to belong to the RSDLP, of which the various factions were equally important elements. He stated his willingness to work with any faction, depending upon which most answered the needs of the moment at any particular instance. Indeed, Trotsky accepted that 'hegemony' in the party would go to whomsoever 'is best able, by its distinctive features, to fulfil the demands of the current period' (Trotsky 1994: 132).

It is perhaps quite natural therefore that when Trotsky joined Bolshevik ranks in the summer of 1917, there was no statement about how contradictory views on organisational matters were now being resolved. There was no admission of 'correctness' on either side for the differences of 1903–1904 had soon lost their significance. Trotsky merely joined a faction of the RSDLP that he thought had the correct response to a political crisis. In the instance of joining, however, organisational matters were probably not uppermost in Trotsky's mind. After all, the Bolshevik faction was still far from the centralised model of *What is to be Done?* This was partly a reflection of the state of political flux typical of all parties and movements of Russia at that time. There were no membership lists and fixed loyalties. These changed rapidly, in rapidly changing circumstances, in a society caught up in constant elections and re-elections. It was also a reflection of splits and disagreements within Bolshevik ranks. The Bolshevik Central Committee, for example, had several competing voices within it. There was no single agreed message. On the eve of the October Revolution, Central Committee members felt able to warn the general press of a policy they did not agree with. Furthermore, it is well to remember that the October Revolution was carried out under Trotsky's strategy of relying upon Soviet institutions, rather than a victory of a Leninist vanguard. Indeed, it has been recently argued that in 1917 the Bolsheviks took many of their policies and slogans from the advanced workers, rather than leading the workers as a vanguard (Marot 1994; Smith 1995).

It was in the post-1917 period, after the October Revolution, that the centralised model of party organisation favoured by Lenin finally came into being. In this process Trotsky supported Lenin; in some instances even running ahead of Lenin's centralisation. This was not a simple and coherent process, but proceeded by fits and starts. One aspect of the emergence of a centralised political system was the suppression of competing political parties. Vanguard politics permitted space for only one vanguard. And within the one remaining political party, the Bolshevik or Russian Communist as it was renamed in 1919, there emerged a vanguard in the central bodies. In part this was a consequence of becoming a party of government. The Communist Party had to be a well oiled, centralised and controlled body, with membership lists, annual congresses and conferences, and numerous government and non-governmental organisations to be staffed. In 1919 the Secretariat, responsible for party administration, was reformed, expanded and became increasingly specialised, with separate departments for information, for organisation and instruction of lower organisations, distribution of party workers, and so on. Also in 1919 the party elite was reorganised into small teams of a Politburo and an Orgburo, to conduct the Central Committee's political and organisational business respectively. In March 1921 the Tenth Party Congress accepted a ban on factions. Henceforth it was a crime to organise opposition to the official platform of the Central

Committee. Then in 1922 a post of party General Secretary was created. This position was understood to be of vital importance, for the post-holder would be responsible for ensuring that local organisations carried out Moscow's orders and that the central institutions operated in a smooth and efficient manner.

The emergence of a centralised vanguard party was accompanied by a new official version of how the October Revolution had occurred. In 1920, Lenin's pamphlet *'Left-Wing' Communism: An Infantile Disorder* was published. This sought to establish Bolshevism as the model for all communist parties to emulate. It argued that in 1917 the Bolsheviks had acted as a classic vanguard, providing the workers with theoretical and organisational guidance. Lenin's message was that the type of body he had promoted since *What is to be Done?* is the essential prerequisite to a successful seizure of power. Trotsky was content to meet the requirements of current Leninist thinking. Trotsky abandoned a previous interpretation of the October Revolution as a defensive act forced upon the Bolsheviks by the masses to guarantee rule by the Soviets, to a carefully planned conspiracy.

It is perhaps a little ironic that just as a Leninist model of a party vanguard was actually created, Lenin and Trotsky began to voice concerns about the health of the vanguard. Both discerned a party of bureaucrats ruling over the ordinary membership. The bureaucrats were not inventive and creative, but carrying out orders from above, shoring up their privileges and acting in a tyrannical manner. Lenin and Trotsky's respective solutions to the problem of bureaucratisation did reflect their pre-1917 differences on the nature of vanguard politics.

Lenin's aim was to downsize the administration, specifically to rid it of non-proletarian petty pen-pushers. Those remaining in post should, according to Lenin, be highly knowledgeable and well trained, and subject to constant re-examination and quality control. Lenin's remedy for bureaucratisation was the creation of small, specialised centres of expertise to guide the further course of the revolution. As his intellectual biographer has recognised:

[Lenin's prescriptions] rested entirely upon the exemplary qualities of what he recognised to be a tiny handful of able, devoted, totally incorruptible men grouped in one exemplary all-powerful institution. Here, at last, was the Jacobin solution, the rule of the men of Virtue. (Harding 1981: 302)

Trotsky thought that the party should put more responsibility upon the proletarian core of the ordinary membership. Allow them to take up positions in political and economic management, to have genuine choice in party elections, and to have full freedom of criticism within the party. Trotsky's answer to the problem of bureaucracy within the vanguard was thus to call for genuine inner-party democracy.

Once again, however, Trotsky's position was not far removed from that of Lenin's. Trotsky offered no concrete proposals of how genuine inner-party democracy would operate. He proposed no model of inner-party pluralism or of a broader form of socialist pluralism. On the contrary, Trotsky continued to insist upon the primary role of a communist vanguard. Trotsky thus refused to take his anti-bureaucracy campaign outside the ranks of the Central Committee. In moments of blind loyalty he declared that 'in the last analysis the party is always right, because the party is the sole historical instrument that the working class possesses for the solution of its fundamental tasks' (Trotsky 1975: 161).

Even when he was expelled from the Communist Party and from the Soviet Union, Trotsky argued that the decisive factor in determining the outcome of a proletarian revolution was the leadership offered by the vanguard, along strict Leninist lines (Trotsky 1974b: 41–42; Thatcher 2003). The problem of the rise of fascism in Germany and elsewhere, for example, was reduced to the incorrect leadership offered by Stalin. With Trotsky in command a communist Germany would have stood alongside a communist USSR. In a diary entry of the mid-1930s, Trotsky made the October Revolution contingent upon Lenin's presence. No Lenin, no revolution. There could be no greater recognition or tribute to the role not only of the intellectual in politics, but of the super-intellectual.

When Trotsky founded the Fourth International it was as a vanguard body. Its genius in understanding world history was premised, however, upon the qualities of its leadership. Under the guidance of the Fourth International, Trotsky envisaged the world proletariat establishing pan-continental Soviet regimes across Europe, the Americas and Asia as stepping-stones to the creation of a world socialist federation. The Trotskyist movement itself, however, would find it hard to survive first without Trotsky, and then the competing factions grouped around competing leaders. The Fourth International remains as a small, but significant aspect of revolutionary politics that operates on the margins of the world's political orders.

Conclusion

There is a tension in Marx's conception of the socialist revolution. On the one hand, there are texts in which the workers' liberation is to be conducted by the workers themselves. Perhaps the most famous example of this is in the preamble to the rules of the First International: 'The emancipation of the working classes must be conquered by the working classes themselves' (Marx and Engels 2000b: 622). On the other, there is also a notion of a communist vanguard, whose special knowledge of the 'march of history' guarantees for itself the role of leadership. In the *Manifesto of the Communist Party*, for example, we read of communists who 'have no interests separate and apart from the proletariat as a whole' (Marx and Engels 2000a: 255). This tension is also evident in the debates in Russian socialism around the structure and nature of the party and its relationship to the working class.

Lenin emerges as a 'vanguardist' *par excellence*, arguing for an intellectual vanguard composed of professional revolutionaries, organised hierarchically. Trotsky appears to defend the workers' self-emancipation, prioritising a leadership from within the working class, having far more rights of dissent. These two views clashed most notably at the polemics that surrounded the Second Congress of the RSDLP. For some historians the history of pre-1917 Russian socialism points to the dominance of Trotsky's conception of the revolutionary process, in which intellectuals serve as auxiliaries to the workers who resolve current issues of the socialist movement. Lenin's model of the RSDLP was not achieved before 1917; indeed it took several years after 1917 for the Leninist vanguard organisation to establish itself.

This version of events has something to commend itself, although it does overlook some similarity in outlook between Lenin and Trotsky in the pre-1917 period. For just as there are two Marxs on the relationship between socialist intellectuals and the masses, so there are two Trotskys, and even perhaps two Lenins. For Lenin and Trotsky a socialist intellectual had an 'advanced' consciousness. They shared many assumptions about the role of the socialist intellectual in politics and in the move towards socialism in particular. Intellectuals could offer either ideological guidance or mystification to the workers. It was the duty of a revolutionary social democrat to take the workers to a socialist consciousness.

It was in establishing and defending a communist state, however, that Lenin and Trotsky's preference for the tutelage of intellectuals over the masses was crystallised in its most extreme form. They came to express worries about the condition of the vanguard, and offered differing remedial advice, but the centrality of a vanguard was not questioned. Ultimately Lenin and Trotsky prioritised the role of the vanguard of socialist intellectuals over the masses. Lenin and Trotsky seemed blind to the likely undemocratic consequences of vanguard leadership, that an elite body, whether of professional revolutionaries or conscious workers, would rebuff any democratic controls from below as opening the floodgates to 'lower' forms of consciousness. Each promoted the tutelage of the socialist intellectuals over the masses via an assumed unity between class and party (Miliband 1977).

In the post-1917 period Trotsky agreed fully with the notion that leadership of Lenin's type was needed to stage a socialist revolution. Furthermore, Trotsky rejected any suggestion that a Leninist vanguard produced the undemocratic politics typical of Stalin's USSR, that Lenin's organisational model led to Stalinism (LeBlanc 1990). Trotsky did not return to the objections against Lenin set out in *Our Political Tasks*. Instead, Trotsky accepted that without a correct vanguard leadership of the wise, there could be no socialism. If the vanguard was thrown off course, it needed to be corrected by another vanguard from the 'proletarian core'. There was no firm definition of what this 'proletarian core' would consist of, other than agreement with views held by Trotsky. The opposition Trotskyist movement, therefore, mirrored the hierarchical control typical of the Stalinist communist parties.

Lenin and Trotsky produced their views on the role of the socialist intellectual in the socialist movement with Russian conditions uppermost in mind. Their views came to dominate Marxist politics more broadly precisely because they managed to hold power in Russia and exert such influence over the formation of communist parties across Europe. The communist parties of the Third International, for example, signed up to a Leninist vanguard model of party organisation. It was a model of Marxist politics also adopted by Trotsky's Fourth International.

Although some commentators stress a Marx that believed in the proletariat's self-emancipation (Draper 1971; Geras 1986), the conflict in his thought between self-acting workers and a vanguard of intellectuals was resolved in Russian Bolshevism in the latter's favour. This aided representations of Marxism as undemocratic, as a utopia that promised liberation but delivered a dictatorship.

Notes

1. See, for example, 'To the Workers of the Semyannikov Factory (1895)'; 'To the Working Men and Women of the Thornton Mill (1895)'; and 'Draft and Explanation of a Programme for the Social Democratic Party (1895/1896). All of these documents are conveniently translated in Harding and Taylor (1983).
2. This study claims that Lenin did not establish close relations with workers, that the strike movement of the 1890s in St. Petersburg was led by a labour elite, not socialist intellectuals, and that the key feature of the capital's working-class movement of the time was the divergence of interests between

workers and socialist intellectuals. Some Russian socialists drew the conclusion that the workers were best placed to know their own interests. Lenin, however, drew the conclusion that 'if labour would not become involved in politics of its own free will, then politics had to be brought to it from the outside by a Social Democratic party elite' (Pipes 1990: 125).

References

Deutscher, I. (1954) *Trotsky: The Prophet Armed*, Oxford: Oxford University Press.

Draper, H. (1971) 'The Principle of Self-Emancipation in Marx and Engels', in R. Miliband and J. Saville (eds), *The Socialist Register*, London: Merlin, 81–109.

Geras, N. (1986) *Literature of Revolution*, London: Verso.

Harding, N. (1981) *Lenin's Political Thought 2*, Basingstoke: Macmillan.

Harding, N. and Taylor, R. (eds) (1983) *Marxism in Russia: Key Documents 1879–1906*, Cambridge: Cambridge University Press.

Khrustalev-Nosar, G. (1906) 'Istoriia Soveta Rabochikh Deputatov (do 26 Noiabria 1905)', in *Istoriia Soveta Rabochikh Deputatov*, St. Petersburg, 45–169.

Knei-Paz, B. (1978) *The Social and Political Thought of Leon Trotsky*, Oxford: Oxford University Press.

LeBlanc, P. (1990) *Lenin and the Revolutionary Party*, London: Humanities Press International.

Lenin, V. I. (1977) *Selected Works 1*, Moscow: Progess Publishers.

Marx, K. and Engels, F. (2000) 'The Communist Manifesto', in D. McLellan (ed.) *Karl Marx: Selected Writings*, Oxford: Oxford University Press, 245–271.

Marx, K. and Engels, F. (2000) 'Circular Letter', in D. McLellan (ed.) *Karl Marx: Selected Writings*, Oxford: Oxford University Press, 620–622.

Marot, J. E. (1994) 'Class Conflict, Political Competition and Social Transformation', *Revolutionary Russia*, 7(2), 111–163.

McKean, R. B. (1990) *St. Petersburg Between the Revolutions*, London: Yale University Press.

Miliband, R. (1977) *Marxism and Politics*, Oxford: Oxford University Press.

Pipes, R. (1963) *Social Democracy and the St. Petersburg Labor Movement, 1885–1897*, Cambridge, MA: Harvard University Press.

Pipes, R. (1990) *Russian Revolution 1899–1919*, London: HarperCollins.

Read, C. (1996) *From Tsar to Soviets: The Russian People and Their Revolution, 1917–1921*, London: UCL.

Smith, S. A. (1995) 'Rethinking the Autonomy of Politics', *Revolutionary Russia*, 8(1), 106–116.

Swain, G. (1983) *Russian Social Democracy and the Legal Labour Movement, 1906–1914*, Basingstoke: Macmillan.

Thatcher, I. D. (2003) *Trotsky*, London: Routledge.

Thatcher, I. D. (2005) 'Late Imperial Urban Workers', in I. D. Thatcher (ed.), *Late Imperial Russia: Problems and Prospects*, Manchester: Manchester University Press, 101–119.

Trotskii, N. (1906) 'Sovet i prokuratura', in *Istoriia Soveta Rabochikh Deputatov*, St. Petersburg, 1906, 311–323.

Trotsky, L. D. (n.d.) *Our Political Tasks*, London: New Park Publications.

Trotsky, L. D. (1974a) *The Intelligentsia and Socialism*, London: New Park Publications.

Trotsky, L. D. (1974b) *Writings of Leon Trotsky 1938–39*, New York: Pathfinder.

Trotsky, L. D. (1975) *The Challenge of the Left Opposition (1923–1925)*, New York: Pathfinder.

Trotsky, L. D. (1994) 'In Defence of the Party', Glasgow: *Journal of Trotsky Studies*, 2, 61–174.

Trotsky, L. D. (1997) 'Doklad sibirskhkh delagatov', *Trotsky Collection Volume 1*, Tokyo: Trotsky Institute of Japan, 100–146.

White, J. D. (2001) *Lenin: The Practice and Theory of Revolution*, Basingstoke: Palgrave.

3
Gramsci and the Intellectuals: Modern Prince Versus Passive Revolution

Peter Thomas

Gramsci is the Marxist theorist *par excellence* of the Intellectuals. Marx and Engels sketched out perspectives for a theory of the social position and efficacy of intellectuals with their analysis of the historical emergence of the division of labour and critique of the deleterious role of 'ideologists' as (conscious or unconscious) defenders of the status quo (most notably, in the *German Ideology*). The *Communist Manifesto* went on to note the class transition of certain types of intellections in periods of revolutionary upheaval. However, writing before the Dreyfus affair in which the term 'Intellectual' was established for the first time as a key word of modern political discourse, Marx and Engels did not offer a comprehensive theory of the structural role of intellectuals in modern societies. Other Marxists have developed themes related to specific aspects of the question of the intellectuals. Brecht's entire intellectual practice, for example, can be regarded as developing a multifaceted aesthetico-philosophical meditation on the potentials for *eingreifendes Denken* (intervening thought) by a new type of intellectual engaged in a practice of dialectical pedagogy; Sartre, from a different perspective, saw the contradictions between the class origins of certain types of intellectual and their ostensible commitment to truth as being resolved in practices of political commitment and solidarity; Critical Theory, in varying forms, from Adorno and Horkheimer to Marcuse to Habermas, posited the intellectual as the privileged site of critique and repository of the best elements of the Marxist tradition in an epoch dominated by the failure of the revolutionary project and the emergence of an increasingly totalitarian and repressive post-war society. No other theorist, however, whether consciously affiliated to the Marxist tradition or not, has offered such comprehensive theorisations of the question of the intellectuals as Gramsci, ranging from detailed historical analyses of their emergence and function in modern societies, their economic and political determinations and their relation to other social practices and categories. These are all united within not only a proposal for the future development of Marxist theory and politics, but a new definition of the historical determinateness and political efficacy of all philosophy and intellectual practice. Viewed from this perspective, we could go beyond the initial affirmation of this essay and declare Gramsci to be *the* theorist of the intellectuals *tout court*.

Within Anglophone Marxism, the most visible of Gramsci's formulations regarding intellectuals have undoubtedly been the categories of the traditional and organic intellectuals. Following upon the 1971 publication of *Selections from the Prison Notebooks* (the first volume to make a significant number of Gramsci's carceral researches widely available in English in a thematically organised form, including a section dedicated to the theme of the intellectuals), these categories were diffused throughout Anglophone Marxism and the broader Anglophone intellectual culture as a central element of what Chantel Mouffe described in 1979 as the reign of 'gramscism' (Mouffe 1979: 1). Cultural Studies, in particular, lying at the crossroads of the Anglophone humanities and social sciences, benefited from the reception of Gramsci at a moment when it was entering a consolidating, institutional phase of development. As Stuart Hall has noted on numerous occasions, Gramsci's category of the organic intellectual, and his own personal example, seemed to offer the fledgling discipline a model for the integration of political commitment with a serious intellectual research project (Hall 1992: 281).

More recently, Gramsci's theorisations of the intellectuals have been challenged by alternative approaches with more tangential relations to the Marxist tradition. The concept of the 'specific intellectual', for example, associated with Deleuze and Foucault, has been widely perceived as more useful for grasping the disciplinary and control procedures of the neo-liberal new world order (cf. Foucault 1980: 128); one particularly influential cultural studies critic has gone so far as to argue for 'Foucault's much greater "useability" [than Gramsci's] in the contexts in which, today, intellectual work has and needs to be done' (Bennett 1998: 62). Nevertheless, in a period in which the wisdom of the rash dismissal of Gramsci along with all things Marxist as 'superannuated' is slowly beginning to be questioned, it may perhaps be timely and salutary to return to the letter of Gramsci's texts with a view to determining the continuing relevance of his researches for contemporary politics and social theory. Such a return necessarily involves placing Gramsci's treatment of the question of the intellectuals within the overarching structure of the theoretical laboratory of the *Prison Notebooks*, as the horizon within which their integral meaning becomes visible.[1] For 'the intellectuals' constitute not merely one theme indifferently arranged alongside others which can be untimely ripped from their context without significant conceptual loss. On the contrary, Gramsci's theorisation of the role of intellectuals in modern societies constitutes the point of departure for his initial historical researches, and occupies a central theoretical position in his subsequent reformulation of the fundamentally political status of philosophy within the Marxist *Weltanschauung*. The full significance of categories such as the traditional and organic intellectuals, therefore, only becomes apparent when they are considered in the context of both the historical conjuncture and the theoretical problematic in which they emerged, and to which they were designed as concrete political responses.

The guiding thread that organises all of Gramsci's carceral researches can be succinctly characterised as *the search for an adequate theory of proletarian hegemony in the epoch of the 'organic crisis', or 'passive revolution', of the bourgeois 'integral state'*. Gramsci appropriated the concept of 'passive revolution' from Vincenzo Cuoco. He transformed it, in the first instance, in order to provide an analysis of the distinctive features of the Italian *Risorgimento* (Q1, 44).[2] However, it soon became clear to Gramsci that the concept could have a more general significance and be used to indicate the road to modernity taken by those nation states lacking in the radical-popular 'Jacobin moment' which had distinguished the experience of the French revolution and, further, to signify the particular pacifying and incorporating nature assumed by bourgeois hegemony in the epoch of imperialism. As Domenico Losurdo has argued:

> Beginning with the defeat of the workers and popular classes in June 1848 and further with that of 1871, a phase of passive revolution begins, identifiable neither with the counter-revolution nor, even less, with the political and ideological fall of the dominant class. The category of passive revolution is a category used in the *Prison Notebooks* in order to denote the persistent capacity of initiative of the bourgeoisie which succeeds, even in the historical phase in which it has ceased to be a properly revolutionary class, to produce socio-political transformations, sometimes of significance, conserving securely in its own hands power, initiative and hegemony, and leaving the working classes in their condition of subalternality. (Losurdo 1997: 155)[3]

'Wandering between two worlds, one dead, the other powerless to be born'[4]: if the bourgeois passive revolution of Gramsci's time was still able to produce limited forms of historical progress, its logic of disintegration, molecular transformation, absorption and incorporation nevertheless remained dedicated to one goal: prevention of the cathartic moment[5] in which the subaltern classes cross the Rubicon separating a merely 'economic-corporative' phase from a truly 'hegemonic' phase. In other words, the goal of the passive revolution was to stop the subaltern social layer becoming a genuine class, agent and actor within history.[6]

This policy of 'permanent structural adjustment' *avant la lettre* was thrown into crisis by the Russian Revolution of 1917, whose significance was immediately understood by the young Gramsci, famously saluting it as *'The Revolution against "Capital" '*. In so far as the Soviets demonstrated the return of a concrete possibility of an alternative modernity to that of a continual passive revolution by a degenerating bourgeoisie, it necessarily produced a crisis of confidence in existing regimes and gave stimulus to subaltern movements on an international scale. This was particularly the case in the two Western European countries in which passive revolution had been the rule rather than the exception for social transformation and modernisation in the later half of the nineteenth century, Italy and Germany, both immediately wracked by profound social and political upheavals. The subsequent rise of Fascism in Italy and the crushing of the revolutionary workers' movement in the Weimar Republic (ultimately paving the way for the emergence of National Socialism) were essentially attempts to manage this crisis by exaggerating and intensifying the logic of the pre-antediluvian status quo (acceleration of 'revolution' from above, closer integration of the state and civil society, abolition of previous limited forms of independent political expression and organisation of subaltern groups). If these reactionary movements succeeded in rebuffing a combatative workers' movement, they nevertheless introduced elements of risk, division and explicit conflict into the passive revolutionary project that destabilised its fundamental presuppositions. Indeed, the very 'success' of Fascist reaction intensified the structural crisis of bourgeois hegemony, producing an *Ausnahmezustand* (state of exception) which would not be resolved with a return to the dull compulsion of (relatively) stable parliamentary and institutional incorporation until after the Second World War when the various national bourgeoisies had marched their respective working classes through rivers of blood. Gramsci's response to this crisis, from the years of *Ordine nuovo* in the Turin workers' movement, through the founding years of the PCI (Italian Communist Party), his intense polemics with Bordiga and direct involvement in the work of the International, to the early years of the still fragile Fascist regime, right up until his imprisonment and his final precarceral text (*The Southern Question*), was of a singular and consistent nature. He attempted to translate one of the central terms of the Russian revolutionary experience and Lenin's political theory and practice in particular – to wit, that of *gegemoniya* (hegemony) – into a theory adequate to grasp the specific conditions obtaining in the West and to construct the forms of proletarian hegemony suitable for overthrowing them. This remained the leit motif of the entire *Prison Notebooks'* project, despite or because of its (only seemingly) fragmentary nature; but when Gramsci begins to write his first notebook in 1929, over two years after his initial arrest, it was developed within a new theoretical problematic which had a decisive significance for grasping the political function of the intellectuals and the distinctive nature of proletarian hegemony.

'Formation of the groups of Italian intellectuals: development, attitudes (*atteggiamenti*)' was the third theme which Gramsci wrote in his first prison notebook (on 8 February 1929) (significantly, it had been immediately proceeded by the theme, 'Development of the Italian bourgeoisie until 1870').[7] In the early phases of his research, Gramsci continually returns to the theme of the intellectuals from various perspectives, including those derived from previous researches in the Marxist tradition into the general consequences of the division of labour and the deleterious role of 'ideologists/ideologues' (under the rubric of Lorianism – cf. in particular Q1, 31–63). Nevertheless, his central concern in these early notebooks remained the same as that of *The Southern Question*: a determination of the historical and structural specificity of the Italian nation state, the combined and uneven development of Italian capitalism (particularly between the industrial north and the still predominantly rural south), consequent formation of distinct types of intellectuals within the Italian social formation (Q3, 39), and absence of radical-popular Jacobin moment producing an organic fusion between the people and intellectuals (who had remained, by and large, in the cosmopolitan role descending from the Renaissance (Q3, 63)). From the outset Gramsci announced the perspective which shaped all of his considerations on the question of the intellectuals: 'The term intellectual must be taken to mean not only those social strata who are traditionally termed intellectuals, but in general the whole social mass that performs functions of organization in the broad sense: whether in the realm of production, culture or public administration: they correspond to the non-commissioned officers and to the lower ranks of officers in the army' (QI, 43).[8] Later, he added the following central formulation:

> The intellectuals have the function of organising the social hegemony of a group and its domination at the level of the state, that is, the consensus given by the prestige of their function in the productive world and the apparatus of coercion for those groups which neither actively nor passively 'consent', or for those moments of crisis of command and of leadership in which spontaneous consent suffers a crisis. From this analysis there results a very large extension of the concept of the intellectuals, but only in this way does it seem to me to be possible to arrive at a concrete approximation to reality. (Q4, 49)

This expanded concept of the intellectuals is symptomatic of and can only be understood within a new theoretical problematic, progressively clarified throughout the *Prison Notebooks*, but present from the outset: that of the 'integral state'.[9] The initial stimulus for this 'expanded' definition of the state was Gramsci's well-known characterisation of the differential types of (bourgeois) state formation in Russia and Western Europe: 'In the East, the state was everything, civil society was primitive and gelatinous; in the West there was a just relation between state and civil society and in the trembling of the state one noticed immediately a robust structure of civil society' (Q7, 16). It soon became clear to Gramsci, however, that an adequate comprehension of this 'just relation' required an expanded concept of the state *as such*, the higher, more advanced form making visible the secret anatomy of the lower. This expanded concept of the state was crucial for grasping the distinctive logic of the passive revolution, its persistent, structural capacity for incorporating subaltern energies, limiting them to merely 'economic-corporative' moments within the existing institutions and preventing them from progressing to their own political (i.e. potentially hegemonic) forms. According to this concept, the state (in its integral form) was not to be limited to the machinery of government and legal institutions (the state understood in a strict or limited sense, 'political society', in opposition to 'civil society'). Rather, the concept of the integral state was intended as a dialectical unity of the moments of both civil society and political society, a 'historical block' of the base and the superstructures[10], the terrain upon which social classes compete for social and political leadership or hegemony over other social classes; a hegemony guaranteed, 'in the last instance', by capture of the legal monopoly of violence embodied in the institutions of political society.[11] 'The State is the entire complex of practical and theoretical activities with which the ruling class not only justifies and maintains its dominance, but manages to win the active consent of those over whom it rules' (Q 15, 10). Within such an integral state, in the institutions of civil society where hegemony is contested just as much as those of political society where it is consolidated and guaranteed, the intellectuals of opposed social classes play a decisive role (varying according to the particular nature of that class's hegemony) of leadership, articulation of interests and coordination of initiatives of the ideologies which arise upon a given mode of production and are the forms in which 'men become conscious of this conflict [between classes] and fight it out' (MECW 29, 262).[12] There is no 'organisation without intellectuals', Gramsci declared (Q11, 12), thereby raising the implicit question of the particular types of intellectual corresponding to particular types of organisations.

The expanded concept of the intellectuals within an expanded concept of the state had two important consequences. First, it permitted Gramsci to resist a reductive economistic analysis of the question of intellectuals based upon their class background (a tendency which has not been absent in certain traditions within Marxism, particularly in its Stalinist and Maoist formations). Rather, he comprehended the intellectuals on the basis of their actual function in the reigning relations of production and their political correlates. 'He comprehended them not primarily from the circuit of capital as a professional group or according to the measure of their self-image as great intellectual heroes, but rather, under the aspect of their organising function in the ensemble of social relations and division of labour' (Demirovic and Jehle 2004: 1268–1269). Gramsci's class analysis of the intellectuals was therefore of a fundamentally political nature: intellectuals may be determined, in the first instance, by their position in the relations of production (though in a highly mediated form)[13], but their class position *qua* their social function as intellectuals is only realised to the extent to which they are 'organically' fused with the political aspirations of a class, rather than deduced from their personal class origins.

Second, with the emphasis upon social and political organisation rather than specific intellectual activity, Gramsci explicitly rejected a theory according to which intellectuals form a homogenous social group distinct from social classes, or even an independent class. 'The intellectuals do not form an independent class, but each class has its intellectuals' (Q1, 44).[14] Rather than a horizontal relation between intellectuals across classes, Gramsci argued that there existed a vertical organisation of intellectuals of varying ability and efficacy (and varying degrees of political consciousness of their roles) within classes, according to the previously quoted metaphor drawn from the ranks of military officers. This vertical relation extends across the (artificial) division between political society and civil society, so that there is a closer relation between intellectuals of the same class performing seemingly distinct functions, than there is between intellectuals of different classes engaged in similar activities.[15] If a horizontal relationship predominated within the logic of the passive revolution, 'an atmosphere of solidarity of all intellectuals' (Q1, 44), this was to be explained as a function of the hegemonic position of one class, subordinating and exerting influence on all other subaltern social layers, including their intellectuals.

It is in the context of this multi-faceted analysis that the categories of the traditional and organic intellectuals receive their meaning. In both instances, Gramsci highlights the intimate relation between these figures and transformations of the mode of production, but, equally, stresses that they are subject to a decisive *political* mediation. Thus, if 'Every social group, born on the original terrain of an essential function in the world of economic production, creates at the same time organically one or more ranks of intellectuals', it is nevertheless the case that such organic intellectuals of the new class gain their 'homogeneity and consciousness of their own function'– that is, become genuinely organic to the new class *qua* class – 'not only in the economic, but also in the social and political field' (Q12, 1–A text; Q4, 49). However, both the constitutively intellectual and political nature of these organic intellectuals' activity, *qua* intellectuals and *qua* organisers of their class, was usually obscured, according to Gramsci, by an already existing intellectual order. 'But every "essential" social group, emerging into history from the preceding economic structure and as an expression of its (i.e. this structure's) development, has found, at least up until now, pre-existing social categories which appear as representatives of a historical continuity uninterrupted even by the most complicated and radical transformations of social and political forms' (Q12, 1). These 'traditional intellectuals' were in fact the organic intellectuals of a previously emergent and now consolidated and dominant social class, unwilling, at best, or, at worst, unable, to recognise their continuing political function. (Gramsci's immediate reference was the situation of the intellectuals of the Catholic Church in Italy, seemingly independent of social classes, but originally 'organically linked to the large land owning sections of the aristocracy'). 'Since these various categories of traditional intellectuals feel with an *"sprit de corp"* their uninterrupted historical continuity and their "qualification", they posit themselves as autonomous and independent from the dominant social group' (Q12, 1). A preliminary political task of the organic intellectuals of an emerging social group, therefore, was to contest the prestige enjoyed by the traditional intellectuals, the projection of their own image as that of the intellectuals *tout court*. It was by means of this that they posited their own specific activities and priorities as defining the very nature of intellectual activity and its location in the social relations as such (thus Gramsci's continual insistence upon the criteria of organisation and social function for defining the intellectuals, rather than the nature of intellectual activity).

Such was the condition confronted by the new organic intellectuals of the workers' movement in Gramsci's Italy, in a culture dominated by the traditional intellectual Benedetto Croce. Croce seemed to be elevated up into some Olympian zone above the fray of immediate politics where his 'philosophy of freedom' patiently and inexorably elaborated itself – the all too finite evidence of fascist reaction and regression notwithstanding. Such was Croce's and similar figures' dominance of the terrain of 'intellectuality' that it had become difficult even to recognise the organic intellectuals of an emerging but still subaltern social class as 'intellectuals' at all. Gramsci comprehended this element of Croce's seemingly 'merely' intellectual practice *politically*. Albeit in a highly mediated form, Croce's organisation of an intellectual order claiming its autonomy from immediate politics in fact played an important role in guaranteeing the continuance of contemporary bourgeois hegemony. By means of its established prestige and consequent power of attraction for new initiatives, Croce's doctrines produced

> perhaps the greatest quantity of 'gastric juices' to assist the process of digestion. Set in its historical context, the context of Italian history, Croce's work appears to be the most powerful mechanism for 'conforming' the new forces to its vital interests (not simply its immediate interests, but its future ones as well) that the dominant group possesses, and I think that the later has a proper appreciation of his utility, superficial appearances notwithstanding. (Quoted in Buci-Glucksmann 1980: 21)

Croce was not merely 'a constructor of ideologies for governing others' (Ibid.); with his dominance of the definitions of intellectual practice, he was a 'realiser of the passive revolution' (Frosini 2003: 56), actively preventing others from constructing ideologies in order to govern themselves.

Armed with his concept of the integral state as the terrain on which competing classes contested for social and political hegemony, however, Gramsci was well placed to understand the transformation of these once organic intellectuals into traditional intellectuals and their subsequent dominance of definitions of intellectual activity as themselves products and symptoms of the hegemony of the class whose interests they served and organised (whether consciously or not). They were the necessary complements, at the level of social agents, of the 'speculative' phase of thought which accompanied the achieved hegemony of a social class, the form in which a class refined its 'ideology' (intimately bound to its current class interests) and presented it as 'philosophy' (generally valid, across class boundaries, and with a purchase on the future). At a decisive moment in the *Prison Notebooks* (in Notebook 11, the notebook in which Gramsci presented his most detailed proposal for a 'philosophy of praxis'), Gramsci posed two questions which redefined the nature of philosophy as the *Weltanschauung* of a class, and thus, also, the status of those whose task it was to organise and diffuse such a *Weltanschauung* in the concrete forms of the various superstructures:

1. Is the 'speculative' element essential to every philosophy, is it the form itself which every theoretical construction as such must assume, that is, is 'speculation' a synonym for philosophy and theory?
2. Or must the question be posed 'historically': the problem is only a historical problem and not a theoretical one in the sense that every conception of the world, in a determinate historical phase, assumes a 'speculative' form which represents its apogee and the beginning of its dissolution? Analogy and connection with the development of the state, which passes from the 'economic-corporative' phase to the 'hegemonic' phase (of [active] consent). It can be said that every culture has its speculative or religious moment, which coincides with the period of complete hegemony of the social group which it expresses, and maybe coincides precisely with the moment in which the real hegemony is dissolved at the base, molecularly, but the system of thought, precisely because of that (in order to react to the break-up) is perfected dogmatically ... Criticism must therefore resolve speculation into its real terms of political ideology, of an instrument of practical action (Q11, 53).

In order for the workers' movement to counter the logic of the bourgeois passive revolution, it needed to elaborate its own hegemonic apparatus, within the relations of production as well as in the superstructures, a hegemonic apparatus not merely antagonistic to that of the bourgeoisie, but really distinct from it, in a relation of real contradiction. At the level of philosophy, this involved opposing the ruling class's restricted, speculative 'owl of Minerva' with a new conception of philosophy, posed in 'realistic' and 'concrete historical' terms capable of a wide diffusion among all subaltern layers: a 'philosophy of praxis' oriented to the future and a new social order. At the level of the intellectuals, those whose role it was to articulate and organise such a new popular *Weltanschauung*, it called for the creation of a qualitatively new type of intellectual which would be both adequate to the specific tasks of the emerging class, and capable of exercising hegemony on the terrain of 'intellectuality' over and against the already established traditional intellectuals of the dominant class. 'The assimilation and "ideological" conquest of the traditional intellectuals', Gramsci argued, will be 'quicker and more effective the more the given group elaborates simultaneously its own organic intellectuals' (Q12, 1). The elaboration of these intellectuals, Gramsci repeatedly acknowledged (e.g., Q4, 55), would involve a long and tortuous process, for reasons both internal to the political development of the working class movement in its totality (structurally consigned to a subaltern position within the bourgeois state, its own distinctive group of intellectuals would be developed only insofar as the class as a whole struggled to emerge from its 'economic-corporative' phase and exercise genuine class-based hegemony), and because of the power of attraction and incorporation exercised by the 'organic intellectuals of the passive revolution' through their dominance of the existing intellectual order.

Nevertheless, the question remained: what would be the nature of these organic intellectuals, the features which would distinguish them from the existing traditional intellectuals and permit them both to exercise hegemony within the intellectual order (thus neutralising the role played by figures such as Croce as organisers of the passive revolution in the superstructures) and to make an adequate contribution to the distinctive social forms which would be necessary to forge proletarian hegemony? In order to answer this question, it is necessary to consider an alternative line of historical and theoretical research that had accompanied Gramsci's consideration of the question of the intellectuals from the beginning of the *Prison Notebooks*. Central to this had been Gramsci's condemnation of the enduring cosmopolitanism of the Italian intellectuals and their failure to assist in forging a national-popular unity – the absence in the Italian *Risorgimento* of the 'Jacobin moment' that distinguished the French

Revolution. Gramsci traced this failure back to the particular model of intellectuality that had emerged in the Renaissance, counterposing it to the more thoroughly popular experience of the Reformation.[16] Occurring earlier, the (Italian) Renaissance had elaborated a sophisticated intellectual culture superior to that which accompanied the later (Germanic) Reformation, a more popular experience of spiritual and moral reform which only much later, in German Idealism (and, ultimately, Gramsci suggested, in its transformation in the Marxist tradition), had generated a comparably sophisticated higher intellectual order (cf. Q4, 3). The Renaissance, however, for all of its strengths, had not been able to establish any organic relation with the masses, either before its heyday or after; when intellectuals formed in that tradition were confronted by the emergence of the Reformation, their attitude was one of detachment and incomprehension (Gramsci's continual reference was Erasmus's condemnation of Luther: *'ubicumque regnat lutheranismus, ibi literarum est interitus'* (Q4, 3; Q16, 3, i).

   This was precisely the tradition of intellectuality continued, in a modified form, during the *Risorgimento* in the nineteenth century and by Croce in the early twentieth century. Their relationship to the masses necessarily remained 'bureaucratic' and 'formal'; they were structurally incapable of making the transition from knowledge (*sapere*) to comprehension (*comprendere*) to feeling (*sentire*), and vice versa; 'the intellectuals become a caste or priesthood (organic centralism)' (Q4, 33). In effect, they were the 'specific intellectuals' of their own time, remaining on the terrain of 'technique' and unable to progress to a political comprehension of their social function of leadership and organisation. Viewed in a historical perspective, Gramsci argued, these intellectuals were the modern inheritors, in a suitably laical form, of the relationship of merely formal unity between the intellectuals and the masses established by the Roman Catholic Church. In this case, the intellectuals had been seen as custodians of ideas (theology), enjoying the privilege of certain innovations within doctrinal limits, while the masses were denied any active participation in the social intellectual order, left in their condition of retarded development, superstition and prejudice (Q11, 12, iii).[17] Similarly, for the organic intellectuals of the passive revolution and particularly in Croce's philosophic system, the intellectuals were responsible for the various moments of truth, comprehended under the concept of 'philosophy'; to the masses was left only 'ideology', compromised by its involvement in practical affairs.[18]

   The new organic intellectuals and new intellectual order envisaged by Gramsci broke decisively with this tradition. For the intellectuals organically linked to the proletariat's hegemonic project, it did not suffice to make 'individual "original" discoveries'; rather, their role was much more one of being 'permanent persuaders' (Q4, 72–Q12, 3), critically diffusing already discovered 'truths' as the basis for a new society (Q11, 12). They attained their status as intellectuals not as specialists in any particular field of knowledge, but rather, as 'leaders' (Q4, 72), or 'organisers of a new culture' (Q12, 1). 'The position of the philosophy of praxis is antithetical to this Catholic [position]', and thus, implicitly, also to that of Croce and similar figures. It 'doesn't tend to leave the "simple people" in their primitive philosophy of common sense, but rather, to lead them to a superior conception of life. If it affirms the exigency of contact between the intellectuals and the simple people, it is not in order to limit scientific activity and in order to maintain a unity at a low level of the masses, but precisely in order to construct an intellectual-moral block that renders politically possible a mass intellectual progress and not only of small groups of intellectuals' (Q11, 12, iii). Whereas the traditional intellectuals contributed to the passive revolution by denying to the masses the access to the intellectual resources they needed in order to engage in an expanding dialectic of activity and consciousness, these permanent persuaders would find their intellectual resources precisely in their organic integration with the masses, in a reciprocal relationship of 'democratic pedagogy' in which the intellectuals would be at least as often 'the educated' as 'the educators'.[19] They would be intellectuals who were 'organically the intellectuals of these masses', working out and making coherent the principles and problems which the masses had posed in their own practical activity, and thus building a cultural and historical block (Q11, 12, iii).[20]

Gramsci famously characterised this cultural and historical block, echoing Machiavelli, as a 'modern Prince' (Q8, 21; Q13, 1), or the fusion of a qualitatively new type of political party and oppositional culture that would gather together intellectuals (organisers) and the masses in a new political and intellectual practice, 'organising the organisers'. Bourgeois hegemony, particularly in the form of the passive revolution, was characterised by a state of continual 'disinformation', deception, pedagogy-as-discipline and exclusion; it was imposed from above and did not aim to reduce the distance between organisers and the organised – on the contrary, it erected institutional and structural barriers to such expansive democratic practice. The 'modern Prince', on the other hand, or the adequate institutional form of proletarian hegemony, was nothing more than an 'active and effective expression' of the process of formation of a 'national-popular collective will' and 'intellectual and moral reform' (Q8, 21).[21] Intensifying the expansion of the social functions of intellectuals that had occurred in the modern world, it instituted a form of pedagogy-as-democratic practice, continually striving to reduce the distance between its 'intellectuals' and the broader popular masses. At its limit, all members of the 'modern Prince' were to be considered as intellectuals, not merely in the sense that 'there are no non-intellectuals' (Q12, 3), but in the integral sense that they would all perform the social function of organic intellectuals of their class, that is, 'organisers', 'permanent persuaders', 'constructors of a new and higher form of civilisation'.

Just as its Machiavellian predecessor, Gramsci's 'modern Prince' remained no more than a proposal for the future, not a concrete reality, in his time – and in our own.[22] It is one of the measures of the extent to which Gramsci remains our contemporary that the theory of the intellectuals and the qualitatively new conception of intellectual practice that he forged in a Fascist prison cell remain today a horizon for our own intellectual and political practice in the epoch of neo-liberal passive revolution. For whatever the substantial differences between Gramsci's theoretical, political and cultural contexts and our own, his insights into the forms of a possible proletarian hegemony retain today their fertility for further theoretical and practical investigation, awaiting the energies and initiatives of a reviving working class movement which alone will be able to confirm and to transform them in practice. Gramsci's theory of the intellectuals challenges us to take up his necessarily incomplete project: Valorisation of existing intellectual practices organic to the working class movement, organisation of a new intellectual order, diffusion of practices of democratic pedagogy and construction of the institutional forms adequate to their expansion – in short, the formation of a 'modern Prince' on the changed terrain of an aggressive neo-liberal postmodernity.

Notes

1. In this sense, the commencement of the English translation of Valentino Gerratana's integral critical edition of the *Prison Notebooks* by Joseph Buttigieg in 1992 constituted a landmark in Anglophone Gramscian scholarship. The completion of this ambitious multi-volume undertaking will undoubtedly open a new season of Gramscian scholarship within Anglophone Marxism, richer and subtler than the first because the distinct literary and conceptual challenges of the *Prison Notebooks* will be able to be adequately confronted. As several passages decisive for the present study have not yet been translated in the English critical edition, all quotations have been taken from the Italian critical edition edited by Valentino Gerratana, *Quaderni del carcere*. Translations

are my own. References are to individual notebooks and numbered notes: thus, for example (Q12, 1), refers to *quaderno* (notebook) 12, note 1.

2. Gramsci originally used the term 'revolution without revolution', adding 'passive revolution' at a later date in the margins. Elsewhere, he employed the term 'royal conquest' and not 'popular movement' (Q3, 40).

3. Cf. also the following argument of Pasquale Voza: 'The concept of passive revolution, born as a radical re-elaboration of the expression of Cuoco, is always posited, even when it refers to the *Risorgimento*, as a concept valid for connoting and interpreting the mode of formation of modern states in nineteenth century continental Europe' (Voza 2004: 195).

4. Matthew Arnold, *Stanzas from the Grande Chartreuse.*

5. Gramsci's initial discussion of the concept of 'catharsis' took place as a critique of Croce's aesthetics, particularly as Croce deployed it in his reading of the tenth Canto of Dante's *Inferno* (Q4, 78–88). However, it subsequently became a decisive term in Gramsci's political vocabulary, used to indicate the structural conditions which determine the capacity of a class to emerge from subaltern passivity and elaborate its own concrete political initiatives. 'The term "catharsis" can be employed to indicate the passage from the purely economic (or egoistic-passional) to the ethico-political moment ... from being an external force which crushes humans, which assimilates them and makes them passive, the structure is transformed into a means of freedom, into an instrument for the creation of a new ethico-political form, into the origin of new initiatives. Fixing the "cathartic" moment thus becomes, in my view, the point of departure for the whole philosophy of praxis' (Q10 II, 6).

6. This was precisely the position of Lenin, one of Gramsci's central points of reference throughout the *Prison Notebooks*: 'From the standpoint of Marxism the class, so long as it renounces the idea of hegemony or fails to appreciate it, is not a class, or not yet a class, but a *guild*, or the sum total of various guilds ... It is the consciousness of the idea of hegemony and its implementation through their own activities that converts the guilds as a whole into a class' (Lenin 1963: 231–232).

7. On the 19th of March 1927, in a letter to Tatiana Sucht, Gramsci had previously listed four themes for further study; in the first position was research into the history of Italy in the nineteenth century, with particular reference to the formation and development of Italian intellectuals.

8. Cf. Gramsci's famous criterion that 'All men are intellectuals ..., but not all men have the function of the intellectuals in society' (Q12, 1).

9. For the most comprehensive discussion of the concept of the 'integral state' and the central role of the intellectuals within it, see Buci-Glucksmann (1980), particularly 19–118. Cf. also Rottger (2004). Anderson (1976) is the most well-known critique of this concept.

10. Gramsci comprehended 'the superstructures' (in the plural) in a non-reductive or epiphenomenal sense – that is, he viewed the superstructures not as mechanically derived from an originary 'base', but as constituting a dialectical unity or 'historical block' with the dominant relations of production, the means by which they were organised, guaranteed, and made to endure. This was a central element of his refutation of Croce's critique of Marxism as a not so disguised neo-Platonism for whom the economy was a type of demiurge. On the theme of Gramsci's critical relation to Croce, see Frosini (2003, 54–56, 123–134).

11. It is necessary to stress this element, against interpretative traditions, from Italian proponents of a 'historical compromise' to Eurocommunists to contemporary advocates of a nebulously defined radical democracy, which have attempted to confine Gramsci's theory of hegemony to a war of position in the trenches of civil society. It is only within the problematic of the integral state as a dialectial unity of both civil society and the state (understood in a limited sense) that Gramsci's theory of proletarian hegemony becomes comprehensible, as a theory of the political constitution of an alliance of subaltern classes capable of exercising leadership over society and against its class antagonist, necessarily progressing to the dismantling of the state machinery which provides the ultimate (coercive) guarantee for the bourgeoisie's (consensual) hegemony.

12. Alongside the *Theses on Feuerbach*, Gramsci translated Marx's 1859 *Preface* to the *Contribution to the Critique of Political Economy* in an early period of his incarceration. It constituted a touchstone throughout the *Prison Notebooks*, a text to which Gramsci continually returned in order to gain new theoretical insights.

13. 'The relationship between the intellectuals and the world of production is not immediate, as occurs for the fundamental social groups, but is "mediated" in different grades, by the entire social fabric, by the complex of superstructures, of which the intellectuals are precisely the "functionaries" ' (Q12, 1).

14. Cf. also the following passage: 'In order to analyse the social functions of the intellectuals it is necessary to research and examine their psychological attitude (*atteggiamento*) toward the great classes that they [the intellectuals] place in contact in diverse fields' (Q1, 43).

15. 'The methodological error with the widest diffusion seems to me to be that of seeking this essential characteristic in the intrinsic features of the intellectual activity and not instead in the system of relations in which it (or the grouping which embodies it) is found in the general complex of social relations. In truth: (1) the worker isn't specifically characterised by manual or instrumental labour ... but by this labour in determinate conditions and in determinant social relations' (Q4, 49). Similarly, Gramsci implicitly suggests, the intellectual should not be specifically characterised by intellectual labour, but by the position of this intellectual labour in determinant social relations.

16. Gramsci made an explicit comparison between the double opposition Renaissance-*Risorgimento*/Reformation-French Revolution on numerous occasions. See, for example, the following: 'the Reformation is related to the Renaissance as the French Revolution is to the *Risorgimento*' (Q3, 40).

17. Gramsci noted another failure to create any organic link between the intellectuals and the masses in previous philosophies of immanence, a philosophic and political limitation which he argued needed to be overcome in the new philosophy of 'absolute immanence', that is, the philosophy of praxis (Q11, 12).

18. Gramsci went further and suggested that the limited (and limiting) unity between intellectuals and popular classes of the Catholic Church was in fact superior to the purely bureaucratic relation to popular initiatives implicit in Crocean and modern Italian idealist philosophy (in Gentile's 'actualism', the relation was explicitly secured by the institutions of the Fascist state).

The Catholic Church at least attempted to integrate the lower orders into a (more or less) 'organic unity'; idealist philosophy, on the other hand, contented itself with a merely formal relation to the masses and was unable to elaborate the concrete institutional forms necessary for a genuinely comprehensive *Weltanschauung* – a limitation most noticeable in its failure to challenge the role of religious education in schools.

19. Gramsci's translation of the *Theses on Feuerbach* in the preparatory phases of researches was decisive for this perspective of democratic pedagogy, the third thesis in particular.

20. At one stage, Gramsci went so far as to define this new type of intellectual as a 'democratic philosopher' who 'is convinced that his personality is not limited to his own physical individual, but is an active, social relation of transformation of the cultural environment' (Q10, II, 44).

21. Valentino Gerratana underlines this aspect of Gramsci's conception of the distinctive nature of proletarian hegemony, noting that 'While for the hegemony of a class that tends to conceal the antagonism of interests it is sufficient to attain a passive and indirect consent – and this is the normal form of political consent in democratic-bourgeois or authoritarian regimes-, in the perspective of the hegemony of the proletariat "it is a question of life and death – Gramsci writes – not passive and indirect consent, but that which is active and direct, the participation therefore of individuals, even if that provokes an appearance of disaggregation and of break-down" (Q15, 13)' (Gerratana, 1997: 126).

22. Gramsci's concept of the 'modern Prince' cannot, therefore, be reduced to a mere metaphor for already existing political institutions or parties. Rather, like Machiavelli's 'concrete "phantasy" ' (Q8, 21), it was posited as the non-existing element necessary to fill the constitutive lack of the present, in order to open it to the future. The political party, Gramsci argued, was the historically given form in which the decisive elements of organisation, unification and coordination had already begun to occur. Its re-elaboration into a non-bureaucratic instrument of proletarian hegemony, however, required an ongoing dialectical exchange with the popular initiatives from which the modern Prince emerged and into which it sought to intervene. 'The modern Prince, the myth-Prince, cannot be a real person, a concrete individual. It can be only an organism, a social element in which the becoming concrete of a collective will, partially recognised and affirmed in action, has already begun. This organism is already given by historical development; it is the political party, the modern form in which gathers together the partial, collective wills that tend to become universal and total' (Q8, 21).

References

Anderson, P. (1976) 'The Antinomies of Antonio Gramsci', *New Left Review*, 100, 5–79.

Bennett, T. (1998) *Culture: A Reformer's Science*, London: Sage.

Buci-Glucksmann, C. 1975 (1980) *Gramsci and the State*, D. Fernbach (trans.), London: Lawrence and Wishart.

Demirovic, A. and Jahle, P. (2004) 'Intellektuelle' in *das historisch-kritische Wörterbuch des Marxismus* 6/11, W. F. Haug (ed.), Hamberg: Argument, 1267–1286.

Foucault, M. (1980) *Power/Knowledge: Selected Interviews and Other Writings 1972–1977*, C. Gordon (ed.), New York: Pantheon.

Frosini, F. (2003) *Gramsci e la filosofia*, Roma: Carocci.

Gerratana, V. (1997) *Problemi di metodo*, Roma: Editori riunti.

Gramsci, A. (1975) *Quaderni del carcere*, V. Gerratana (ed.), Torino: Einaudi.

Hall, S. (1992) 'Cultural Studies and its Theoretical Legacies', in L. Grossberg, C. Nelson and P. Treicher (eds), *Cultural Studies*, New York: Routledge, 277–294.

Lenin, V. (1963) *Collected Works* 17, Moscow: Progress.

Losurdo, D. (1997) *Antonio Gramsci dal liberalismo al 'comunismo critico'*, Roma: Gamberetti.

Marx, K. and Engels, F. (1975–) *Marx-Engels Collected Works* (MECW), London: Lawrence and Wishart.

Mouffe, C. (ed.) (1979) *Gramsci and Marxist Theory*, London: Routledge.

Rottger, B. (2004) 'integraler staat', in *das historisch-kritische Wörterbuch des Marxismus* 6/11, W. F. Haug (ed.), Hamberg: Argument, 1254–1266.

Voza, P. (2004) 'Rivoluzione passiva', in F. Frosini and G. Liguori (eds), *Le Parole di Gramsci*, Roma: Carocci, 189–207.

4

'Unhappy Consciousness': Reflexivity and Contradiction in Jean-Paul Sartre's Changing Conception of the Role of the Intellectual

Leon Culbertson

Jean-Paul Sartre articulated two distinctly different conceptions of the role of the intellectual. He cited the events of May–June 1968 as central to the precipitation of circumstances that necessitated a move from the *classic* to the *revolutionary* intellectual (sometimes also referred to by Sartre as the 'leftist' or 'new' intellectual). This chapter will argue that it would be a mistake to regard a specific set of political events as *solely* responsible for bringing about this alteration in Sartre's position. The chapter will attempt to place Sartre's changing conception of the role of the intellectual within the wider context of his own pre-reflective 'fundamental project' as an intellectual. The chapter will explore the dialectical relationship between Sartre's abandonment of literature as a bourgeois art form in favour of existential biography, his political writing and action and his changing conception of the role of the intellectual. This will be done in a manner that is broadly consistent with the dialectical nominalism he developed in the *Critique of Dialectical Reason*. The themes of contradiction and reflexivity will be highlighted to illustrate the dialectical understanding Sartre's own work can give of his conception of the role of the intellectual.

In short, Sartre faced fundamental contradictions in all the areas considered here. His praxeis[1] can be understood as attempts to transcend those contradictions. His praxis was deviated by the inertia of the situation in which he existed at any given time, creating new constraints and conditioning future praxis. Sartre's attempts to transcend the contradictions of his situation are therefore reflexive. In thinking about the intellectual Sartre is engaged in a reflexive act; he is thinking about his *own* role as much, and perhaps more so, than anyone else's role. The issue of the role of the intellectual is not simply an abstract theoretical problem for Sartre; it is a deeply personal and concrete *dilemma*.

It is this emphasis on the role of Sartre's thought on the intellectual in *his own* project *as* an intellectual that marks this chapter as distinctly different from the others in Part I of this text. The other chapters look to the thought of different Marxist thinkers with a view to illuminating Marxist thought on the role of the intellectual as a whole by considering specific features of the work of each thinker. While this chapter broadly attempts to do the same, the point which I take to be most significant from that exercise in relation to Sartre is the need to pay much closer attention to the role of the intellectual as a concrete historical individual with a complex past, individual project and deeply entrenched prejudices and theoretical blind spots. The concrete situation of the *individual* intellectual is not the result of individual caprice, or of any form of determinism, but is rather a complex product of the dialectical interaction of a unique individual orientation towards the world and shared social, historical, cultural and political constraints which condition that orientation *from birth*, not from the age at which one is old enough to vote or earn wages.[2]

It must be acknowledged that the issue of Sartre's fundamental project and the degree to which this can be characterised as reaching a concrete manifestation in his role *as* an intellectual is complex and requires far closer attention than is possible here. If space had permitted, consideration would also have been given to Sartre's philosophical work, particularly his political philosophy and ethical thought. What will be provided here is an overview of a way of thinking about Sartre's own conception of the role of the intellectual and a dialectical sketch of *some* of the relevant terrain.

Sartre's abandonment of literature

Sartre's post-war politicisation is first evident in his advocacy of 'committed literature', but Flynn (1979) points out that, 'it appears that at the very time he is elaborating a theory of committed literature in *What is Literature?* Sartre is himself losing confidence in the power of art to change men's situations' (Flynn 1979: 162). This is a fundamental contradiction faced by Sartre in his adoption of the role of an intellectual.

Although Sartre was born in 1905, his upbringing left him inculcated with the bourgeois ideology of pre-1848 France. The primary instrument for, and expression of, such inculcation was literature.[3] Yet, as Scriven (1984) notes, 'Sartre's writing activity is ostensibly an attempt to radicalise literature, to engage literature in the socio-political events of the contemporary world, an attempt to undermine the image and practices of the traditional writer' (Scriven 1984: 10). This is a fundamental contradiction, which Sartre never fully succeeded in escaping. Sartre's biographies of nineteenth-century bourgeois writers such as Baudelaire, Mallarmé and Flaubert are the product of his fascination with the culture and ideology into which he was indoctrinated as a child (see Scriven 1984: 13).

For Sartre, literature appeared universal, and therefore classless, prior to the fall of the July Monarchy in 1848. Literature was a central part of the universal ideology of the advancement of mankind. This, however, was challenged by the emergence of class-consciousness after the events of 1848 and the continuing development of science. While God had been 'obliged to retire back to Heaven' (Sartre 1974a: 234) by the end of the seventeenth-century, by the mid-late nineteenth-century this 'Hidden God' was now a Dead God. With the death of God came the decline of the universal ideology of literature. This was followed by a period where the acquiescence of writers in the ideological, and consequently material, march of bourgeois capitalism was so complete that they effectively said nothing for 40 years prior to 1900. Literature became an entrenched, institutionalised, alienating myth, through which the reader was indoctrinated in 'squalid nonsense' (Sartre 1967b: 112). It should be remembered, however, that this is not simply an objective analysis conducted by a twentieth-century writer blessed with hindsight. Sartre uses the expression 'squalid nonsense' in describing how *he himself* was for a long time persuaded of the emancipatory potential of bourgeois literature and art for art's sake.

If, as Scriven (1984) claims, 'bourgeois literary criticism exists in order to consecrate literature as the quintessence of bourgeois ideals, while masking its class origins beneath a conciliatory universal rhetoric' (Scriven 1984: 16), then that is certainly not what Sartre felt literature *should* be. As Caute (1998) points out: 'The thesis [of *What is Literature?*] is clear: literature, properly employed, can be a powerful means of liberating the reader from the kinds of alienation which develop in particular situations. By this process the writer also frees himself and overcomes his own alienation' (Caute 1998: ix). For Sartre, literature is not a universal, classless practice. Yet there is a clear contradiction between

Sartre's position and the concrete practices of his own writing at least prior to 1940 and possibly even as late as the mid-1950s. This is exactly the opposite of what we might reasonably expect from Sartre given his view of literature. In fact, his mature view of literature was slow in developing. Prior to 1940 he detached literature from politics and the social and historical situation in which he existed. The contingency of existence as described in *Nausea* was given significance by Sartre's idealistic faith in bourgeois literature. It would be an oversimplification to regard 1940, or even the Second World War, as the point at which Sartre saw the light and changed his position on literature. Rather, he changed his position on literature (and politics and the role of the intellectual) as part of a gradual process.

Scriven (1984) has argued correctly that the late 1940s and early 1950s should be viewed as a period of transition. The emergence of the notion of 'committed literature', which is most clearly articulated in *What is Literature?*, and exemplified in a move towards existential biographies (*Baudelaire, Saint Genet and Mallarmé, or the Poet of Nothingness*) was not the terminal point of Sartre's *volte-face*. Committed literature allowed Sartre to continue with all the forms of writing he had engaged in before, with the addition of existential biography. This would not change until the end of the 1950s.

Scriven argues that committed literature attempts to fuse class struggle and bourgeois literature and the result is the subordination of class struggle to the established myth of Literature. He concludes that, 'there is a sense in which the residual aspects of Sartre's pre-war ideological mystification are still present in his post-war theory of committed literature' (Scriven 1984: 18). Even Lyotard correctly identifies the same contradiction and effectively accuses Sartre of bad faith (roughly, self-deception) in his adoption of the role of the intellectual as a means of escaping confrontation of the contradiction. He claims: 'A doubt began to undermine the redemptive role he has accorded to the writer ever since the revelation that befell him in his captivity. Yet he did not elaborate that doubt, but rather rid himself of it by shifting from the writer's vocation to the "intellectual's" [sic] an identical responsibility for curing the world of alienation' (Lyotard 1986: xi).

Counter to Scriven's interpretation Sartre claims, in an interview with Simone de Beauvoir in 1974, that the growing role for politics in his life did not diminish the value of literature because 'political action ought to build up a world in which literature could be free to express itself' (de Beauvoir 1985: 167). He also claims that at the time of his *rapprochement* with the Communist Party in the early 1950s (1952–56) – precisely the time that Scriven claims Sartre was in a transitional phase which would lead to his abandonment of literature – he was 'dedicated to literature' (de Beauvoir 1985: 167). Despite this, however, Sartre claimed in 1971 that, 'there is a sense of style in *The Words* because the book is a farewell to literature: an object that questions itself must be written as well as possible' (Sartre 1977b: 111).[4] While it may be a matter of historical importance whether the interpretation outlined by Scriven (1984) is correct or not, the central issue here is whether there was in fact a fundamental contradiction. Not only does this appear to be true, but also Sartre's claim that there was 'no more literature' (Sartre 1977b: 131) and description of *Words* (published in 1963) as a 'farewell to literature' suggests that Sartre was fully aware of the contradiction.

Clearly, literature, politics, philosophy and the role of the intellectual are not discrete issues in relation to Sartre's life; they are dialectically linked in a synthetic whole and do not in themselves exhaust any description we might give of that whole. What are given here are really descriptions of the same contradictions from different perspectives.

Sartre's political writing and action

During the 1930s Sartre was not a member of any political organisation, nor did he adopt a public position in any of the major political events of the time. This is in contrast to many other French intellectuals during this period. Despite spending the academic year 1933–1934 in Berlin, Sartre wrote nothing on the rise of Nazism, or indeed, any other political events of the time. While he did have political opinions, he kept them private and tended to view political events from a purely theoretical perspective (see Drake 2003: 30).

When asked if he had ever been tempted to join the International Brigades in Spain, Sartre admitted that 'it never even occurred to me' (Sartre 1978: 46).[5] He regarded his commitment at this point as purely a theoretical one because he had not suffered at the hands of fascism or the bourgeoisie, both of which he detested. For Sartre, the existence of the bourgeoisie was essential for him to have something to rail against.

Sartre had adopted the project of the life of a writer and during the 1930s there was no place for political commitment in Sartre's conception of that role. During the 1930s and early 1940s Sartre's individualism and 'preference for the oblique communication proper to imaginative literature and the fine arts' (Flynn 1979: 158) prevented him from becoming politically active. Despite this, Sartre did feel that political engagement was something he could foresee for himself.

Prior to the Second World War Sartre's sympathy for the working class was outweighed by his view that there was a conflict between Marxism and individual freedom. Reflecting on this period Sartre claimed that 'every man is political. But I did not discover that for myself until the war, and I did not truly understand it until 1945' (Sartre 1977a: 44–45). He continues:

> Before the war I thought of myself simply as an individual. I was not aware of any ties between my individual existence and the society I was living in. At the time I graduated from the Ecole normale, I had based an entire theory on that feeling. I was a 'man alone', an individual who opposes society through the independence of his thinking but who owes nothing to society and whom society cannot affect, because he is free. That was the evidence on which I based everything I believed, everything I wrote, and everything I did in my life before 1939. During the whole period before the war I had no political opinions, and of course I did not vote. I was very interested in the political speeches of Nizan, who was a Communist, but I also listened to Aron and other Socialists. As for me, I felt that what I had to do was write, and I absolutely did not see writing as a social activity. (Sartre 1977a: 45)

Sartre claimed that the war divided his life in two, marking a 'transition from youth to maturity' (Sartre 1977a: 48). For the first time Sartre's own freedom had been negated. This made him aware of the material constraints on freedom, and both intentional and unintentional reciprocity. He was led to re-evaluate his conception of *his own* role as a writer. While this did not lead him to determinism, it did lead to an appreciation of the situated nature of freedom in concrete reality. It was only a short step from this philosophical awareness to an appreciation of the need for political engagement. Freedom is always constrained and constraining – freedom always comes with responsibility. For Sartre, the key responsibility was that of exercising, through political commitment, the freedom to which he was condemned.

Sartre displayed this change of heart in the early 1940s. He wrote and staged the play *Bariona, or the Son of Thunder*,[6] which had the theme of resistance, while in a prisoner of war camp in Trèves. The play was performed on Christmas Day 1940. In March 1941, following his release/escape[7] from the prison camp, he was instrumental in the formation of a resistance group called *Socialisme et Liberté* (Socialism and Freedom).[8] He also staged another resistance play called *Les Moches* (*The Flies*) in

Paris in 1943. Even the frequently cited slogan – 'Hell is Other People' (Sartre 1955: 47) – from *Huis Clos* (*No Exit*) in 1944 is as much a comment on totalitarianism as it is on individualism.[9]

Adopting political commitments is one thing, but that does not mean that those commitments were always wise. Birchall (2004) is acutely aware of this. For example, he claims that 'Sartre undoubtedly made some colossal misjudgements about the nature of Stalinism' (Birchall 2004: 2), and 'made many rash and imprudent claims' (Birchall 2004: 3).[10] Sartre conceded that he had made many mistakes, but claimed that these were not 'mistakes of principle' (de Beauvoir 1985: 400). He claimed in 1974 that he was still 'wholly in agreement' with his past (de Beauvoir 1985: 400).

Responding to de Beauvoir's enquiry as to which mistakes Sartre made, he replies: 'Not having joined in violently and wholeheartedly with certain people when I was of the right age to do so' (de Beauvoir 1985: 400). Sartre is referring here to the non-Communist left. Contrary to other claims he made that such a thing did not exist in France prior to 1968, Sartre is acknowledging that he did not do all that he could have done to strengthen his connections with such groups. He notes that, 'to the left of the Communists there were groups that challenged the official communism and that were sometimes right on a great many points. I did nothing to get to know them. I let everything that was to the left of the Communist Party drop until '66' (de Beauvoir 1985: 400).[11]

It is Sartre's mistakes which reveal a contradiction at the heart of his political commitments. As Birchall (2004) recognises: 'There were great weaknesses in Sartre's political stance. All too often he made choices in terms of the short-term alternatives available, and ended up siding with the big battalions of the established left rather than looking to the longer-term potential in the situation, though to his credit he did so primarily out of a belief that without the mass of the working class nothing could be achieved' (Birchall 2004: 4).[12] Birchall may wish to give credit to Sartre for the principle which motivated his actions, but the fact is that Sartre was wrong and within a few years he would have a philosophical understanding of that fact in the form of his 'Theory of Practical Ensembles' in volume one of the *Critique of Dialectical Reason*, and perhaps more importantly, his discussion of the deviation of collective praxis in the unfinished volume two of the *Critique*. These philosophical insights, however, came largely as a result of the apparent contradiction in his approach to Stalinism throughout much of the 1950s. Birchall (2004) correctly identifies this contradiction in claiming that Sartre chose the Stalinist PCF in favour of the anti-Stalinist left because the PCF constituted a far larger group and for Sartre the larger the group, the more likely it was to have an impact on the present situation. The smaller groups of the anti-Stalinist left could not, in Sartre's view, affect the present; to choose them would have been to resign himself to the idea that change could not come *at that time*. While he acknowledged the strength of the arguments made by the anti-Stalinist left, Sartre chose the practical option in an attempt to affect the situation in which he found himself. His hope was that anti-Stalinism would eventually have the strength to replace the PCF (Birchall 2004: 7).

Flynn (1979) gives a similar explanation in claiming that Sartre felt that, at that particular time, the Communist Party was a necessary vehicle for political action on the part of French workers (and presumably also French intellectuals as a consequence of their need to communicate with the workers). For Sartre, this was a necessary compromise *at that time*, but one that he entered into strictly on his own terms. Hence, his claim in *The Communists and Peace* that: 'The purpose of this article is to declare my agreement with the Communists on precise and limited subjects, reasoning from *my* principles and not *theirs*' (Sartre 1968b: 68 – original emphasis).

The approach Sartre took to political commitment following May–June 1968 shows some similarities with that which led him into such a mess over Stalinism and the PCF, yet it also shows a distinct difference. Like his political action during the 1950s, the late 1960s and 1970s saw Sartre siding with groups with whom he could never agree on more than *certain* principles. The obvious example here is Sartre's involvement with the Maoists. Sartre was prepared to lend his support despite disagreements. The significant difference, however, was the fact that Sartre no longer felt that the only hope lay in a large, structured organisation like the PCF.[13]

The issue of the role of the intellectual synthesises the contradictions faced by Sartre as viewed from the perspectives of literature and politics. Unsurprisingly, therefore, Sartre's conception of the role of the intellectual changed. However, Sartre described this change as resulting from the events of May–June 1968. Yet the fundamental contradictions outlined below suggest that those events identified the need for such a change, yet the need had always been there. In addition, the new conception of the role of the intellectual advocated by Sartre was, in at least his own case and possibly more generally, a fundamental impossibility.

Sartre's 'unhappy consciousness': Two conceptions of the intellectual

The classic intellectual

Sartre draws a distinction between 'technicians of practical knowledge' (Sartre 1974a: 238) and classic intellectuals. They are both members of the same occupations, but function differently. Technicians of practical knowledge are 'implicitly entrusted with the task of transmitting received values'. They exploit the authority of their specialised knowledge to 'camouflage dominant ideology as scientific laws' (Sartre 1974a: 238). Sartre claims that because knowledge is practical it is incorrect to regard classic intellectuals as those who work exclusively with their intelligence. He does not define classic intellectuals solely in terms of their profession, but he does regard them as those who employ 'techniques of practical knowledge' (Sartre 1974b: 286). While classic intellectuals employ techniques of practical knowledge, they are distinct from technicians of practical knowledge because they employ those techniques in quite a different way.

Sartre illustrates this distinction with the example of scientists working on atomic fission to improve their nation's atomic arsenal. If those scientists collectively act to alert the public to the danger of atomic weapons, then they become classic intellectuals rather than technicians of practical knowledge. The key elements here are the fact that they move outside their area of expertise, they exploit either their notoriety or their authority as 'experts', and they protest on the basis of value judgements rather than technical grounds (see Sartre 1974a: 230–231). While the technician of practical knowledge perpetuates dominant ideology, the classic intellectual challenges such ideology. They both achieve their respective goals by virtue of their acknowledged expertise.

Sartre notes, however, that there is a fundamental contradiction to the role of the technician of practical knowledge. The aim of the knowledge developed by such individuals is the good of all, whether he or she is a writer, a scientist, a teacher or an engineer. However, the same contradiction faces all technicians of practical knowledge:

> The totality of their [technicians of practical knowledge] knowledge is conceptual, that is to say universal, but it is never used by *all* men; it is used, in the capitalist countries, *above all* by a certain category of persons belonging to the ruling classes and their allies. Thus the application of the universal is never universal, it is particular; it concerns *particular people*. (Sartre 1974b: 286)

So the procedure by which the technician of practical knowledge works, and the way that he or she gains knowledge is *universal*, yet such technicians are objectively tied to the ruling class. The knowledge gained by the technician of practical knowledge is not of universal benefit. On the contrary, such knowledge benefits *particular* classes. The awareness on the part of an individual of the fact that the universal enterprise is actually in the interest of a particular group is what Sartre refers to (borrowing an expression from Hegel) as 'unhappy consciousness' (Sartre 1974b: 287). It is this 'unhappy consciousness' that characterises the intellectual *qua* intellectual. The key distinction here is between the technician of practical knowledge who is unaware of the contradiction inherent to their role (and therefore reproduces dominant ideology), and the classic intellectual who is aware of the contradiction and acts to challenge dominant ideology as a result of this awareness.

It would be wrong to imply that Sartre thought more highly of the classic intellectual than the technician of practical knowledge. While his comments on the technician of practical knowledge are disparaging,[14] his comments on the classic intellectual are vicious:

> Who listens to them? In any case, they are intrinsically weak – they *produce* nothing and possess nothing but their salary to live on, which prevents them from standing up for themselves in civil society, let alone political society. Intellectuals are thus ineffective and unstable; they compensate for their lack of political or social power by taking themselves for an elite qualified to deliver judgement on everything – which they are not. Hence, their moralism and idealism (they think as if they were already living in the distant future and pass judgement on our times from the abstract point of view of posterity). (Sartre 1974a: 229)

Sartre argued that intellectuals should show solidarity with those engaged in struggle in whatever manner possible. During the period between 1945 and 1968 he wrote a great number of political articles for both French and international publications, particularly *Les Temps modernes*, the journal he founded in 1945 with Simone de Beauvoir and Maurice Merleau Ponty. He also conducted numerous interviews with the national and international media. He took part in political discussions, 'was a signatory to an open letter to the President of the Republic, and engaged in polemics with other intellectuals' (Drake 2003: 33). In addition he was a signatory to countless manifestos, regularly made public speeches, wrote a number of prefaces to books with political themes, 'was the author of a number of reportage and gave countless press conferences' (Drake 2003: 33).[15] Despite this activity Sartre concluded, following the events of May–June 1968, that a new role was necessary for the intellectual; he referred to this as the 'revolutionary intellectual'.

The revolutionary intellectual

Sartre came to regard the contradiction faced by the classic intellectual as ultimately insurmountable by the praxis of such intellectuals. He claimed that, 'organization of demonstrations by committees cannot in itself alter the very kernel of the nature of the intellectual in our society, as someone who is condemned to be in perpetual contradiction, in so far as he does the opposite of what he wants to do and helps to oppress the people he should want to liberate' (Sartre 1974b: 289).[16]

For Sartre, May 1968 was not the result of intellectuals becoming aware of a contradiction and wishing to surpass that contradiction; it was the result of students who had an understanding of the situation and were adamant that they did not want to be like the classic intellectuals. In many cases students had completely broken with their role as 'apprentice intellectuals'. Instead they had taken jobs in factories in an attempt to eliminate the distance that separated them from the proletariat. In time, this led to a change in their use of language to the point that they no longer spoke the language of the intellectual. The problem faced by Sartre was that his age made such a transformation almost impossible. The best he could hope for was a compromise.[17] He claimed that there had been an abandonment of the idea that intellectuals 'speak' to the proletariat. The role of the intellectual was no longer the production of theories. It was necessary to forge 'a direct relationship with those who demand a universal society, i.e. with the masses' (Sartre 1974b: 292). Sartre was not optimistic about the role that could be played by those who were established as intellectuals prior to May 1968, regardless of their age at the time. He saw little hope of re-educating intellectuals and cited the individualism of most intellectuals as an insurmountable problem. He identifies the 'ideological interests' (Sartre 1974b: 292) that intellectuals have as a result of the works that they have already produced. The idea here is not simply that if an individual has identified with a position they are not inclined to change. What Sartre has in mind is based on the notion of the 'practico-inert', the material consequences of previous praxis. Works published by intellectuals are 'real, material objects'; they are the 'objectification' of the individual (Sartre 1974b: 292). This creates an inertia that must be transcended, altered or accepted. Regardless of which is chosen by the individual, the existence of such work makes the intellectual 'different from the man who, let us say, punches tickets on the underground all day' (Sartre 1974b: 293). Sartre points out that 'you have a past that you can't repudiate. Even if you try to, you can never repudiate it completely because it's as much part of you as your skeleton. This gives rise to a problem – what can you ask of a forty-five year old who already has an extensive production behind him?' (Sartre 1974b: 292).

Sartre often claimed that as there was no equivalent to the ultra-left prior to May 1968, it would have made no sense for an intellectual to work in a factory in the 1930s or 1940s. At that point the only option was to join the Communist Party or, if one did not agree with the party, become a fellow traveller.[18] Sartre claims that the task which must occupy the intellectual post-1968, is that of placing what he or she has learned 'directly at the service of the masses' (Sartre 1974b: 294). This means that intellectuals must have an understanding of what Sartre refers to as the 'concrete universal',[19] because it is this approach to the general ideas of intellectuals that the masses need (Sartre 1974b: 294).[20]

After May 1968 Sartre faced a major problem because not only was he a classic intellectual who was aware of the need to change completely his role, but he was engaged in the project of writing *The Family Idiot*, his 2801 page *unfinished* existential biography of Gustave Flaubert.[21] This project had been an ambition of Sartre's for around 25 years and he had been working on it for 15 years. It made no sense to Sartre to abandon the project, yet he recognised that it illustrated the fact that he had changed very little as a result of the events of May–June 1968; he remained a classic intellectual. The problem with the *Flaubert* was that it was an example of 'intellectual knowledge' which the masses had 'neither the time nor the means' to tackle, at that historical juncture (Sartre 1974b: 295).[22] Sartre notes:

> There is certainly something ambiguous here, and I felt it while composing the book. On the one hand, the fact that I deal with someone from the nineteenth century and am concerned with what he did on June 18, 1838, can be called an escape. On the other hand, my aim is to propose a method on which another method can be constructed, and that, in my opinion, is contemporary. Also, when I look at the content, I have the impression that I am escaping – and perhaps this is somewhat the case – and when, on the other hand, I look at the method, I have the feeling that I am of the moment. (Sartre 1977b: 131)

Sartre continues, however: 'I am certain that if I were fifty today, I would not begin the *Flaubert*.'[23] Sartre regarded himself as having been radicalised 'in another direction' (Sartre 1974b: 296) between May 1968 and becoming director of *La Cause du peuple* in 1970. This radicalisation did not prevent Sartre from continuing with *The Family Idiot*, and it certainly did not mean that he agreed with the Maoists on very many issues, but it was still (in his eyes) a commitment 'to the side of the people' (Sartre 1974b: 296).

The contradiction here is clear. Sartre cannot be the revolutionary intellectual that he claims the historical situation requires, precisely, because he has produced the work which in many ways has brought him to the point where he is able to identify the need for the revolutionary intellectual. Had he not already been an intellectual then perhaps he could have adopted the necessary role, yet had he not been an intellectual already it is unlikely that he would have been able to identify the need for the revolutionary intellectual. Also, Sartre continues to work on the *Flaubert* despite being faced with the practical problem of intellectuals. One might argue (as Sartre was aware) that in working on *The Family Idiot* he was simply avoiding facing the problem of the role of the intellectual.[24] Sartre's claim that the method employed in the book is of great value at that historical juncture, even if the topic of the book is a form of escape simply doesn't answer the objection here. Sartre's assumption is that the *Critique of Dialectical Reason* is a work which addresses the issues necessary to solve the problem of the role of the intellectual, but this is clearly not the case. If the revolutionary intellectual has to communicate effectively with workers the *Critique* is not the way to do it. The *Critique* is rarely appreciated by philosophers and political theorists, let alone workers; its length and complexity are not conducive to a wide readership. The real contradiction is that Sartre rarely met workers and did not understand them. The problem is not, as Foucault claimed, that Sartre is a man of the nineteenth century trying to think of the twentieth, but that he is a bourgeois intellectual trying to understand workers.[25]

The dialectical intelligibility of the development of Sartre's conception of the intellectual

An approach broadly consistent with Sartre's existential psychoanalysis – exemplified in his existential biographies of Baudelaire, Genet, Mallarmé, Tintoretto, Flaubert, and his own autobiography, *Les Mots* (*Words*) – would regard Sartre's adoption of the role of an intellectual as related to his role as a writer. The role of a writer was pre-reflectively adopted as a means of giving significance to the contingency of his Being. The origins of this 'original project' (Sartre 1958: 565) are to be found in Sartre's childhood. Yet Sartre quickly finds that his fundamental project faces a contradiction. As Scriven (1984) points out: 'Sartre begins practising literature at a historical juncture at which, more than any previous time, the literary institution is being radically called into question. ... Literature is impossible at the moment at which Sartre begins to write'. Literature was impossible at this time because it had become 'an oppressive ideological force, an alien institution which makes unreasonable demands on writer and public alike' (Scriven 1984: 19).

Sartre experienced an alienating and lonely childhood in which he was immersed in the culture of the French bourgeoisie under Louis-Philippe and inculcated with those values (despite having been born in 1905). Central to this was a particular conception of the nature and role of literature. During the 1930s he faced the contradiction outlined by Scriven. The Second World War politicised Sartre, but as Birchall notes, this was not purely an external determinant.[26] On the contrary, Sartre encountered the Second World War from a particular perspective because of the material constraints imposed by the praxis of his childhood and early adulthood. His transcendence of those constraints in the concrete historical situation of the Second World War did not lead to an abandonment of literature, but the emergence of the concept of committed literature. This was as much the creation of a new role for himself (the committed writer) as it was the creation of a new form of culture (committed literature); Sartre's praxis was reflexive.

Sartre's 'involvement' with Stalinism and the PCF ultimately demonstrated to him that there was a contradiction in his conception of the committed writer. This contradiction has been highlighted by Birchall (2004) – the working class could not succeed through the Party and if the Party were the only way that the working class could achieve anything, then they were unable to make significant changes to their situation. In the course of writing the *Critique*, Sartre identified the root of the problem in his discussion of the 'Theory of Practical Ensembles' and the deviation of collective praxis. His analyses of the French and Russian Revolutions move him much closer to understanding the problems faced by the working class in contemporary capitalist economies (although not necessarily to understanding the working class themselves). The deviating impact of structure within a group is a fundamental contradiction which can only be overcome through a form of perpetual revolt found in the concept of the 'group-in-fusion' (the spontaneous formation of an unstructured group in the face of a shared threat).[27] This insight marks a change in Sartre's political involvement – he became much more willing to make alliances regardless of the size of the group and the specifics of their ideology. Sartre was prepared to lend his support to groups with which he did not necessarily agree on more than some basic fundamental principles. In this sense, Sartre's political activity of the late 1960s and 1970s is a prototype of the anti-capitalist movement which has emerged since the late 1990s. Anti-capitalist demonstrations could be viewed as examples of the formation of groups-in-fusion because the whole group is a spontaneous gathering despite the fact that many of the individual groups which comprise the larger gathering are highly organised.

The events of May–June 1968 reveal another contradiction, however. Despite having some understanding of the deviation of collective praxis and a basic idea of the best strategic approach to the instigation of social change, it became apparent that a fundamental re-thinking of the role of the intellectual was required. Not only was a new form of intellectual necessary, but Sartre could not be one of those new intellectuals because of the practico-inert product (material consequences) of his previous praxis (his ideological interests – the weight of his published work and public pronouncements). True to the spirit of the view found in the *Critique* that true totalisation is impossible and that all totalisations are open-ended 'de-totalised totalities, Sartre ends his life with new questions and new ideas (regardless of one's opinion of the status of *Hope Now*, a text of recorded discussions between Sartre and his secretary, Benny Lévy, which are often regarded as a manipulation of the ailing Sartre by Lévy). Sartre found that social and political existence was as contradictory as that he had outlined in the ontology of *Being and Nothingness*.

It is easy to view Sartre's political writing and action, whether overtly philosophical or practical (of course, everything was always both simultaneously), as driven by a strategic aim – a free socialism, yet that would be to neglect the reflexive dimension which Sartre was always so careful to try to preserve in his accounts of the praxeis of others. Sartre's political involvement is as much a quest to found his contingent existence – ultimately in the role of the intellectual – than it is a drive to destroy capitalism. The two dimensions are dialectically linked and cannot be considered fully in isolation from one another. Of course, Sartre found exactly what he always knew he would find – his existence could not be contained in the role of the intellectual. While he implied that the reason for this was that he was too old to adopt the new role of the revolutionary intellectual, he was perhaps a little guilty of bad faith here. He was continually pre-reflectively aware that the new intellectual would have no more success in founding his or her existence than Sartre had himself.

Conclusion: reflexivity and contradiction

Sartre regarded the intellectual as facing a fundamental contradiction. Intellectuals rarely originate from the working class and always speak a language of abstract generalisation. Clearly this is not very helpful if one wishes to assist the working class. This contradiction is found in Sartre's own lack of concrete engagement with workers, which rendered him hopelessly optimistic about the privileged insight of the working class and the salience of the morality of their praxis. Furthermore, this optimism is inconsistent with his own position in much of his published work, particularly *Search for a Method* and *Critique of Dialectical Reason*. Sartre's philosophical writing struggles constantly with contradiction: Praxis deviated by the inertia of matter and the praxis of others, the unity and reciprocity of collectives lost to structure and organisation, the 'singular' or 'concrete universal' and human existence which 'is what it is not and which is not what it is' (See Sartre 1958: 58, 63, 67 and 68; 1999: 211). By the 1970s Sartre found himself escaping reality while claiming to be wholly contemporary in working on *The Family Idiot*. In his political commitments Sartre was also pulled in different directions – he never agreed with the PCF yet he sided with them for years and he assisted groups with whom he had only very general agreement despite the fact that his ethical thought insisted on the importance of particularism. If this is not confusing enough, Sartre began writing literature as literature became impossible to write.

The identification of contradiction presents us with nothing but questions. Some understanding of Sartre's action is provided by sensitivity to the fact that the praxis described here is *Sartre's* praxis. *He* lived *this* contradiction, and his praxis aims at the transcendence of the concrete situation in which he found himself at each historical juncture. In understanding this we not only begin to make sense of a life (and see a larger project unfolding), but also come to appreciate that Sartre's thought on the role of the intellectual is not just another topic among many, but reflexive praxis with the goal of giving significance to Sartre's own concrete contingent existence.

Notes

1. The correct transliterated Greek spelling of the plural of praxis is praxeis, not praxes, see McBride (1991: 233).
2. This is a criticism Sartre makes of Marxist thought. He claims: 'Today's Marxists are concerned only with adults; reading them, one would believe that we are born at the age when we earn our first wages. They have forgotten their own childhoods. ... [E]verything seems to happen as if men experienced their alienation and their reification *first in their own work*, whereas in actuality each one lives it *first*, as a child, *in his parents' work*' (Sartre 1968a: 62).
3. Scriven (1984) points out that: 'Writing for Sartre was not one activity among many. It was *the* privileged activity which gave shape and substance to his personal existence. Existence was synonymous with the act of writing' (Scriven 1984: 10).
4. Responding to the question: '*You hardly see anything more than a mini-praxis in literature today?*' Sartre replies: 'Yes. But anyway, there is no more literature' (Sartre 1977b: 131).
5. Also see Sartre (1977a: 46–47).
6. An English translation of the play can be found in Contat and Rybalka (1974b: 72–136). Also see Contat and Rybalka (1974a: 410–413).
7. The Stalag in which Sartre was held captive contained many civilians who had been picked up by German soldiers. The civilians were to be repatriated. All that was required was a reservist's pay book (easily forged) and a plausible reason why you would have been discharged as unfit for service. Sartre took advantage of his near-blind eye and claimed he suffered from dizzy spells. This was sufficient to gain his release. See de Beauvoir (1965: 478–479).
8. *Socialisme et Liberté* lasted less than nine months; Sartre soon turned his attention back to writing.
9. See Contat and Rybalka (1974a: 97–98) on misinterpretations of the play.
10. Birchall (2004: 4) also refers to Sartre's 'many tactical judgements and misjudgements'.
11. Sartre claimed on a number of occasions that prior to 1968 there was nothing to the left of the PCF (*Parti communiste française*) in France. Birchall (2004, 5–6) demonstrates that this is simply untrue and that there is absolutely no way that Sartre could have been unaware of a collection of groups which, despite lacking homogeneity, had some influence on French left-wing politics. Birchall cites the following: Organisations of 'orthodox' Trotskyism; dissident Trotskyists such as the group *Socialisme ou barbarie*; anarchists and syndicalists, particularly those connected to the journal *La Révolution prolétarienne*; the left of the socialist party (originally *gauche révolutionnaire*, later *Parti socialiste ouvrier et paysan* and prior to a move to the right in the late 1940s there was a far left element in the SFIO (*Section française de l'internationale ouvrière*); 'those surrealists who did not follow Aragon into Stalinism'; the independent left press (publications such as *Combat, Franc-Tireur, France-Observateur*, and in a qualified sense, *L'Express*); *nouvelle gauche* in the 1950s and its successor *Parti socialiste unifié* (PSU) in the 1960s and 'a number of individuals who had emerged from the Trotskyist movement' (Pierre Naville, Maurice Nadeau, Gérard Rosenthal and David Rousset).

12. In *The Communists and Peace* Sartre claims that 'The Party is the very movement which unites the workers by carrying them along towards the taking of power. How then can you expect the working class to repudiate the C.P.? It is true that the C.P. is nothing outside of the class; but let it disappear and the working class falls back into the dust' (Sartre 1968b: 130). He also claims: 'Today, [1952] a worker in France can express and fulfill himself only in a class action directed by the C.P.' (Sartre 1968b: 131).

13. See de Beauvoir (1985: 3–127) for an account of Sartre's political commitments and action during the 1970s.

14. The technician of practical knowledge is: 'Born, in general, into the middle ranks of the middle classes, where from earliest childhood a particularist ideology of the ruling class is inculcated in him, while his work invariably ranges him in any case with the middle classes. This means that in general he has no contact whatever with workers: in fact he is an accomplice to their exploitation since, after all, he lives off surplus value. In this sense his social being and his destiny come to him from without: he is a middle man, a middling man, a middle class man. The general ends towards which his activities lead are not *his* ends' (Sartre 1974a: 239).
Sartre also points out that 'the ruling class determines the number of technicians of practical knowledge in accordance with the dictates of *profit*, which is its supreme end. It decides at the same time what fraction of surplus value it will devote to their salaries, in keeping with the level of industrial development, the state of the business cycle, and the appearance of new needs'. (Sartre 1974a: 237)

15. I am indebted to Drake (2003: 33) for a concise summary of the myriad of related activities that Sartre regarded as appropriate to his role as a committed intellectual.

16. Sartre notes that in May 1968 many intellectuals remained classic intellectuals and that these people 'failed at the outset to understand that this was a movement contesting themselves. Some of them were visibly confounded, and cherished a nagging hostility to the events of May when suddenly they felt the movement was contesting *them* in their capacity as *intellectuals*, whereas until then the intellectual had always been there to help others, to be available – the natural person to provide the theories, the ideas' (Sartre 1974b: 289). Drake (1997) turns this accusation on Sartre himself, claiming that Sartre's interventions in support of the students were examples of the praxis of the classic intellectual. Sartre was external to the events and was a 'supporter' rather than a 'player'. Drake also claims that Sartre did not fully understand the significance of the events as they occurred and 'failed to perceive (until later) that the events represented a challenge to *him*' (Drake 1997: 44).

17. This is how Sartre viewed the situation, but it is questionable how accurate this really is. While Sartre may have accurately assessed his own situation, it seems likely that he was rather over-optimistic in relation to the success of the students who attempted to form a new relationship with the proletariat.

18. Birchall (2004) challenges this claim. See n. 11 above.

19. Sartre coined the apparently oxymoronic neologisms of the 'concrete universal' and the 'singular universal' to illustrate his view that the general is incarnated in the particular.

20. Sartre claims that: 'While learning the language of the masses they [intellectuals] can give a certain expression to the techniques they possess. For example, I think that a newspaper today that is created for the masses should comprise a certain proportion of intellectuals and a certain proportion of workers, and that the articles should be written neither by the intellectuals nor by the workers, but by both together. The workers explain what they are and what they are doing, and the intellectuals are there to understand, to learn and at the same time to give things every so often a certain type of generalization'. (Sartre 1974b: 294)

21. Scriven (1984, 103) asks whether the *Flaubert* is 'Marxism or onanism?' and notes that '*L'Idiot de la famille* is too long, too large and too weighty by anybody's standards. ... Practically nobody has read it.' (1984: 105). Caws quips that 'the book sometimes feels that it is quite as long as the life with which it deals' (1984: 192).

22. In 'On The Idiot of the Family', an interview with Michel Contat and Michel Rybalka first published in *Le Monde* on 14 May 1971 and translated in *Life/Situations: Essays Written and Spoken*, Sartre is questioned about the apparent contradiction in his self-professed political commitment and his abandonment of volume two of *Critique de la raison dialectique* in favour of completing *L'Idiot de la famille*. While Sartre cites age and the volume of reading necessary to complete the *Critique* as reasons, there is something of a mistake in the way that the problem has been presented because *both* the *Critique* and the *Flaubert* are examples of intellectual knowledge unsuitable for communication with workers. See Sartre (1977b).

23. He concedes that 'this is the practical problem, which I have not yet resolved very well: how can a political writer make himself understood by a popular audience while carrying out an idea to the very end? In my opinion the new style of intellectual must give everything to the people today. I am sure one can go far in this direction, but I do not yet know how. ... It is also clear that the leftists are not very preoccupied by theory. What interests them – even the intellectuals among them – is to discuss an action that has been carried out and to draw lessons from it or to discuss another action still to be carried out' (Sartre 1977b: 132).

24. It seems likely that Sartre worked on the *Flaubert* as a way of understanding himself.

25. As Anderson (1993) points out, Sartre 'never had ... any close relations with members of ...[the working] class, let alone with those who actually lived in poverty' (Anderson 1993: 136). Consequently Sartre had a romantic view of the values, morality and general perspective of the working class.

26. Despite Sartre's claim that, 'every man is political, ... But I did not discover that for myself until the war, and I did not truly understand it until 1945' (Sartre 1977a: 44–45), Birchall (2004) argues correctly that 'It was not the war that made Sartre the committed writer, but rather the interaction between the experience of war and Sartre as he had already developed. What he saw depended on what he was already looking for. Every French person was affected by the Occupation, but not every French person was Sartre' (Birchall 2004: 13).

27. As it lacks an organisational structure, the group-in-fusion constitutes only a temporary means of overcoming alienation. It is a limited resolution of the problems encountered by individual praxis.

References

Anderson, T. C. (1993) *Sartre's Two Ethics: From Authenticity to Integral Humanity*, La Salle, IL: Open Court.

de Beauvoir, S. (1965) *The Prime of Life*, P. Green (trans.), Harmondsworth: Penguin, 1965.

de Beauvoir, S. (1985) *Adieux: A Farewell to Sartre*, P. O'Brian (trans.), Harmondsworth: Penguin.

Birchall, I. H. (2004) *Sartre Against Stalinism*, Oxford: Berghahn.

Caute, D. (1998) 'Introduction', in J-P. Sartre, *What is Literature?*, London: Routledge, vii–xvii.

Caws, P. (1984) *Sartre*, London: Routledge and Kegan Paul.

Contat, M. and Rybalka, M. (1974a) *The Writings of Jean-Paul Sartre Volume One: A Biographical Life*, R. McCleary (trans.), Evanston: Northwestern University Press.

Contat, M. and Rybalka, M. (1974b) *The Writings of Jean-Paul Sartre Volume Two: Selected Prose*, R. McCleary (trans.), Evanston: Northwestern University Press.

Drake, D. (1997) 'Sartre and May 1968: The Intellectual in Crisis', *Sartre Studies International*, 3 (1), 43–65.

Drake, D. (2003) 'Sartre: Intellectual of the Twentieth Century', *Sartre Studies International*, 9 (2), 29–39.

Flynn, T. R. (1979) 'L'Imagination au Pouvoir: The Evolution of Sartre's Political and Social Thought', *Political Theory*, 7 (2), 157–180.

Lyotard, J-F. (1986) 'A Success of Sartre's', in D. Hollier (ed.), *The Politics of Prose: Essay on Sartre*, Minneapolis: University of Minnesota Press, xi–xxii.

McBride, W. L. (1991) *Sartre's Political Theory*, Bloomington, IN: Indiana University Press.

Sartre, J-P. (1955) *No Exit and Three Other Plays*, S. Gilbert and L. Abel (trans.), New York: Vintage Books.

Sartre, J-P. (1958) *Being and Nothingness: An Essay in Phenomenological Ontology*, H. E. Barnes (trans.), London: Routledge.

Sartre, J-P. (1963) *Saint Genet: Actor and Martyr*, B. Frechtman (trans.), New York: George Braziller.

Sartre, J-P. (1965) *Nausea*, R. Baldick (trans.), Harmondsworth: Penguin.

Sartre, J-P. (1967a) *Baudelaire*, M. Turnell (trans.), New York: New Direction.

Sartre, J-P. (1967b) *Words*, I. Clephane (trans.), Harmondsworth: Penguin.

Sartre, J-P. (1968a) *Search for a Method*, H. E. Barnes (trans.), New York: Vintage.

Sartre, J-P. (1968b) *The Communists and Peace, With a Reply to Claude Lefort*, P. R. Berk (trans.), New York: George Braziller.

Sartre, J-P. (1974a) 'A Plea for Intellectuals', in J-P. Sartre, *Between Existentialism and Marxism*, J. Matthews (trans.), London: New Left Books, 228–285.

Sartre, J-P. (1974b) 'A Friend of the People', in J-P. Sartre, *Between Existentialism and Marxism*, J. Matthews (trans.), London: New Left Books, 286–298.

Sartre, J-P. (1974c) 'Bariona, or the Son of Thunder', in M. Contat and M. Rybalka (eds), *The Writings of Jean-Paul Sartre Volume Two: Selected Prose*, R. McCleary (trans.), Evanston: Northwestern University Press, 72–136.

Sartre, J-P. (1977a) 'Self-Portrait at Seventy', in J-P. Sartre, *Life/Situations: Essays Written and Spoken*, P. Auster and L. Davis (trans.), New York: Panteon, 3–9.

Sartre, J-P. (1977b) 'On *The Idiot of the Family*', in J-P. Sartre, *Life/Situations: Essays Written and Spoken*, P. Auster and A. Davis (trans.), New York: Pantheon, 109–132.

Sartre, J-P. (1978) *Sartre by Himself*, R. Seaver (trans.), New York: Urizen.

Sartre, J-P. (1981) *The Family Idiot: Gustave Flaubert 1821–1857*, five volumes, C. Cosman (trans.), Chicago, IL: The University of Chicago Press.

Sartre, J-P. (1991a) *Critique of Dialectical Reason Volume One, Theory of Practical Ensembles*, A. Sheridan-Smith (trans.), London: Verso.

Sartre, J-P. (1991b) *Critique of Dialectical Reason Volume Two, The Intelligibility of History*, Q. Hoare (trans.), London: Verso.

Sartre, J-P. (1991c) *Mallarmé, or the Poet of Nothingness*, E. Sturm (trans.), University Park, PA: The Pennsylvania State University Press.

Sartre, J-P. (1998) *What is Literature?*, B. Frechtman (trans.), London: Routledge.

Sartre, J-P. (1999) *The War Diaries: Notebooks from a Phoney War 1939–1940*, Q. Hoare (trans.), London: Verso.

Sartre, J-P. and Lévy, B. (1996) *Hope Now: The 1980 Interviews*, A. van den Hoven (trans.), Chicago, IL: The University of Chicago Press.

Scriven, M. (1984) *Sartre's Existential Biographies*, New York: St. Martin's Press.

5
Althusser: Intellectuals and the Conjuncture

Warren Montag

The notion of the intellectual is nearly absent from Althusser's work, a fact all the more striking in that this notion occupied an important place in the reflections of such contemporaries as Raymond Aron and Jean-Paul Sartre, and such predecessors as Antonio Gramsci. His many critics on the Left would undoubtedly confer a symptomatic value on this near absence: Was it not precisely his failure to reflect on his own social position which allowed him to produce his highly 'intellectualised' Marxism, in which authentic Marxist thought was mingled indistinguishably with such 'academic' figures as Freud and, most notoriously, the incomprehensible Spinoza? Althusser's relative disinterest in the category of the intellectual raises other questions, as well: Is there not a striking paradox in the fact that Althusser's 'hypercritical' approach to philosophy, as Derrida put it, the approach which refuses to place anything off limits, even that which is the necessary, if 'mystical,' foundation for criticism itself (that which is thus 'undeconstructible'), would fail to account for the position of the subject of the enunciation of the critique (which would be one way of thinking about the intellectual) (Derrida 1994: 90)?

Of course, it would be possible to compose an 'Althusserian' response to such questions and argue (with no doubt a certain justification) that exactly because the category of the intellectual (his social origin and function, his necessity or superfluity, his duties and rights) was so often and so vividly discussed it would be difficult in such a context to say something new and more importantly effective. In addition, it would be all the more unlikely that Althusser himself, at least after the publication of *For Marx* and *Reading Capital* in 1965, could say anything about the intellectual that his audience would not read as autobiographical and hence a self-justification (even if this took the form of a denunciation of intellectuals as if to say, 'I'm not like all the others,' – the very hallmark, he would say later, of the petty bourgeois intellectual). And certainly Althusser believed in the effectivity of silence, a silence that makes one's adversaries uncomfortable in that it allows their accusations to echo shrilly in the void until they fade away. Rather than begin with either a denunciation of Althusser (as so much writing about him does), or a defence, it may perhaps prove more productive (to the extent that our objective is to understand his work) to ask at the outset what is the effect of this absence, how and to what extent it is not merely an accidental omission, but a determinate one that makes Althusser's theory what it is. Such a procedure would not, of course, prevent us from reading this relative absence as a symptom, but it cautions us not to assume that we know in advance precisely of what this absence is a symptom.

The few points at which Althusser discussed the question of the intellectual in his better known works are notable for the fact that rather than interrupting the general silence about this question, they can easily be read as its continuation by other means. The language Althusser uses, the concepts he invokes, is ostentatiously orthodox, drawn from the most sterile and empty lexicon of the Party that he would describe as an Ideological State Apparatus. His statements are perhaps an enactment of the maxim he attributed to Pascal: 'kneel down, move your lips in prayer and you will believe' (Althusser 2001: 2 (translation modified)). Thus, to dismiss Althusser's treatment of the subject as simply banal or uninteresting would be to miss its liturgical character, the sense in which it is the fact of adherence or conformity to prescribed forms itself that is foregrounded in his statements. We may take as an example his response to Maria Antonietta Macchiocchi in an interview published in *L'Unità* in 1968: 'You know what Lenin said about "intellectuals." Individually certain of them can be (politically) convinced and courageous *revolutionaries*. But in their majority, they remain "incorrigibly" petty bourgeois in their ideology. Gorky himself was for Lenin, who admired his talent, a *petty bourgeois* revolutionary. To become "ideologues of the working class" (Lenin), "organic intellectuals" (Gramsci), intellectuals must undertake a radical revolution in their ideas: a long, painful, difficult re-education. An exterior and *interior* struggle without end' (Althusser 1971: 12).

In part, these statements appear to exhibit all the characteristics of the ritual self-denunciation required by the two ideological apparatuses that in sequence dominated his life: the Catholic Church and The French Communist Party. Althusser took great pleasure and comfort in such rituals: from his constant self-criticism to its final caricature in *The Future Lasts Forever* where it is no longer the fact of being the petty bourgeois intellectual who requires the ritual of confession, but the fact that he was nothing more than the impersonation of an intellectual, a fraudulent version of what was itself a contemptible figure. In a sense, he produced his own little drama of the unhappy consciousness which feels real only when it is the object of contempt and abjection. But even in this passage there are signs of a less Christian view of the intellectual. Althusser himself produced a comic reading of the 'struggle without end' of the petty bourgeois intellectual against his own 'class instincts' which, as Althusser explains a few lines later, reassert themselves as soon as they are 'overcome' (Althusser 2001: 2 (translation modified)). This is the figure that he evokes at the beginning of *Philosophy and the Spontaneous Philosophy of the Scientists*: a character out of one of the Beckett plays that Althusser so passionately admired who, having fallen down, picks himself up only to tumble into a hole. It is worth noting that in the comic version, there exists no Other in relation to whom the philosopher is corrupt or abject, and therefore no sin and no absolution. This is the Althusser who would write that 'we who have no religion, not even the religion of our theory and still less that of the ends of history … must speak paradoxically of error without truth and deviation without a norm' (Althusser 1998: 240). Perhaps these few words represent Althusser's attempt to dramatise the movement of error without truth and deviation without a norm by depriving it of any nostalgia or longing.

These last reflections may help us account for the crude determinism of Althusser's response to Machiocchi, a determinism otherwise unworthy of the theoretician of overdetermination and trenchant critic of every form of the base-superstructure model. Althusser, perhaps more than any other self-defined Marxist philosopher, thought and wrote about the strategy of philosophy and his models were Lenin, Machiavelli and, above all, Spinoza. He claimed to have discovered in Spinoza an 'astonishing contradiction': 'this man who argues *more geometrico* with definitions, axioms, theorems, corollaries, lemmas and deductions and therefore in the most "dogmatic" way in the world was an incomparable liberator of the mind' (Althusser 1992: 468). Nor did Spinoza's dogmatism consist in the form of his philosophy alone:

> For Spinoza began with God! He began with God and was really (I believe in accordance with the entire tradition of his worst enemy's comments) an atheist (like Da Costa and so many other Portuguese Jews of his time). A supreme strategist, he began by infiltrating the primary stronghold of his adversary, or by installing himself there as if he were his own adversary, and therefore beyond suspicion of being

the adversary of his adversary, and repositioning the theoretical fortress in order to turn it against itself as one might turn its cannons against its own occupants. (Althusser 1992: 468)

These reflections may help us account for the fact that the determinism that allows him to condemn the petty bourgeois intellectual recurs in other texts from the same period. A contemporaneous text, 'Lenin and Philosophy' (February 1968) offers a similar analysis, but supported by a historical example taken from the history of the Bolshevik party: 1908, a period of 'disarray among the "intellectuals," including among the Bolshevik intellectuals' (Althusser 2001: 11). A group of the latter, the Otzovists, in the grips of bourgeois ideology, specifically empirio-criticism, claimed, no doubt in all sincerity, to offer a Left-wing critique of the Bolshevik strategy of participation in parliament, 'but these leftist proclamations concealed rightist theoretical positions' (Althusser 2001: 12). Althusser went on to summarise Lenin's position that philosophy professors are 'petty bourgeois intellectuals functioning as so many ideologists inculcating the mass of student youth with the dogmas – however critical or post-critical – of the ideology of the ruling classes' (Althusser 2001: 18).

Even one of his best-known works, 'Ideology and the Ideological State Apparatuses,' written a year later, in 1969, conceives of what Althusser once called the social formation as a system whose coherence is so absolute that the only result of its functions can be its own reproduction: the superstructure assures the reproduction of the relations of production. Not only are we thus at antipodes with the materialism of the encounter that he was simultaneously developing elsewhere, but the very notion of history is foreclosed. As Michel Pêcheux noted (Pêcheux 1982), historical transformation cannot be explained on the basis of the model of ideological subjection that Althusser develops. What does this mean for the intellectual, a figure who, it must be noted, has little place in the ISAs essay or in the manuscript from which it was excerpted? The vast majority, of course, have no other function than to sanctify the existing state of things and do so consciously and in good conscience. The minority who choose to join the working class in its struggle against Capital (but what determines them to do so, especially given the hold of class instinct, derived in turn from class position?), desire to be other than what they are but their relation to the workers' movement (which itself necessarily plays little role in Althusser's account of the reproduction of the relations of production) can never be anything other than one of permanent, being structural, exteriority. The intellectual thus understood is condemned to a perpetual struggle against the whispering within of class instinct, an instinct whose ruses are numberless, whose forms are legion. The intellectual is heroic insofar as and for as long he resists that which finally cannot be resisted. One triumphs over the force of class instinct and class position only through sacrifice and self-denial, through voluntary subjection to the discipline of an external apparatus.

These postulates so notable for a moralism (which one might be tempted indeed to call petty-bourgeois) not commonly associated with Althusser, expressed in the idiom of a certain Stalinist tradition, however, produce some surprising effects. As Althusser argued in relation to Spinoza: the most extreme philosophical dogmatism can produce (or be made to produce) the most extraordinarily liberating effects. His meditations on philosophical strategy, and not simply his own, but even more importantly, that of his adversaries led him to conclude that the very resistance Marxism provokes in the dominant ideology does not merely or most importantly take the form of attacks and criticisms from a position outside of Marxism. The critics of Marxism such as Aron or Popper are far less effective than the adversary who far from denouncing Marxism 'ends up penetrating it' to revise it from within, not only claiming to be Marxist, manipulating its terms and concepts, but more importantly sincerely believing itself to be so. Such revisionist currents may be marked by the importation of 'foreign' ideas into Marxism (e.g., existentialism or rational choice theory), but they may well draw their arguments from and appeal to the authority of Marx, Engels and Lenin alone. It was for this reason, of course, that Althusser's analysis of Marx, and of the complexity proper to Marx's corpus, proved far more controversial than his work on Montesquieu or even Freud. In fact, one might go further and draw from Althusser's first critics the charge (however inchoately formulated) that if the most cunning form taken by petty bourgeois ideology is not that of an attempt to refute Marxism, but precisely that of Marxism itself in the form of a return to the early Marx (just as Bernstein was a privileging of a certain late Engels), the distinction between the self-described Marxist and non-Marxist is called radically into question. In fact, as more than one critic insinuated by means of a reference to structuralism, if petty bourgeois ideology can emerge within Marxism on the basis of textual references to Marx himself, if 'objective' anti-Marxists can pose as its advocates and champions, would the inverse not be logically true as well? In this way, Althusser could be understood as arguing, or at least making possible the argument that Marxism, or a philosophy objectively allied with it by virtue of its subversion of the dominant forms of thought, could emerge in the heart of non-Marxist or even anti-Marxist thought. If the latter is true, then the distinction between philosophy written in the idiom of Marxism, using certain of its categories and concepts, and philosophy written without the slightest reference to these idioms, except perhaps to reject them as meaningless, appears null. We might even go further: if the most effective attacks on Marxism originate within it, depending on the circumstances, the only possible way to combat them might well be by making a detour outside of Marxism.

Indeed, Althusser's preface to *For Marx*, entitled 'Today,' appears precisely to suggest such notions. In his analysis of the theoretical 'poverty' of the French Communist Party (PCF), of all the 'form of bourgeois domination' that 'long deprived the French workers' movement of the intellectuals indispensable to the formation of an authentic theoretical tradition,' the most pernicious was 'a reflex "workerist" distrust of intellectuals' (Althusser 1969: 25). This distrust was not derived, rightly or wrongly, from the petty bourgeois position of intellectuals, but from the specific nature of the French bourgeoisie and their struggles against 'the feudal class' (Althusser 1969: 25). In particular the anti-clericalism of the bourgeoisie and of their state meant that 'French intellectuals ... felt no vital need to seek their salvation at the side of the working class' (Althusser 1969: 25). The effects of this trajectory were double: on the one hand, an intelligentsia 'steeped' in an idealism and positivism without real opposition and a workers' movement bereft of allies among the intelligentsia.

Of course, one might argue that if only the intellectuals had been forced by historical circumstances to rally to the workers' movement, the 'French poverty' would never have existed: one might merely point to the very different histories of the German or Russian movements: that there was no French Marx or Lenin, or even a Luxemburg or Kautsky, was due entirely to the specificity of the class struggles in France, which allowed intellectuals to remain in the stagnant atmosphere of petty bourgeois ideology. But this explanation of the French poverty was by itself insufficient: to it must be added 'another national reason' (Althusser 1969: 25), that of French philosophy as a whole. For not only was there no French Lenin, neither was there a French Husserl. Althusser pointed to the 'pitiful history of French philosophy in the 130 years following the Revolution of 1789', a history of 'incredible ignorance and lack of culture', the only exception to which was Comte (Althusser 1969: 25). Even if things had begun to improve in the last 30 years, 'the burden of a long century of official philosophical stupidity' (Althusser 1969: 25–26) continued to weigh on the French workers' movement. This is what Althusser would call 'the theoretical vacuum' (Althusser 1969: 26) of French politics.

It may now appear not only that Althusser's Communist critics were right in their suspicions about him, but that the case is even worse than they guessed. Marxism, it seems, can develop a theory adequate to its practice only to the extent it recognises that it does not exist in a vacuum, but is surrounded by non-Marxist philosophies with which it remains in constant communication and on which it may rely in order to combat the non-Marxist tendencies that arise in Marxism itself and which are in turn allied with other opposing non-Marxist philosophies. The distinction between the two is not simply blurred, it is thus revealed to be a fiction which, moreover, primarily serves the dominant forms of thought. In fact the question posed to Althusser by Machiocchi in the 1968 interview (and which was in fact written by Althusser) was 'why is it generally so difficult to be a Communist in philosophy?' (Althusser 2001: 2). Althusser would arrive at this position, which meant surrendering the project of a Marxist philosophy, although already implicit in the preface to *For Marx*, with great difficulty.

However ironic it may seem, all the evidence suggests that it was nothing less than a sustained reading of Lenin that led Althusser to these very unorthodox and, in certain ways, unprecedented positions. In December of 1967 as he was composing 'Lenin and Philosophy', he wrote a long self-reflective letter to Franca Madonia. It is important to state at the outset that this letter no more represents the 'real' Althusser than any other document he wrote and must be read with the same caution and care as any of his texts. This new-found interest in and more pertinently appreciation of Lenin is all the more striking in that five years earlier Althusser had expressed to the very same correspondent a very different estimate of Lenin:

> I am reading Lenin's theoretical texts on philosophy. God, it's weak. I have verified once again that Lenin, an incomparable political clinician, an incomparable practical theoretician (in the sense of reflection on concrete situations, concrete historical problems) is a weak theoretician when he rises above a certain level of abstraction. ...
> When he does theory, he thinks he's doing theory, but in fact has only defined and stated practical concepts, that is, concepts with which one can wage hand to hand combat (combat au corps à corps), tactical concepts for immediate defense, full contact combat at close quarters, as we say ... while real theory assumes something other

than tactical concepts, that is, properly theoretical and 'strategic' perspectives. (Althusser 1998a: 306)

Five years later, without referring to the letter itself, but to the work contemporaneous with it, especially the essay 'On the Materialist Dialectic', Althusser would denounce the conditions of his prior denunciation of Lenin, coming close to developing a theoretical justification of the very notion of 'practical theoretician' with which he had reproached Lenin. He reports to Madonia that while writing an 'article for the Soviets', (an article, 'The Historical Task of Marxist Philosophy' currently available only in English translation), that 'something began to change and I am able to account for an entire series of phenomena that had remained a mystery to me: the reactions provoked by my published works in the different milieux they reached' (Althusser 1998a: 754). Reading Lenin allowed him to understand for the first time the 'objective effects' of some of his most notable definitions of philosophy. Of these 'the most important from the point of view of its effects', was 'philosophy is the Theory of theoretical practices' (Althusser 1998a: 755). Althusser argues that there exist two possible ways of reading this statement: '(1) philosophy is the Science of sciences (the Theory of theoretical practices) or (2) philosophy is immanent in the sciences (the theoretical practice of theoretical practices)' (Althusser 1998a: 755). While this definition of philosophy was correct insofar as it 'showed the privileged relation of philosophy to the sciences', it was false insofar as it remained silent about 'the other relation that defines philosophy' (Althusser 1998a: 775), its relation to ideologies which are in turn sites of class struggle. Althusser argues that this constitutes philosophy's organic relation to politics.

In this way Althusser has rejected his earlier critique of Lenin and has denounced the very pretension to rise above class struggle in theory, the aversion to the hand to hand combat in close quarters, mired in the specificity of the concrete conjuncture, forced to use any and every tactical concept at one's disposal, as quintessentially 'petty-bourgeois', the hallmark of the figure of the intellectual as scorned by Lenin. There can no longer be any pretence of speaking about philosophy, or even of constructing a Marxist philosophy. The latter would be no more than another version (Left in form, Right in essence) of 'the theoretical denial of its own practice' that Althusser would soon come to see as constitutive of philosophy as such, a paradoxical Marxism indeed that would dematerialise itself by constituting a transcendental dimension from which it could speak of the totality of which it is not a part. To reject such an idealism, to be a Marxist in philosophy rather than a Marxist philosopher, is not simply to affirm the practical state of one's own philosophy, but the modes and operations proper to this practice.

In fact, in 'Lenin and Philosophy,' there appears to be an organic link between the denunciation of the intellectual and the demand that philosophy recognise and theorise the specific struggle that constitutes it. A year earlier Althusser in the lecture that would later be published in *Philosophy and the Spontaneous Philosophy of the Scientists* had described the 'comic spectacle' of the philosopher who tells us, in all modesty, that he is nothing less than 'the specialist of the "totality" ' (Althusser 1990: 80). The specialist of the totality was once the spokesperson for the universal which transcends the egoism of individuals believing themselves to be dissociated even as they fabricate a universal community unawares. It was he who would recall their participation in this community, which conferred a transcendental meaning upon empirically particular acts: that which the individual desires for himself who 'must' (and, properly understood, does) desire for all others. Today, for someone like Habermas, the self-declared heir to the unfinished project of the Enlightenment, the universal in whose name he speaks no longer exists, as it did, for Kant and Hegel, in opposition to the disaggregated world of competing individuals, but instead in opposition to a world of disaggregated and competing collectivities (or Gemeinschaften – a word which also pluralises the universal). The intellectual thus understood speaks for the community of all communities, the sphere of all public spheres, rising above partisan struggles between separate interest groups. What is comic about such a position, the position of the universal and the transcendental, which the specialist of the totality occupies? Like a cartoon character running in mid-air, he speaks only as long as he remains ignorant of positionlessness; to point out the absurdity of speaking from nowhere (which is to say, everywhere) is to send the philosopher crashing to the ground, his ground, his position, the position that he occupied all along, except in his own imagination. In this sense the affirmation of the universal is simultaneously a denial not only of one's own position, but of the practical existence of philosophy itself. It was precisely Lenin's great merit, according to Althusser, to have demonstrated that all philosophy is partisan, participating in a struggle for ideological domination and all the more when it denies such participation, a denial that is revealed to be nothing more than a ruse to gain the advantage. As Hobbes said, in war force and fraud are the cardinal virtues.

Does this not then commit Althusser to a kind of relativism, a relativism of positions or even perspectives which not only must posit a totality in relation to which the plurality of positions must be judged 'partial,' but further renders all positions equivalent insofar as they are equidistant from the truth that is the whole. But Althusser's thought refuses to be confined to the alternatives of the universal and the particular and the whole and its parts. First, not all positions are equivalent: 'one cannot see everything from everywhere;' historical reality becomes knowable and more importantly known 'only on the condition that one occupies certain positions and not others in the conflict' that defines a given moment (Althusser 1996: 111). This in turn requires that the philosopher knows that he occupies a place in the space of philosophy not only different from others but in opposition to others who once occupied or seek to occupy that place. The philosopher most 'know' that is, not only passively perceive but actively think through the struggle in which he has engaged and must continue to engage.

If Althusser's earlier remarks ridiculed the pretensions of philosophy to speak of the totality, he will go on to theorise its humiliation at the hands of Lenin. For if philosophy can and does occupy, that is, both conquer and defend, certain positions against a legion of adversaries at stake is neither the truth nor the totality. Philosophy does not even produce knowledge; it invents nothing and discovers nothing. In 'Lenin and Philosophy', he will go so far as to say that 'the history of philosophy is annulled in the nothing (le rien) that it produces' (Althusser 2001: 38). Althusser presents the formulas from the unpublished lectures to the scientists delivered in 1967. In its propositions or theses, philosophy does not simply or primarily speak in the commonly accepted sense of the term; instead, it acts. It does so by 'drawing lines of demarcation' (Althusser 1971: 61) which make visible a difference or an antagonism. Its action or intervention, however, 'is well and truly the philosophical nothing whose insistence we have postulated, since effectively a line of demarcation is nothing, not even a line, not even a trace but the simple fact of demarcating, and therefore the void of a distance taken' (Althusser 2001: 38). Even worse, philosophy never steps outside of itself, but always operates in and on philosophy. Would this not represent the idealism, and paradoxically, the intellectualism with which Althusser's critics reproached him? In fact, Althusser's theses represent on the one hand a narcissistic wound to philosophy: it is reduced to demarcation and thereby to nothing and deprived of its profundity and pathos. On the other hand, however, if the line of demarcation that philosophy draws is nothing, 'that nothing is not null' (Althusser 2001: 37). For at stake in its irreducible, 'eternal' existence are scientific and political practices; it is nothing less than the battlefield in which the fate of these practices will be decided.

But the humiliation of the intellectual at Althusser's hands is not yet complete. What I have repeatedly called the 'absence' of the intellectual from his work, but which might more accurately be called its marginalisation, the deliberate placing of the intellectual at the margins, is without doubt a commentary on the practice of intellectuals, a confronting of this practice as it imagines itself with its own reality and the production of an uncomfortable discrepancy. But it is also a commentary on a conception of the intellectual, which perhaps Althusser himself did not entirely escape (as is indicated in his rejection of the universalistic 'Theory of theoretical practices'), which played an important role in the history of Marxist thought. From Marx and Engels to Kautsky and the Lenin of *What is to be Done* there exists a notion (perhaps never present in its pure form – even in Kautsky) of the intellectual, product of the capitalist division of labour, which frees him from manual labour, granting him the opportunity to think openly, a fact that will lead a certain number of such intellectuals to discover the scientific basis of Marx's critique of capital. In fact, this very freedom will allow them to develop this science and then communicate it to the proletariat, whose perspective is necessarily limited by the material conditions of its existence and the imperatives of its struggle against the exploiting class. This notion of the division of labour and of the place of the intellectual or philosopher within it can be found word for word in the chapter 1 of Adam Smith's *Wealth of Nations* from which it was taken by Marx and those who followed him without critical scrutiny. Its crude economism, which has wreaked a great deal of havoc in the history of the socialist and communist movements, serves with equal facility to justify both intellectualist and workerist arguments.

It is here that Althusser's work on ideology, in particular, his insistence that ideology cannot be thought as an ideal reflection of the economic infrastructure assumes its relevance. If intellectuals are free from manual labour they are by no means free in any meaningful sense to think and to argue, to choose if they will to take the side of the working class. Instead, every intellectual thinks and speaks from within a determinate apparatus, governed by its practices and rituals in both speech and action. The figure of the intellectual is supplanted by that of the journalist or the professor, speaking under compulsion from within the apparatuses of the media or of academia (or of a political party – even a Communist Party).

The very possibility of the intellectual thus defined opposing the mechanisms of discipline that bring him to life and compel him to speak is determined not by the will of the individual, but by the always shifting balance of forces in the struggle without end the play of which may bend, twist and crack these apparatuses, making it possible to 'think otherwise'. But even this possibility will be lost if the intellectual retreats into a religion of theory, a temptation often difficult to resist when the alternative not only offers no assurances, but when to assess the balance of social forces correctly may well mean acknowledging a defeat that could last a generation. But to take Althusser seriously is to accept that thinking in and through the conjuncture (however sobering an experience it may be) is not only a better alternative to the various forms of theoretical denial, it is the only alternative.

References

Althusser, L. (1969) *For Marx*, London: Verso.
Althusser, L. and Balibar, É. (1997) *Reading Capital*, London: Verso.
Althusser, L. (2001) *Lenin and Philosophy*, New York: Monthly Review Press.
Althusser, L. (1994) 'Spinoza', in *L'avenir dure longtemps*, Paris: Editions Stock/IMEC, 467–467.
Althusser, L. (1996) *Writings on Psychoanalysis*, Jeffery Mehlman (trans.), New York: Columbia University Press.
Althusser, L. (1990) *Philosophy and the Spontaneous Philosophy of the Scientists*, London: Verso.
Althusser, L. (1998a) *Lettres à Franca (1961–73)*, Paris: Stock/IMEC.
Althusser, L. (1998b) 'Histoire terminée, histoire interminable', in Y. Sintomer (ed.), *Solitude de Machiavelli*, Paris: PUF, 237–246.
Derrida, J. (1994) *Specters of Marx*, London: Routledge.
Pêcheux, M. (1982) *Language Semantics, Ideology*, New York: St. Martin's Press.

6
T. W. Adorno as a Critical Intellectual in the Public Sphere: Between Marxism and Modernism

Gerard Delanty

Theodor W. Adorno (1903–1969) is now widely recognised as one of the most important Marxist public intellectuals and German philosophical and political thinkers of the twentieth century. Adorno was central to the development of the Frankfurt School, or simply critical theory, a movement that played a formative role in the rise of Western Marxism (as a nuanced alternative to the Marxist claims of Leninism, Stalinism and Trotskyism) and came to be one of the main influences on the so-called cultural turn in the human and social sciences in 1980s. He defined the role of an active public intellectual, engaged in social and cultural analysis that was articulated beyond the university, evidenced by his numerous radio talks and newspaper articles, essays and interventions in the German public sphere. At the same time his work dissolved the boundaries that previously separated the disciplines of sociology, psychology and philosophy and influenced decades of social research (Adorno 1970–1986). His major works – especially the seminal *Aesthetic Theory, Negative Dialectics, Dialectic of Enlightenment* and *Minima Moralia* – his writings on modernist aesthetics, his critique of popular culture, his dialogue with Walter Benjamin and his reflections on the Holocaust continue to be of interest and relevance to contemporary public debates, whether focused on the nature of 'left' (Marxist) thinking (Jameson 1967, 1971), the need to address the cultural in social and political thought (Jameson 1990) or ethical questions around the nature of the human subject (Bernstein 2001).

Yet at the time of his death in 1969, Adorno was criticised by Marxists and radicals as being a conservative or bourgeois modernist in his alleged belief that capitalism had eradicated critical potential, save that which could be found in high culture, and in his disdain for mass culture. Arguably, the renewed interest in Adorno from post-Marxist and postmodern thinkers speaks against his intellectual and political radicalism rather than for it. This chapter is concerned to make a considered appraisal of Adorno's significance as a critical left-wing intellectual, and so add something to understandings of what a critical left-wing (Marxist?) intellectual is.

The central argument advanced here is that a considered understanding of Adorno has to begin with his belief that he was living in a world without meaning. The role of the critical intellectual therefore was not to create or recover meaning, but to demonstrate the limits of existing ways of thinking. This was the basis of Adorno's so-called immanent approach to critique, the attempt to demonstrate the contradictions inherent in reality and offer people a critical language. As a critical intellectual, Adorno aimed less to provide moral or spiritual leadership than to show the limits of the prevailing modes of thought and reason, and at the same time to provide people with forms of consciousness and critical categories with which they can use to approach self-consciousness (Adorno 1998: 300). It is in this sense that Adorno can be seen as a political intellectual, that is, one who was less concerned with a particular political ideal or mode of social organisation. His concern rather lay with the cultural structures of public debate and self-understanding. The political nature of this style of intellectual activity was therefore more indirect or mediated than direct. It was a concept of critique deeply embedded in the German philosophical notion of reason as self-reflection, where reason is more or less equated with critique. The specific way in which Adorno accomplished this was through the Hegelian-Marxist method of immanent critique, the attempt to demonstrate the inner contradictions within reality. The assumption underlying this approach was the dialectical constitution of reality as a self-creative process. Although some of his work suggests he abandoned this approach – the pessimistic exercise of the *Dialectic of Enlightenment*, for example – there is ample evidence of a basic adherence to the immanent approach to critique. Thus, the role of the intellectual for Adorno could be seen to reside in the function of bringing to consciousness contradictions in reality in order that the historically most progressive form of consciousness can emerge.

The argument presented here is that Adorno was neither exclusively a Marxist nor a bourgeois modernist, but an iconoclastic left-wing thinker who came to be the leading critical public intellectual of the Holocaust for the post-war German public sphere. As he remarked in one of the last of his many radio talks in 1969: 'Critique is essential to all democracy. Not only does democracy require the freedom to criticise and need critical impulses. Democracy is nothing less than defined by Critique' (Adorno 1998: 281).

Marxism and critique

Adorno was by inclination a critical thinker rather than being driven by particular political concerns or movements. His critical predisposition attracted him to Marxism, in which he found a framework for critical theory, though there is little doubt that his status as a Marxist thinker is ambivalent. However, Adorno resolutely resisted right-wing thinkers and was close to Marxism on many issues. Like Gramsci he recognised both the role of ideas in modern politics and the autonomy of culture, but unlike Gramsci he was less inclined to see the role of the intellectual in terms of giving expression to an emerging self-consciousness. For Adorno, the task of the intellectual was considerably more nuanced and indirect. His view was that there were no normative-political positions from which the intellectual could speak.

In a period of some 30 years Adorno progressively refined Marxism to create his own unique philosophy. This was more a philosophical 'style' as Adorno never established a formal system. His essayist and polemical style was reflected in his most advanced work, *Negative Dialectics*, published in 1966, only three years before his death (Adorno 1973). This was Adorno's major philosophical treatise, an extraordinarily difficult, stylistically obscure text in which Adorno's own use of the concept of negative dialectics is not always clear or consistent. The entire work can be read as a series of reflections on the philosophical nature of critical thinking.

Negative dialectics – with its emphasis on non-identity thinking – was an alternative to what he perceived to be the false moment of positivity in Hegel and in Marx. Hegelian dialectics culminated in a moment of positivity in absolute mind coming to know itself in a phenomenological process that was entirely intellectual. For Marx, the overcoming of the class conflict in the founding of a new societal model represented the fulfilment of dialectics. Negative dialectics was a rejection of these tendencies towards what Adorno regarded as identity thinking in favour of a recovery of what he perceived to be the genuine radicalism of dialectics. Given the contemporary salience of identity, Adorno's work is a powerful caution as to its limits. In place of a simple model of identity, Adorno argued for a self-reflective kind of thinking, which might be the basis of an alternative identity for society more generally. To recover the negative within dialectics was the aim of Adorno's entire philosophical method and the basic *animus* of his critical theory of society, which was intended to be a permanent critique of the present.

Negative dialectics can be seen as a foundation for an ethics of intellectual resistance. Adorno embodied this role of resistance, although in view of his critics he intellectualised it to a point that it lost its political effectiveness. As Martin Jay has pointed out, his unrelenting resistance to institutional systems and to the existing forms of socialism meant that he was destined to the isolation that characterised many left-wing intellectuals in the first half of the twentieth century (Jay 1984b: 16). Where politics appeared to be universally conformist, for Adorno the intellectual could represent a form of opposition that could keep the political space open. Underlying this conception of the intellectual was a very Marxist belief in the utopia of revolutionary change. However, it must be appreciated that for Adorno politics alone was insufficient and the isolation of the intellectual, epitomised in the condition of exile, confirmed this tendency to see the intellectual as someone whose autonomy came at the price of their isolation, as is evident in his remarks about intellectuals in *Minima Moralia* (Adorno 1974: 28). But this did not detract from an abiding belief that the intellectual had a role to play: 'The fact that the term "intellectual" came into disrepute at the hands of the of the National Socialists seems to me just one more reason to use it in a positive sense: the first step toward self-reflection would be to stop cultivating vagueness as a higher ethos and stop slandering enlightenment, and instead resist the baiting of intellectuals, no matter what disguise it might take' (Adorno 1998: 21). Adorno's defence of the role of the intellectual was most apparent in his criticisms of anti-intellectualism in modern life, especially in the anti-intellectualism he saw within the teaching profession.

Susan Buck-Morss has drawn attention to Adorno's use of non-identity and the anti-systematising influence of Benjamin, who also impressed upon Adorno a sensitivity to the momentary and the particular. It was in the 'concrete particular', she argues, rather than in the universal that Adorno located negative dialectics and where, as suggested by Ernst Bloch who exerted an influence on Adorno, a measure of utopianism might be possible (Buck-Morss 1977). Adorno was not adverse to the idea of utopia, insofar as this was a critical alternative to the status quo. However, the concept had a less central role than it had for other critical theorists, such as Bloch and Herbert Marcuse. As is especially evident in his inaugural lecture, 'The Actuality of Philosophy', Buck-Morss argues

Adorno brought critical theory towards a form of cognition in which the 'non-intentional' would figure but in a way that so-called bourgeois philosophy (Idealism, Dilthey's hermeneutics, Husserl's phenomenology, existentialism) reduced to an affirmative stance (Buck-Morss 1977). Truth lay not in the subject or in the object but in their non-identity.

There is little doubt that his preoccupation was with philosophical concerns and, was limited when it came to devising a social scientific methodology that adequately reflected his critical philosophy. Yet, although not a sociologist by training, Adorno has had a significant impact on the methodology of the social sciences since the early 1970s. *The Positivist Dispute in German Sociology* reshaped the original social theory of the Frankfurt School, reflecting the origins of Adorno's philosophical approach in the context of the Frankfurt School's attempt to link philosophy and social science (principally sociology and psychology).

Agnes Heller has commented that the positivist dispute was a decisive turning point in Germany sociology (Heller 1978). In her view it reflected an attempt to reconnect sociology to the German philosophical tradition, if this connection proved limited. The attempt to reorient German sociology away from American positivistic social science revealed considerable common ground between the antagonistic positions of Adorno and his chief protagonist in the German positivist dispute, Karl Popper, since both shared a common rejection of empiricism. In his desire to reject any sociology that accepted without critique the accounts of the world of people, Adorno could not develop a truly radical sociology. Nevertheless, there is a hint that by the late 1960s Adorno, perhaps in response to the student movement, was moving beyond the extreme pessimism of *Negative Dialectics*, the basic idea of which was that the moment for emancipation has been missed. The positivist dispute was in fact a misnomer, since much of the debate was in fact a debate between Popper and Adorno and is better described as a debate about critical theory and neo-positivism, as represented by critical rationalism. For both Popper and Adorno, critique was the essence of science, but for the latter critique is immanent. The idea of immanent critique was never fully developed within his social science thinking, and only attained fruition in the form of cultural critique or a critique of ideology.

This is evident in Adorno's difficulties with empirical social research, when his concept of culture did not lend itself to measurement and his philosophical approach was poorly equipped for the purpose of social research. When Paul Lazerfield employed the exiled Adorno in Princeton in 1938 to undertake empirical research on radio music (see Morrison 1978), the ensuing project was a failure due not least to the Adorno's disdain for empirical research and, in this case, the research object. Adorno was horrified at the prospect of having to use what he regarded to be reified methods to understand reified thought. Further, he was unable to understand contemporary communication, a point that was revealed in an episode in the Princeton project when it became apparent that people remember news better when they hear it on the radio rather than in print. Explaining this as 'paradoxical', he betrayed his mandarin assumption that reading is culturally superior to the audio-visual forms of mass communication. Ironically when Adorno returned to Germany in the 1950s he used the medium of the radio for interviews and lectures.

When Adorno moved with Horkheimer in 1941 to California, any serious interest in linking philosophy to sociology was abandoned in favour of a cultural critique of modernity. Few developments in Marxism were more consequential, however, than Adorno's re-direction of the dialectical heritage into the domain of culture and Western Marxism in the direction of a critique of ideology. As with postmodernist Marxist intellectuals, Adorno recognised that some of the most important social struggles in late modernity were to be fought out in the domain of culture into which capitalism had penetrated, bringing about a more complete kind of reification than had previously been the case.

Adorno as a public intellectual of the Holocaust

One of Adorno's seminal texts was the *Dialectic of Enlightenment (DE)*, written with Max Horkheimer between 1939 and 1944 in California. It was in many ways a departure from the earlier thinking of the Frankfurt School, which had attempted to develop a postpositivist social science aimed at identifying progressive and critical reason (Adorno and Horkheimer 1972). Adorno's wider philosophical approach was not entirely reflected in this work, with its characteristic aphoristic and rhetorical style. Robert Hullot-Kentor, one of Adorno's major translators, has noted on the complicated history of the book that there can be little doubt that the book bears the predominant influence, stylistically and intellectually, of Adorno, who succeeded in getting the book republished against the wishes of Horkheimer (Hullot-Kentor 1989). Despite his modernist contempt for popular culture (which critics have claimed disguised his conservatism) Adorno had a radical mind and lacked the conformism of his co-author, who disapproved of birth control and dissonant music. Hollot-Kentor claimed the disagreement over the book's fate was not an isolated incident but involved a deeper difference between the two authors on the critical task of the intellectual. For Adorno, this was an uncompromising attempt to bring about social change by means of raising the general level of public debate through self-reflection. Adorno was sceptical that public opinion alone without the presence of critical intellectuals such as himself could rise above the level of nationalist self-indulgence or what he called the false-consciousness of ideology.

This is a work over which views differ. Richard Rorty condemned the *DE* for its political message, which, with Bernard Yack, he calls 'left-wing Kantianism': the view that humanity is suppressed by the institutions of modern society (Rorty 2000; see Yack 1997). Rorty's highly sceptical reading sees *DE* as having a corrupting influence on contemporary thought. This is broadly speaking the position of Habermas, for whom Adorno's view on modernity allowed no room for emancipatory developments (Habermas 1984, 1987). Such criticisms are undoubtedly valid on a surface reading or from the vantage point of a different philosophical and political perspective. Albrecht Wellmer, one of Adorno's German followers and a representative of the second generation of critical theory, sees *DE* as a quasi-literary work rather than as a philosophical or theoretical work (Wellmer 2000). Wellmer is struck by the poetic power of the work which is one of those rare books that allows numerous readings and whose theoretical weakness may be the source of its strength. It should read, he argues, as a collection of fragments 'of brilliant insight, of condensed metaphors and aphorisms, written when the real horrors of history even surpassed those depicted and predicted by the authors' (Wellmer 2000: 18–19).

A different reading suggests less left-wing Kantianism than a Hegelian-Freudian Marxism. Joel Whitebook for instance argues that the central category in *DE* is sublimation (Whitebook 2000). If this is so, then, there is a possible solution to the impasse for which the work has generally been criticised. With its implicit connection with dialectical progression, there is the suggestion that the dialectic of enlightenment is not closed to the positive concept of reason that announced the book in the early pages. Axel Honneth, who has played a significant role in reshaping critical theory after Habermas, argues that there is one key aspect of the *DE* that is still relevant, namely its concern with social pathologies (Honneth 2000). Although under the different circumstances of the present time, such pathologies will be viewed differently, it is important to see that Adorno and Horkheimer were addressing an important question. Honneth sees a wider 'world disclosing critique' in their approach, a form of social criticism that aims at evoking new ways of seeing the world. In the *DE* this was precisely what was attempted and explains why the authors avoided an appeal to truth claims as such.

Few themes capture Adorno as an intellectual more than 'Damaged Life' – the famous theme of *Mimina Moralia* (Adorno 1974). This work concerns the theme of exile in America and homelessness, which typifies the intellectual as someone who occupies a certain distance from life itself. Habermas, in a dismissive comment, has commented that Adorno was always 'out of place' unable to adjust to exile and later to post-war Germany (Habermas 1983). Leo Lowenthal, a fellow exiled critical theorist who was acquainted with Adorno in his American exile, commented on his 'naïve unfamiliarity with the real world' (Leowenthal 1984). Adorno was never prepared for his departure from the comfortable and protected life of the pre-war German upper Jewish middle class and never adjusted to living in the United States. The sense of homelessness dominated his writing, especially *Miminia Moralia*, written in California, 1944–1947 shortly after the writing of the *Dialectic of Enlightenment* and of which it was a continuation.

Many critics have noted, however, that Adorno also saw the positive side to America and when he returned to Germany he was a changed person, seeing European cultural modernity in new light (see Jay 1984a). If an earlier Germany shaped his view of America, he saw post-war Germany on his return there from the perspective of his American exile. Indeed, as Hohendahl argues, many of Adorno's criticisms of America were not substantially different from those of the American left. In any case when he returned to post-war Germany, Adorno's approach changed, although his polemical style remained much the same (Hohendahl 1992).

For Adorno, anti-Semitism and the Holocaust represented a major crisis in modernity. He was above all the intellectual of the Holocaust (see Müller-Doohm 2005). As a public intellectual in post-war Germany, Adorno's major contribution was in establishing a critical discourse in the direction of denazification. In one of his most important essays, originally a talk given in November 1959, 'What Does Coming to Terms with the Past Mean?', Adorno attacked the political complacency of Adenauer's Germany on the question of German guilt and the neutralisation of atonement. He reminded the German public that 'National Socialism lives' but in a different form. He considers 'the continued existence of National Socialism *within* democracy potentially more threatening than the continued existence of fascist tendencies *against* democracy' (Adorno 1986: 115). In this piece Adorno displays his role as a critical intellectual by challenging the audience to think critically about the relation to the recent past and thereby to create a critical self-reflective consciousness. This stance can be compared with the bourgeois contemplative position, which he attacked in 1967 in his famous essay on 'Cultural Criticism and Society', which concluded with the claim that 'To write Poetry after Auschwitz is barbaric'. The result is that critique must face this challenge, which traditional bourgeois culture is unable to address. 'Critical intelligence cannot be equal to this challenge as long as it confines itself to self-satisfied contemplation' (Adorno 1984: 34).

He was equally critical of the fanaticism of elements in the left, unpopular with the militant left and regarded as too conservative by the student movement. Adorno knew the distinction between democracy and dictatorship and opposed the militants in their equation of the democratic state with capitalist hegemony. The space that Adorno occupied, and which marked democracies off from dictatorship, was the free space of critical thought. There is some evidence to suggest that at this time Adorno had accepted that there were limits to his bleak view in *DE* and *Negative Dialectics* of a world without intrinsic meaning. His interventions into public debate would not make much sense if he did not believe in the possibility of social and political progress. It was clearly his view that post-war Germany was very different from the kind of society from which he fled in 1933. However, it was also his position as a critical intellectual in the public sphere that the German public must confront their guilt by ways other than simply moral reproach. Adorno adopted a rhetorical style of political engagement that was designed to shock and provoke the public into confronting the past (Müller-Doohm 2005; Savage 2005).

Modernist or Marxist?

Adorno's most enduring work was *Aesthetic Theory*. Unable to find truth in real life Adorno looked to the aesthetic sphere. In *Aesthetic Theory*, published in 1970 one year after his death, we find an elaborate defence of modernist art and literature and the basis of his cultural critique of mass culture (Adorno 1987). The chief characteristics of this are autonomy, de-aesthetisation, form and redemptive negation. The de-aesthetisation of art refers to its dissonance, its refusal of the bourgeois and ideological aspiration for beauty, and its fragmented, as opposed to harmonious, nature. According to Richard Wolin, in *Aesthetic Theory* Adorno is at his most utopian in his view that philosophy comes into its own in aesthetics

(Wolin 1979, 1990). If the utopian impulse was compromised in *Negative Dialectics*, it is given more voice in the intersection of art and philosophy. Wolin connects this to a redemptory function in Adorno's aesthetics, indicating a 'prefiguration of reconciled life' and 'concrete utopian projections'. Insofar as art is de-aesthetised it can offer a critique of society from whose conventions and values it has distanced itself. The critical power of art consists of its ability to rise above the immediacy of the social and to resist its unmediated incorporation into daily life, a thesis that was the subject of his protracted critical dialogue with Benjamin. It was Adorno's conviction that any attempt to assimilate art into life would be its dissolution. The price of critique was distance. Art must not compromise its autonomy from politics without opening itself to manipulation. This of course meant that art had to be contemplated under the conditions of privatistic consumption, since mass reception was by its very nature problematical in Adorno's eyes. As evidence of the false realisation of art in life, he cited Western mass culture and Soviet realism. Thus art cannot be committed to in the sense of Lukács, Sartre or Brecht; ultimately it can be realised only on the purely aesthetic level. For Adorno art was a symbolic and cognitive container of a world that could not be immediately realised. The key to its autonomy is the aesthetic form itself. What he admired in modernism, including the modernist avant-garde, was that content was subordinated to form; there could be no political message independent of form. The more abstract form was, the more it could resist reification.

The critical reception of *Aesthetic Theory* must be seen in the context of the politically charged backdrop of the radical political currents of the 1970s, which were very hostile to Adorno. Peter Hohendahl emphasises how the work is rooted in Hegelian philosophy, which leant itself to a philosophy of both negativism and immanent critique, a form of critique that begins with the work of art itself rather than its social context. In his view the conception of the autonomy of art is the key idea in the work (Hohendahl 1981).

Against the claims that he increasingly retreated from politics into aesthetics, it might be said that Adorno's whole conception of the aesthetic was a highly political one. Raymond Geuss makes the point that there was no aesthetic sphere for him to retreat into; rather the internal form of the work of art offers a cognition of the contradictions of the social world (Geuss 1998). In this sense he was embedding a Kantian idea in Marxist-Hegelian philosophy, the idea that form is realised in the cognition of contradictions which cannot be overcome by pure thought alone. It is often forgotten that Adorno was directing his attack against classicism as much as against popular art and that he was broadly favourably disposed to the avant-garde (see Harding 1992). Adorno certainly did not fail to question certain aspects of modernism, which he far from pitted against the regression in listening that he thought was a feature of popular music (see also Huyssen 1983).

One of the main weaknesses in Adorno's aesthetic theory, which led him to extreme views on the relation of art to politics, was his treatment of experience. For Adorno, the reification of experience in capitalism pitted critical negativity against a democratic appropriation of art. From the perspective of reception aesthetics, Jauss argues that Adorno abandoned the question concerning the practice of aesthetic experience (Jauss 1982).

Much of Adorno's thinking on autonomy was influenced by his knowledge and devotion to music. His theory of music was extremely complicated since it aimed to relate music to cultural modernity by immanent critique, with the result that without a technical understanding of music, Adorno's theory of music is not accessible beyond a certain point. An accomplished composer and disciple of the 'new music', Adorno believed that it was in music in particular that the modernist aesthetic – the transformation of social content into technical form which in turn undergoes a dialectical process of transformation – was most perfected. The potential for an emancipation within music dominated his thinking, to the point that while being critical of Wagner, he found certain tendencies in his music to indicate a progressive aesthetic. Adorno was convinced that the potential for this was not fully realised until Schonberg, but was to an extent anticipated by Mahler, who Adorno greatly admired. Adorno is often accused for having a nostalgic view of music as at its best only when it is intellectually demanding and elitist, but in fact Adorno was highly critical not only of regression and fetishisation in popular music but also in classical music (Thomas 1989). For instance, he was devastatingly critical of Stravinisky and certain tendencies even in Schonberg, such as the 12 tone scale, which he saw as regression from the free atonality of the earlier music. The essence of Adorno's theory of music rested on the idea that the resolution of discord and tensions must be refused in order to sunder the relation of music to subjectivity and allow dialectical progression; music that accomplished this was somehow more advanced than music that did not. He saw music constantly in danger of regressing into subjectivity. Adorno saw the signs of such regression in many compositions, for example Wagner's leitmotif which served as a musical form of commodification. What is particularly striking is that Adorno applied commodity analysis to Wagner, about whom he was deeply ambivalent. In his work he found a tension between a descent into myth and innovations in the compositional techniques.

One of the most important theoretical legacies of Adorno was the theory of the culture industry in late capitalism (see Bernstein 1991). His various essays and *DE* were the first attempts to understand popular culture and added to Marxist analysis innovative Weberian and Freudian dimensions. Adorno wanted to show that in advanced capitalism not only is labour alienated but so too is consumption and all of culture. Positions vary as to whether Adorno saw any alternatives to the totally administered society. Although clearly seeing sport as an instrument of domination, a regressive response to instrumental reason and a mindless 'pseudo-activity', Adorno certainly did see in certain aspects of popular culture a certain resistance to domination. For instance insofar as sport belongs to the leisure industry it is connected to the realm of freedom and thus is open to an immanent critique the aim of which is the identification of critical resistances. There can be no doubt that Adorno was open to a more differentiated view of mass culture. Certain aspects of mass culture, however, could never be redeemed, for example popular occultism and horoscopes (Nederman and Goulding 1981). The horoscope is not dismissed because of its irrationality; on the contrary it is criticised on grounds of its reification of rationality. The occult reinforces the regimental and instrumentalised routines of daily life with their messages to accept life, conform and their tendency to hold the individual responsible for their failures. In sum, while contemporary scholarship is generally critical of some of the more extreme ideas in Adorno's writings on popular culture, there is widespread support for a critical social theory of popular culture and agreement that within Adorno's own writings there is a recognition that not all of popular culture is monolithic.

Modernist or postmodernist?

Recent studies suggest a postmodernist direction in the reception of Adorno. Several critics have argued that postmodern themes can be found in Adorno. Peter Dews, for instance, argued that Adorno anticipated poststructuralism (Dews 1991; see also Nagele 1986). However, there can be little doubt that it was Frederic Jameson who popularised the notion that Adorno's thought reflected postmodern concerns. Clearly Adorno's central ideas have a resonance in postmodern thought, for instance his critique of identity thinking, and the particular brand of postmodernism that Jameson represents has a certain affinity with Adorno. His thesis of postmodernism as a cultural logic of late capitalism and at the same time the site of new cultural struggles in not fundamentally at odds with Adorno's immanent approach. However, it is questionable that Adorno in fact can be appropriated in this way. For instance, a postmodern approach to popular culture cannot accept Adorno's strong distinction of high and popular culture, and Jameson must resort to implausible arguments – such as that Adorno never held to such a distinction – in order to deal with such inconsistencies (Osborne 1992). Nevertheless there are clear parallels between Adorno and Michel Foucault, as in, for example, their common concern for the crisis of representation. This is also the position of Axel Honneth, for whom both Adorno and Foucault offer different versions of the critique of instrumental reason (Honneth 2000). Despite all the similarities – the emphasis on non-identity, the deconstruction of concepts – it must not be forgotten that Adorno was a dialectical thinker and a critic of domination and would never have accepted the relativism with which poststructuralism has been associated. While being an anti-foundational thinker concerned with non-identity, he remained Hegelian and in this respect differs from postmodern writers who in their pursuit of non-identity have rejected the entire Hegelian heritage (Dallmayr 1997). Non-identity for Adorno does not entail a total rejection of identity in the sense of 'no identity' but involves the articulation of a self-reflective consciousness.

There can be no doubt that Adorno was a representative of European modernism and cannot be too easily placed within a postmodern frame. In any case the epochal significance of postmodernism can now be seen within an extended modernism.

Conclusion

Adorno's critical approach, which denied any substantive recognition of the good, in the final analysis was limited (Lewandowski 1996). Adorno's view of jazz as encouraging an infantile regression and the expression of people who have been defeated and robbed of their individuality has often been considered racist. Ironically some of his own writings in free atonality are not too distant from jazz, especially in its avant-garde forms (Schönherr 1991). Adorno's misconception of jazz revealed a deeper lack of understanding of popular culture more generally. With the emergence of rock, for instance, jazz became less 'popular' and developments within it reveal a developmental process that could partly be accounted for in the terms of Adorno's own aesthetic theory. Not only did he misunderstand jazz, but his aesthetic theory was also ill equipped to accommodate it due to its pervasive concern with form and structural coherence as the container of dialectical progression conceived of in immanent terms (Witkin 2000). The formalistic nature of his aesthetic theory is no longer relevant to current aesthetic practices. This is also evident in his views about film. Unlike Benjamin, Adorno denied the possibility for any type of progressive or revolutionary film, which he saw as a medium that is based on passive reception by the audience, and ignored major differences even between the various studios within the culture industry (see Waldman 1977). The source of the difficulty is the fundamental divide he drew between the masses and intellectuals and between popular and high culture. Yet, despite his lofty contempt for popular culture, Adorno remained a left-wing intellectual. He never sided with the right or took seriously right-wing thinkers. Although his relation with Marxism was ambivalent, it is to this tradition that he properly belongs.

Note

This chapter draws in part from my Introduction to *Theodor W. Adorno*, 4 Vols, edited by Gerard Delanty London, Sage, 2004.

References

Adorno, T. W. (1970–1986) *Gesammelte Schriften*, 20 vols, R. Tiedemann (ed.), Frankfurt: Surmkanp.
Adorno, T. W. (1973) *Negative Dialectics*, E. B. Ashton (trans.), New York: Seabury Press.
Adorno, T. W. (1974) *Minima Moralia: Reflections from Damaged Life*, E. F. N. Jephcott (trans.), London: NLB.
Adorno, T. W. (1984) *Prisms*. Cambridge, MA: MIT Press.
Adorno, T. W. (1986) 'What Does Coming to Terms With the Past Mean?', T. Bahti and G. Hartman (trans.), in G. Hartman (ed.), *Bitburg in Moral and Political Perspective*, Bloomington, IN: Indiana University Press, 114–129.
Adorno, T. W. (1987) *Aesthetic Theory*, Robert-Hullot Kentor (trans.), Minneapolis, MN: University of Minnesota Press.
Adorno, T. W. (1998) *Critical Models: Interventions and Catchwords*, H. Pickford (trans.), New York: Columbia University Press.
Adorno, T. W. and Horkheimer, M. (1972) *Dialectic of Enlightenment*, J. Cummings (trans.), New York: Herder and Herder.
Adorno, T. W. *et al.* (1950) *The Authoritarian Personality*, New York: Norton.
Adorno, T. W. *et al.* (1976) *The Positivist Dispute in German Sociology*, G. Adey and D. Frisby (trans.), London: Heinemann.
Bernan, R. (1977/1978) 'Adorno, Marxism and Art', *Telos*, 34, 157–66.

Bernstein, J. M. (ed.) (1991) *The Culture Industry: Selected Essays on Mass Culture*, London: Routledge.

Bernstein, J. M. (2001) *Adorno: Disenchantment and Ethics*, Cambridge: Cambridge University Press.

Buck-Morss, S. (1977) 'T. W. Adorno and the Dilemmas of Bourgeois Philosophy', *Salmagundi*, 36, 76–98.

Dallmayr, F. (1997) 'The Politics of Nonidentity – Adorno, Postmodernism – and Edward Said', *Political Theory*, 25 (1), 33–56.

Dews, P. (1991) 'Adorno, Poststructuralism and the Critique of Identity', in A. Benjamin (ed.), *The Problems of Modernity*, London: Routledge, 1–22.

Geuss, R. (1998) 'Art and Criticism in Adorno's Aesthetics', *European Journal of Philosophy*, 6 (3), 297–317.

Habermas, J. (1983) 'Theodor Adorno: The Primal History of Subjectivity – Self-Affirmation Gone Wild', in J. Habermas (ed.), *Philosophical Political Profiles*, F. G. Lawrence (trans.), London: Heinmann.

Habermas, J. (1984) *The Theory of Communicative Action*, Vol. 1, T. McCarthy (trans.), London: Heineman.

Habermas, J. (1987) *The Philosophical Discourse of Modernity*, F. Lawrence (trans.), Cambridge: Polity Press.

Harding, J. (1992) 'Historical Dialectics and the Autonomy of Art in Adorno's *Aesthetische Theorie*,' *Journal of Aesthetics and Art Criticism*, 50 (3), 183–195.

Heller, A. (1978) 'The Positivist Dispute as a Turning Point in German Post-War Theory', *New German Critique*, 15, 49–56.

Hohendahl, P. U. (1981) 'Autonomy of Art: Looking back at Adorno's *Ästhetische Theorie*', *German Quarterly*, 54, 133–148.

Hohendahl, P. U. (1992) 'The Displaced Intellectual? Adorno's American Years Revisited,' *New German Critique*, 56, 76–100.

Honneth, A. (2000) 'The Possibility of a Disclosing Critique of Society: *The Dialectic of Enlightenment* in Light of Current Debates in Social Criticism' *Constellations*, 7 (1), 116–127.

Hullot-Kentor, R. (1989) 'Back to Adorno', *Telos*, 81, Fall, 5–29.

Huyssen, A. (1983) 'Adorno in Reverse: From Hollywood to Richard Wagner', *New German Critique*, 29, 8–38.

Jameson, F. (1967) 'Adorno: or, Historical Tropes', *Salmagundi*, 5, 3–43.

Jameson, F. (1971) *Marxism and Form: Twentieth-Century Dialectical Theories of Literature*, Princeton, NJ: Princeton University Press.

Jameson, F. (1990) *Late Marxism: Adorno, or, then Persistence of the Dialectic*, London: Verso.

Jauss, H. R. (1982) 'Sketch of a Theory and History of the Aesthetic Experience', in *Aesthetic Experience and Literary Hermeneutic*, M. Shaw (trans.), Minneapolis, MN: University of Minnesota Press, 3–151.

Jay, M. (1977) 'The Concept of Totality in Lukacs and Adorno', *Telos*, 32, 117–137.

Jay, M. (1984a) 'Adorno in America', *New German Critique*, 31, 157–182.

Jay, M. (1984b) *Adorno*, Cambridge, MA: Harvard University Press.

Knuspit, D. (1975) 'Critical Notes on Adorno's Sociology of Music and Art', *Journal of Aesthetics and Art Criticism*, 33, 321–327.

Lewandowski, J. D. (1996) 'Adorno on Jazz and Society', *Philosophy and Social Criticism*, 22 (5), 103–121.

Lowenthal, L. (1984) 'Recollections of Theodor W. Adorno', *Telos*, no. 61 (Fall), 158–165.

Morgan, W. (1989) 'Adorno on Sport: The Case of the Fractured Dialectic', *Theory and Society*, 17 (6), 813–838.

Müller-Doohm, S. (2005) 'Theordor W. Adorno and Jürgen Habermas – Two Ways of Being a Public Intellectual', *European Journal of Social Theory*, 8 (3), 269–280.

Naegle, R. (1986) 'The Scene of the Other: Theodor W. Adorno's Negative Dialectics in the Context of Poststructuralism', in *Postmodernism and Politics*, J. Arac (ed.), Minneapolis, MN: University of Minnesota Press, 91–111.

Nederman, C. and Guilding, J. (1981) 'Popular Occultism and Critical Social Theory: Exploring Some Thems in Adorno's Critique of Astrology and the Occult', *Sociological Analysis*, 42 (4), 325–332.

Osborne, P. (1992) 'A Marxism for the Postmodern? Jameson's Adorno', *New German Critique*, 56, 171–192.

Rorty, R. (2000) 'The Oversimplification of Politics', *Constellations*, 7 (1), 128–132.

Savage, R. (2005) 'Adorno's Philopolemology: The "Parataxis" Speech as Example', *European Journal of Social Theory*, 8 (3), 281–295.

Schönherr, U. (1991) 'Adorno and Jazz: Reflections on a Failed Encounter', *Telos*, 87, 85–96.

Thomas, C. (1989) 'A Knowledge That Would Not Be Power: Adorno, Nostalgia, and the Historicity of the Musical Subject', *New German Critique*, 48, 155–175.

Waldman, D. (1977) 'Critical Theory and Film: Adorno and "The Culture Industry" Revisited', *New German Critique*, no. 12 (Fall), 39–60.

Wellmer, A. (1985) 'Reason, Utopia and the Dialectic of Enlightenment', in R. Bernstein (ed.), *Habermas and Modernity*, Cambridge, MA: MIT Press, 35–66.

Wellmer, A. (2000) 'The Death of the Sirens and the Origin of the Work of Art', *New German Critique*, 81, 5–19.

Witkin, R. W. (2000) 'Why did Adorno Hate Jazz?', *Sociological Theory*, 18 (1), 145–170.

Whitebook, J. (1993) 'From Schoenberg to Odysseus: Aesthetic, Psychic, and Social Synthesis in Adorno and Wellmer', *New German Critique*, 58, 45–64.

Whitebook, J. (2000) 'The *Urgeschichte* of Subjectivity Reconsidered', *New German Critique*, 81, 125–141.

Wolin, R. (1979) 'The De-Aestheticisation of Art: On Adorno's *Äesthetische Theorie*.' *Telos*, no. 41, Fall, 105–127.

Wolin, R. (1990) 'Utopia, Mimesis, and Reconciliation. A Redemptive Critique of Adorno's *Aesthetic Theory*,' *Representations*, 32, Fall, 33–49.

Yack, B. (1997) *The Fetishism of Modernities*, Notre Dame: University of Notre Dame Press.

Part II

7
Analytical Marxism and the Academy
Jason Edwards

The publication of G. A. Cohen's *Karl Marx's Theory of History: A Defence* in 1978, marked the beginning of a project that would come to be known as analytical Marxism. It flourished during the 1980s alongside its close cousin, rational-choice Marxism, but by the 1990s it was largely defunct. Analytical Marxism was another in a range of responses to a perceived theoretical and political crisis of Marxism in the 1970s. But while at this time many Marxists struggled to try and connect theory and practice in order to inform socialist strategy, the analytical Marxists took a different tack. They rejected the notion that Marxism should be considered principally as a means of analysing and intervening in current social and political conflict, and instead attempted to construct it as a set of empirically testable abstract theses about historical development and collective action. Accordingly, there was little analysis in analytical Marxism of the role of the intellectual in modern capitalist societies. In this chapter, however, I will argue that analytical Marxism does indeed tell us a great deal about the role of the 'intellectual' in contemporary capitalist societies, though more in practice than in its substantive contributions. Nonetheless, by considering the work of G. A. Cohen on history, and Jon Elster on ideology, I shall show how the conceptual and theoretical presuppositions of analytical Marxism enjoin an apolitical, in a specific sense of the term, view of intellectual activity. In part, this apoliticism was a product of the intellectual and political conjuncture in which the Western academy has developed over the past 40 years. But the very concepts and theories that analytical Marxism employed were themselves a component of that conjuncture: they moulded it just as it moulded them.

The leading analytical Marxists, G. A. Cohen, Jon Elster and John Roemer, came from different backgrounds. What they shared in common was an education in Western universities during the 1960s, and some formative commitment to Marxist thought and socialist politics. In the midst of the 'crisis of Marxism' during the 1970s, there was a variety of responses from a new generation of Marxist-influenced thinkers. At the same time, in both North America and Western Europe, the first serious challenges to the post-war order of capitalist societies and the Cold War system of states were emerging. These challenges did not come principally from the 'old' left of organised labour and its political parties, but from movements for civil rights, peace, and the empowerment of marginalised social groups. A central site for these movements and the radical ideas associated with them was the university, with student activism playing the leading role in the protests against the Vietnam War and, in May 1968 in Paris, the events that nearly toppled de Gaulle's administration. While this new student-led radicalism was challenging and, to an extent, changing the face of political and social relations in the West, Marxism was becoming a central intellectual force in academic life. In sociology, economics and some of the humanities, Marxism came close to becoming the mainstream form of analysis. This was not the Marxism of the Soviet Union, the 'diamat' so crudely and programmatically outlined in Stalin's notorious essay, 'Dialectical and Historical Materialism' as a quasi-religious, quasi-metaphysical belief system. The events in Hungary in 1956, and even more so in Czechoslovakia in 1968, had utterly discredited the Soviet variant in the eyes of most Western Marxists. Rather this was a Marxism that was theoretically complex, designed to demonstrate the intricacies of the evolution and structure of the modern capitalist mode of production, and by so doing charting a course towards its revolutionary transformation.

In the 1960s, the most influential of all Marxist thinkers was Louis Althusser. Althusser's main work, to be found in his books *For Marx* and *Reading Capital*, and the famous essay, 'Ideology and Ideological State Apparatuses' (Althusser 1990; Althusser and Balibar 1975; Althusser 1971), was an attempt to clarify a Marxist philosophy that could hold the structural and temporal complexity of the modern capitalist social formation together under the concept of the capitalist mode of production. This audacious effort was welcomed by many younger Marxists who found that 'classical' Marxism, with its emphasis on determination by the economy in the last instance and the proletariat as the exclusive agency of revolutionary transformation, could not account for the social and political relations in modern capitalist and 'communist' societies alike, nor the relations between these societies.

Yet the theoretical confidence of Althusser and those influenced by him had by the early 1970s given way to an assertion of a 'crisis' in Marxism that was of both a theoretical and political order. There can be no question that it was the 'political' crisis that was of greater importance. The movements of the late 1960s, while they had certainly moulded social and political consciousness in a way that would only become clear in the long term, had limited immediate political impact. 'Liberalisation' by Western states in the 1970s fell far short of the demands of the 1968 radicals. Moreover, the traditional working class not only continued to show signs of political conservatism, their radicalism largely confined to trade union activity, but also appeared to be on the wane as a social force. The social composition of wage labour in Western societies was being transformed, though it was a transformation that had been long in the making.

The theoretical and political crisis of Marxism was dealt with in the English-speaking world in a number of ways. The New Left in the United States never had a wholly comfortable relationship with Marxism, finding it insufficient either to explain or prescribe political solutions to problems like racial or gender discrimination and the particular character of American political power. Others found resources in 'heterodox' forms of Marxism, like Trotskyism and Maoism, while others still were to reject ultimately the notion that Marxism could, at least by itself, provide the analytical and political tools for dealing with modern capitalist societies.

It was in this context of the crisis of Marxism that G. A. Cohen worked on and published his *Karl Marx's Theory of History: A Defence*, often seen as the founding text of analytical Marxism. Cohen came from communist background in Canada where he studied as an undergraduate at McGill, before doing his postgraduate work in Oxford and taking up his first lectureship, in moral philosophy, at University College, London (Cohen 1997). Cohen read Althusser in the late 1960s, but Althusser (and indeed 'Western' Marxism in general) had little explicit impact on his work. The dominant influence was rather the kind of analytical philosophy associated with Gilbert Ryle, which flourished in Oxford during the 1950s and 1960s. For Ryle, the purpose of philosophy above all else was to construct logically rigorous arguments that were susceptible of proof (Ryle 1954). While other philosophers in the analytical mode had striven to demonstrate that Marxism as a theory of history and society was incapable of being expressed in a logically rigorous form (Acton 1955), Cohen's goal was to show that historical materialism, as this was developed in Marx's texts, could be so rendered.

As will be seen, Cohen's understanding of historical materialism as a logically rigorous, empirically testable scientific theory provides some important insights into his conception of the relationship between intellectuals and politics. As I will argue, it is a view that is shared by other leading analytical Marxists, and reflects the social and political context in which academic life in Western capitalist societies has developed over the last 40 years. Aside from Cohen, the most prominent analytical Marxists who were embedded in that context were Jon Elster, John Roemer and Adam Przeworski (see Roemer 1982; Elster 1985; Przeworski 1985). All three would come to be identified with a particular current within analytical Marxism, namely rational-choice Marxism. 'Rational-choice Marxism', may seem like an oxymoron, with the theory of rational choice in the social sciences stemming from neo-classical accounts of economic behaviour, which most Marxist economists would reject as ideology. But for the rational-choice Marxists, the strategy of adopting the modern tools of economic and social science was perfectly consistent with the project that had already been announced in Cohen's work. Marxism could be defended as a set of theses within the social sciences, not as a methodology. To test the notion, for example, that there is a tendency for the rate of profit to fall in the long term, one need not adopt the economic presuppositions of the Marxist tradition, and in particular the labour theory of value which to the rational-choice Marxists was false (Roemer 1982; Elster 1985).

Elster, Roemer and the other leading analytical Marxists became academically established in the same institutional and intellectual context, one in which social and political science, particularly in North America, but to some extent also in Western Europe and Scandinavia, has come to be seen by many who practise it as a 'profession'. Academics within these disciplines mainly speak to one another and not to the world at large. The analytical and rational-choice Marxists were a far cry from the Marxist intellectuals of post-war Western Europe, not simply in terms of their lack of overt political engagement, but also in the sense of general public recognition. In part, this is down to an essential element of professionalisation: the creation of a specialised form of knowledge, and vocabulary for accessing it, that is comprehensible only to those who have received a fairly lengthy education within the profession. But the same was true for other Anglophone Marxist intellectuals in the 1960s and 1970s. In general, the academicisation of the Marxist intellectual tells us much about the directions that Marxist thought has taken over the past

40 years. This phenomenon has, however, only rarely been an object of Marxist discourse. But this disregard for what is a central theme in the history of Marxist thought, namely the role of the intellectual in modern capitalist societies, cannot be wholly accounted for by some form of unconscious determination of intellectual activity by contemporary capitalist social formations. It is in large part down to the way in which Marxist intellectuals, or, perhaps more fittingly, academics, have conceived of their enterprise. Nowhere was this more evident than in the work of the analytical Marxists.

Cohen's *Karl Marx's Theory of History* set the tone for the early years of analytical Marxism. As we have seen, Cohen understands historical materialism as capable of being constructed as a logically rigorous and empirically testable scientific theory. Cohen's account of what constitutes the scientificity of historical materialism is, however, elliptical. At times, as in the passage below, it would seem that he wants to defend an old-fashioned positivism:

> The refutation [of the thesis that science is superstructural or ideological] depends on what some will think is a rather simple, and 'pre-Kuhnian', account of science. We would defend such an account, but cannot be obliged to do so here. Here it will suffice to point out that the view accords with nineteenth century conceptions of science, from which Marx did not deviate. (Cohen 1978: 46)

But in *Karl Marx's Theory of History*, it is not always clear in whose voice Cohen is speaking (Marx's or his own), and consequently whether the defence of particular positions is made just in order to render Marx's theory coherent, or because those positions are believed, more generally, to be true.[1] Thus, in an appendix to the book ('Karl Marx and the Withering Away of Social Science'), Cohen criticises Marx's dictum that science is unnecessary where there is no difference between appearance and reality:

> Marx's dictum must be abandoned. If we accept his crude contrast between observation and theory, we may say that scientific explanation always uncovers a reality unrepresented in appearance, but that it only sometimes discredits appearance. Let us call science *subversive* when it does the latter, and *neutral* when it does not. (Cohen 1978: 342)

It is not any clearer here what criterion of the scientificity of a theory Cohen is himself advocating (although the description of Marx's putative belief in a clear distinction between theory and observation as 'crude', provides some indication that Cohen believes this kind of positivism to be at least problematic). But Cohen does make it clear that he himself wishes to defend a view of a society in which there is as little social science as possible, for

> I believe that it is desirable for a person to understand *himself* without relying upon theory. For there is a sense, difficult to make clear, in which I am alienated from myself and from what I do to the extent that I need theory to reach myself and the reasons governing my actions.
>
> The need for a theory of the social processes in which I participate reflects a similar alienation from these processes. Hence a reduced reliance on social science is desirable. This does not, of course, make it possible. The yearning for transparent human relations can be satisfied in part, because we can specify removable social institutions, notably the market, which foster opacity. But it is futile to hope for the total transparency contemplated in the Hegelio-Marxist tradition. (Cohen 1978: 343)

This passage is interesting because it expresses a tension that is evident not only within Cohen's work and analytical Marxism, but in much of the Marxist tradition. On the one hand, Cohen looks forward to a social condition in which the roles of science and theory (and the scientific intellectual) have been much reduced. This constitutes a liberation from abstraction, where one's relations to others can be 'transparent', unmediated by ideas that disguise or distort our real interests and identities as members of the human species. It follows that where social reality was not masked by social appearance, there would be little need for social science. But, Cohen suggests, sometimes *neutral* science does not reveal distortion, but clarifies or takes to a higher level of understanding reality as it appears to us. In this sense, such neutral social science is necessary, even in a communist society. The kinds of potentially 'neutral' science that Cohen cites – linguistics, communication theory and 'in realms of economics which will outlive the market' – indicate that he views neutral science as a largely technical body of knowledge (a productive force, as it were), which help us to understand, and presumably shape the character of social phenomena. We can only hope that such science 'will be generally accessible' (Cohen 1978: 344).

The tension in this view of science is between the picture of a world free from specialised knowledge and social roles, and the belief that such a world is only achievable (and maintainable) given specialised knowledge and social roles. It is a tension that can be located in the work of others who have attempted to establish Marxism on a scientific footing, such as Engels (1978), Plekhanov (1969), Kautsky (1988) and Althusser (Althusser and Balibar 1975). With regard to the latter, Cohen's defence of Marx, and analytical Marxism more broadly speaking, was a great deal more involved in the Althusserian milieu that is often acknowledged. The 'British Althusserians', in particular Barry Hindess, Paul Hirst and their colleagues, had also tried to establish Marxism on a scientific footing. The difference was that they explicitly adopted a very different view of scientific activity to that held by Cohen, and against this standard found Marxism wanting (Hindess and Hirst 1975, 1977; Cutler *et al.* 1977). But unlike this latter group, and the Marxists associated with the *New Left Review* who opposed them, Cohen's engagement with Marxism was distinctly apolitical – in a specific sense of the word. The Marxism of *Karl Marx's Theory of History* is a Marxism of the *longue durée*, which tells us little about current political conditions and what strategy socialists should follow (Lock 1988). In contrast, what came out of the debates in British Marxism in the 1970s, for both the Althusserians and for the remnants of the British New Left, was a view of Marxism as a theory of politics whose role was to analyse the current conjuncture and suggest feasible strategies for transforming capitalist social relations.

While historical materialism has often been regarded as the central and most enduring achievement of Marx and the Marxist tradition, numerous Marxist intellectuals have foundered when it comes to drawing clear political inferences from the theory of history. In the first two decades of the twentieth century, thinkers like Korsch (1970), Lukács (1971), Gramsci (1971), and Lenin (1932), were forced to move away from the economic determinism of 'orthodox' Marxism even if paying lip-service to the notion of determination by the economy in the last instance. Later in the Western Marxist tradition, the Frankfurt School, existential and structural Marxism imported philosophical ideas from outside Marxism in order to salvage historical materialism from what they understood to be, when stated in its crude form, its economic and technological determinism. Cohen's book was a striking riposte to these Marxisms because it set out to defend historical materialism as a general theory of historical and social development that gives priority to technological innovation.

For Cohen, the concepts of historical materialism represent distinct elements of any social order: forces of production, relations of production, economic structure, superstructure. In Marx's theory, or rather in the clearest reconstruction of that theory possible, the forces of production are distinct from the relations of production, the sum of which constitutes the economic structure of society. The legal and political superstructure of a social order is functionally related to the economic structure, ensuring the reproduction of its constitutive relations over time; and, in turn, the economic structure is functionally related to the productive forces, ensuring their continual development. What causes historical and social change, on this model, is not the specific relations that obtain between individuals in the relations of production. Particular class relations and the political manifestations of them are the immediate determinants of transition between social orders, but it is the level of development of the productive forces that ultimately determines the shape of class conflict and the transformative possibilities.

On this understanding of historical materialism, class actors are constrained by the level of development of the productive forces, and the corresponding relations of production that promote their growth, but within these constraints there are numerous possibilities for social and political relations. Accordingly, historical materialism says little about what particular class relations will obtain in a given social order at any given time. Historical materialism in itself tells us nothing of what role intellectuals might play in the particular social order that is contemporary capitalism. The question of political action is not one to be determined at the level of Marx's theory of history, but is, for Cohen, rather a question of what kind of moral decisions social actors can make within the broad class relations characteristic of certain social orders, particularly with respect to the notion of justice (Cohen 1988, chapter 14). It may be that intellectuals can be agents of capitalism, in the sense that they accept and reproduce ideological beliefs that are designed to misrepresent the nature of capitalist class relations. At the same time, however, intellectuals may present socialist challenges to capitalism by recognising, and arguing against, the injustices that are characteristic of capitalist class relations. However, in the latter case this requires that the intellectual is party to the kind of subversive science that demonstrates a gulf between social appearance and social reality, whose demise Cohen had looked forward to in *Karl Marx's Theory of History*.

During the early 1980s, Cohen revised his view of historical materialism, claiming that it may only be true in the 'restricted' sense that economic phenomena will not always explain 'non-economic' phenomena, even if non-economic phenomena do not explain economic phenomena (Cohen 1988, chapter 9). This does not demonstrate that historical materialism, as a theory concerned to explain the development of history and societies according to the growth in human productive capabilities, is false, only that it is a theory with a specific object that does not exhaust the entire range of what is involved in human social life. It follows from this revision of historical materialism that intellectual life need not be determined or explained by material or economic factors. In fact, as Cohen's work from the mid-1980s onwards suggests, the decision to be an anti-capitalist intellectual is entirely moral rather than scientific.

By the mid-1990s then, Cohen and other analytical Marxists had accepted that historical materialism, even where it could be presented as a logically rigorous theory, could only provide limited explanations of its objects, namely historical change and social order, and that it told us virtually nothing about what moral ends socialist should be striving to achieve. But this shift of objects, from history to morality, was not a change engendered by 'discoveries' made by the analytical Marxists as they went about their investigation of historical materialism. Rather, such a switch was made inevitable by the very presuppositions of the analytical Marxist enterprise. From the beginning, Marxism was seen as a collection of theses, some of which could be given logical coherence, others which had to be abandoned at the start (see Elster 1986, chapter 10), and each of which had distinct objects. While, as a set of historical theses, Marxism had some standing, it was simply not possible to describe Marxism as a distinctive moral theory. Of course, Marx employed moral vocabulary in his work, but it is just not credible, as the analytical Marxists fully recognised, to say that Marx believed moral theory was central to his work. If Marxists were interested in morality, they would have to turn to non-Marxist thinkers and concepts to think it. Thus it was, once historical materialism was shown to be of limited relevance to socialist strategy, that Cohen and the other leading analytical Marxists would turn towards moral discourse.

However, the idea that the analytical Marxists failed to entertain from the outset is that Marxism might be seen not as a distinct set of theses with differing objects, nor even a science of historical development and social formations, but rather as a theory whose principal object was not the past, but the present. Cohen's reconstruction of Marx's theory of history takes as its key text the 1859 Preface to *A Contribution to the Critique of Political Economy* (Marx 1992: 424–428) the most programmatic of all Marx's published statements about the nature of his historical method. But Marx's principal work is undoubtedly *Capital* (1990), which is very evidently not designed to test historical materialism as a general theory of human productive development.

Capital is a book that is first and foremost concerned with describing the economic and social relations, or the relations of production, of the capitalist mode of production, and in so describing attending to its possible trajectories and how a transformation to socialism might be effected. Moreover, Marx's most accessible and compelling writing is to be found in his reflections on contemporary politics, most prominently in the *Eighteenth Brumaire of Louis Bonaparte* (1977a) and *The Civil War in France* (1977b). There, and in other places, we see an attempt to analyse the precise character of competing social and political forces in a given context, and what interventions in the context may prove successful for socialists.

In contrast, the literature of analytical Marxism had little if anything to say about present social and political conditions. Certainly, this could not be put down to the lack of qualifications of its main protagonists to write such analyses. Rather, it resulted from the characteristics of the political and intellectual environment in which analytical Marxism developed. The notion that Marxism was in the midst of a 'crisis', a notion that predates analytical Marxism, provides the context in which Marxism needed to be 'salvaged', 'reconstructed', 'recycled' and so on. In this context, analytical Marxism increasingly resembled the kind of 'neutral', as opposed to 'subversive', science of which Cohen had written in *Karl Marx's Theory of History*. It sought not to reveal a gulf between the appearance and reality of capitalism by engaging in a critique of the politics and ideology of current capitalist social relations. Rather, it focussed its intellectual energies on the clarification of theories and concepts, whether in the fields of moral theory, sociology or economics, that might inform such a critique, but which were both on logical and practical grounds separate from it. In both theory and practice, then, analytical Marxism had become an apolitical intellectual activity.

This view of the role of the Marxist intellectual in contemporary capitalist societies differs markedly from that of the most famous Marxist theorist of intellectuals, Antonio Gramsci. Gramsci grounded all intellectual activity in distinct social and historical conditions, with intellectuals falling into one of two categories: the 'traditional' intellectuals, in the pursuit of 'neutral' knowledge, whose function is nonetheless dictated by the historical class relations of a society; and the 'organic' intellectuals, who articulate the interests of specific social classes (Gramsci 1971: 5–14). Gramsci argued that everyone is an intellectual, in the sense that each 'participates in a particular conception of the world, has a conscious line of moral conduct, and therefore contributes to sustain a conception of the world' (Gramsci 1971: 9). Yet, at the same time, 'intellectuals' as a group, whether traditional or organic, perform specific social and political functions. In Gramsci's Marxism, the dominance of a particular class is not simply a consequence of its control of a society's productive forces combined with a monopoly over the state's exercise of coercion; it also rests on the ideological assimilation of the traditional intellectuals by the organic intellectuals of a class, in order to create a 'historical bloc' (Gramsci 1971: 168). Intellectuals, then, come to form part of a social totality in which the production of knowledge is inextricably tied to particular class positions and interests. Gramsci recognised the autonomy of the intellectuals from the economic structure of a society, but at the same time this autonomy is limited by the configuration of class forces in a specific ideological conjuncture.

Apart from Cohen, Jon Elster was perhaps the leading analytical Marxist of the early 1980s. At first sight, Elster's 'Marxism' was of a very different order to that of Gramsci. Elster's early work had focussed on the problem of social explanation in general, and, more narrowly, social explanation in Marxism. Perhaps, even more so than Cohen, Elster was true to the approach of analytical Marxism, holding that Marxism should be considered principally as a set of (potentially) scientific hypotheses. He showed little signs of partisanship in his work on Marx (contrast with the explicit way in which Cohen's first book was a *defence* of Marx's theory of history). The approach that Elster took to Marx in his 1985 book, *Making Sense of Marx*, begins by stripping Marx down to the methodological essentials. Marx, he argues, does provide a valid method for the study of social phenomena, but it is not the 'dialectical' method that so many Marxists have defended. Rather: '[Marx] emphasised the unintended consequences of human action, arguing that they are to be understood in the causal-cum-intentional framework that has become the standard language of the social sciences (Elster 1985: 3).'

Causal explanation of aggregate phenomena in terms of the individual action that goes into them is 'the specifically Marxist contribution to the methodology of the social sciences' (Elster 1985: 4). As Marcus Roberts has pointed out, this is quite wrong – Marx did not pioneer this method, and it is not distinctively Marxist (it was used by, amongst others, Adam Smith) (see Roberts 1996: 29–30). Nonetheless, Elster proceeds to test Marx's substantive theses according to this methodology, finding most of them wanting, and the few that are left in need of important revision, in line with a methodological individualist approach.

One of the aspects of Marx's work that Elster thought worthy of salvation was the theory of ideology (Elster 1986: 199). In order to save it, we must first of all reject those accounts of ideology which employ functional explanation – that is, the explanation of ideological structures in terms of the benefits they confer on social groups or classes – or see ideologies purely in terms of 'emanation' from the economic structure of society (Elster 1985: 460). This approach, *prima facie*, would seem to rule out the kind of explanation of the role of intellectuals that Gramsci had developed. Any account of the ideological function of intellectuals that does not provide 'microfoundations', that is the stipulation of the causes and intentions generating belief formation and dissemination, is to be rejected. Gramsci clearly did not adopt a methodological individualist approach, conceiving ideologies as structures of belief that can be treated as having causal power, and could therefore be regarded as, in themselves, constituting starting points of social explanation.

However, while Elster does not engage directly with Gramsci, he does seek, via his reading of Marx, to defend a similar thesis to that of Gramsci, namely the limited autonomy of intellectuals. Elster wishes to argue that certain world-views developed by ideologists (or what on occasion he refers to as 'intellectuals') have a degree of autonomy from the economic structure. If particular ideas come to be accepted by the ruling class, Elster sees this as an outcome of the operation of a 'filter mechanism': 'Metaphorically speaking, the class shops around for ideological spokesmen until they find someone who has both sufficient prestige among other men of ideas and views sufficiently close to the interest of the class' (Elster 1985: 471). This view does not seem inconsistent with Gramsci's account of the composition of the 'historic bloc'. This also involves a conception of intellectuals, holding to various world-views, who are economically autonomous of the ruling class, but are nonetheless employed by it to cement their ideological hegemony.

Nevertheless, there are major differences between Elster's and Gramsci's approaches. It can be presumed that Elster would reject Gramsci's account of intellectuals on the grounds of its 'functionalism', that is its conception of intellectuals fulfilling specific political functions in order to benefit the economically dominant class. If intellectuals do provide such services, this must be explained in causal-cum-intentional terms. In the absence of deliberate duping on material, status or political grounds, the intellectuals must hold that their beliefs are true *independently* of the social context in which they are articulated and defended. At the same time, members of the economically dominant class may accept the beliefs of the ideologists as true, or may provide support for the ideologists in the knowledge that the dissemination of those ideas serves to maintain their social position and material interests. In any case, according to the rigorous individualism of Elster's methodological position, we cannot understand how ideological beliefs operate independently of causal mechanisms that operate at the level of cognitive psychology (Elster 1985: 476–493).

As several of his critics pointed out, Elster's insistence on 'microfoundations' and individualist explanation, while they might alert us to some of the problems with cruder forms of functionalism in Marxist thought, can only provide a partial account of the explanation of ideology. Elster's account of ideology rests on what Barry Hindess has described as 'a surreptitious structural determination of actor's forms of thought' (Hindess 1988: 23). This is a broader problem with individualist explanation as it is employed in rational-choice theory, which Elster wishes, in part at least, to defend. While Elster does not consider (and here he is on common grounds with Gramsci) ideology as being determined in some crude and direct fashion by class position and interests, he nonetheless claims that the beliefs and desires of the rational intellectual are pre-determined by a given context. Rational intellectuals, in this regard, 'act' in only a very limited sense. They respond in algorithmic fashion to a set of beliefs that have not been formed by them, and to which they unquestioningly submit. In contrast, the merit of Gramsci's approach is to show the extent to which ideological belief is *politically* contestable, in a way which Elster fails to recognise explicitly, and which, in any case, is incompatible with the kind of methodological individualism and rational-choice theory to which he was wedded when writing *Making Sense of Marx*.

In considering Marx's account of ideology, then, Elster seems to embrace the same kind of apoliticism that characterised Cohen's approach to Marx's theory of history. Both thinkers are committed to a view of the individual, and thus those particular individuals who are 'intellectuals', that is one-dimensional. The individual appears in no particular historical context, but at the same time in every one, as a rational prisoner of extra-individual or 'social' forces. What is missing from this analysis is something that has been central to much of the Marxist tradition: that is the attempt to use Marxist concepts in order to understand the differences of particular social formations in specific conjunctural conditions. Cohen, Elster and much of analytical Marxism tended to assume these conditions, and more importantly, in failing to recognise their political contingency, ended up hypostatising them. The point is of particular significance when considering the lack of any serious attempt in analytical Marxism to consider its own intellectual and social context. Analytical Marxism thus failed to explain itself in its own terms.

In this chapter, I have argued that the work of analytical Marxism, while providing for little explicit engagement with the question of the role of the intellectual in contemporary capitalist societies, tells us a great deal about it. In part this is because analytical Marxism was a product of the Western academy as this has emerged over the past 40 years. It has produced scholars whose work is 'professional', in the sense that it is disseminated and discussed only amongst a limited number of relevantly trained people. At the same time, these people represent the first generation of a 'globalised' academy in which individuals move from academic posts in different national contexts with ease and where the academy has come to be increasingly isolated from the social and political conflicts that define these contexts.[2] At the same time, the apolitical view of intellectual activity that the analytical Marxists tended towards can be seen in the very concepts and approaches they adopted. As in much of 'mainstream' Anglophone social and political science, the analytical Marxists failed to relate these concepts and approaches to the ideological and political conjuncture in which they were located. The theory and practice of the analytical Marxists contributed to the misleading impression that the academy has become a site of greater intellectual autonomy over the past 40 years. Yet any reconstructed Marxism in the present must surely pose as one of its central problems the political role of the modern academy and the concepts and theories of its 'intellectuals'.

Notes

1. I'm grateful to David Bates (personal communication) for raising this point.
2. Thus, the leading analytical Marxists, scattered across universities in North America and Europe, used to arrange an annual meeting (usually in Paris) every September (Cohen 1997). Contrast with the way that earlier 'schools' of Marxism had a distinctly national character, or were linked to specific academic institutions.

References

Acton, H. (1955) *The Illusion of the Epoch: Marxism-Leninism as a Philosophical Creed*, London: Routledge and Kegan Paul.
Althusser, L. (1971) 'Ideology and Ideological State Apparatuses', in L. Althusser, *Lenin and Philosophy*, New York: Monthly Review Press, 127–186.
Althusser, L. (1990) *For Marx*, London: Verso.
Althusser, L. and Balibar, E. (1975) *Reading Capital*, London: New Left Books.
Bernstein, E. (1990) *The Preconditions of Socialism and the Tasks of Social Democracy*. Cambridge: Cambridge University Press.

Cohen, G. A. (1978) *Karl Marx's Theory of History: A Defence*, Oxford: Oxford University Press.

Cohen, G. A. (1988) *History, Labour and Freedom: Themes from Marx*, Oxford: Oxford University Press.

Cohen, G.A. (1989) 'On the Currency of Egalitarian Justice', *Ethics* (99), 906–944.

Cohen, G. A. (1995) *Self-Ownership, Freedom and Equality*, Cambridge: Cambridge University Press.

Cohen, G. A. (1996) 'Interview', *Imprints*, 1, 7–25.

Cohen, G. A. (1997) 'Commitment Without Reverence', *Imprints*, 1(3), 23–36.

Cutler, A., Hussain, A., Hindess, B. and Hirst, P. (1977) *Marx's Capital and Capitalism Today*, Vol. 1, London: Routledge and Kegan Paul.

Elster, J. (1985) *Making Sense of Marx*, Cambridge: Cambridge University Press.

Elster, J. (1986) *Karl Marx: An Introduction*, Cambridge: Cambridge University Press.

Engels, F. (1978) 'Dialectics of Nature', in Karl Marx and Frederick Engels, *Collected Works*, Vol. 25, London: Lawrence and Wishart.

Gramsci, A. (1971) *Selections for the Prison Notebooks*, London: Lawrence and Wishart.

Hindess, B. (1988) *Choice, Rationality and Social Theory*, London: Unwin Hyman.

Hindess, B. and Hirst, P. (1975) *Pre-Capitalist Modes of Production*, London: Routledge and Kegan Paul.

Hindess, B. and Hirst, P. (1977) *Mode of Production and Social Formation*, London: Macmillan.

Kautsky, K. (1988) *The Materialist Conception of History*, New Haven, CT: Yale University Press.

Korsch, K. (1970) *Marxism and Philosophy*, London: New Left Books.

Lenin, V. (1932) *State and Revolution*, New York: International Publishers.

Lock, G. (1988) 'Louis Althusser and G. A. Cohen: A Confrontation', *Economy and Society*, 17 (4), 499–517.

Lukács, G. (1971) *History and Class Consciousness*, London: Merlin Press.

Marx, K. (1977a) *The Eighteenth Brumaire of Louis Bonaparte*, in D. McLellan (ed.), *Karl Marx: Selected Writings*, Oxford: Oxford University Press, 300–325.

Marx, K. (1977b) *The Civil War in France*, in D. McLellan (ed.), *Karl Marx: Selected Writings*, Oxford: Oxford University Press, 540–558.

Marx, K. (1990) *Capital*, Volume 1, Harmondsworth: Penguin.

Marx, K. (1992) *Early Writings*, Harmondsworth: Penguin.

Plekhanov, G. (1969) *Fundamental Problems of Marxism*, London: Lawrence and Wishart.

Przeworski, A. (1985) *Capitalism and Social Democracy*, Cambridge: Cambridge University Press.

Roberts, M. (1996) *Analytical Marxism: A Critique*, London: Verso.

Roemer, J. (1982) *A General Theory of Exploitation and Class*, Cambridge, MA: Harvard University Press.

Ryle, G. (1954) *Dilemmas*, Cambridge: Cambridge University Press.

8
Philosophy and Ideology: Marxism and the Role of Religion in Contemporary Politics

Sean Sayers

In this chapter, I will first describe Marx's account of religion and then use it to explore the role of religion in contemporary politics. This has reached an unprecedented level in recent times. How can Marx's work help us to understand this and respond to it?

Marx appears to adopt two quite different kinds of approach to religion. On the one hand, he regards it in traditional philosophical terms; on the other hand he treats it as a form of ideology. There seems to be a tension between these two approaches.[1] Marx's purely philosophical attitude to religion is made clear in his well-known dictum that religion is the 'opium of the people' (Marx 1975b: 244). Marx is a materialist and atheist. He regards religious beliefs as false and illusory. There are no gods, there is no supernatural realm. The physical world is all that there is.

Philosophical materialism and atheism of this sort was not invented by Marx and it is not peculiar to him. Indeed, such ideas can be traced back to the ancient Greeks. They were taken up and developed by Enlightenment thinkers in the seventeenth and eighteenth centuries. The success of the natural sciences in explaining the material world led many at that time to reject religious conceptions as illusory and to maintain that everything that happens can be accounted for in the materialistic terms of the natural sciences. Religious beliefs, according to this view, are fanciful and absurd. They have no valid content. They arise from ignorance and fear of the unknown. They will be dispelled, like a morning mist, by the spreading light of reason and scientific knowledge. According to Hobbes, for example, 'anxiety of the time to come' is one of the main causes of religious ideas.

This perpetual fear, always accompanying mankind in the ignorance of causes, as it were in the Dark, must needs have for object something.

And therefore when there is nothing to be seen there is nothing to accuse ... but some *Power* or agent *Invisible*; in which sense perhaps it was that some of the old poets said that the Gods were first created by humane feare. (Hobbes 1985: 169–170)

Marx, too, rejects religion philosophically. Beyond that, however, his approach is quite different. His primary concern is to understand the role that religion actually plays in peoples' lives and to explain why religious beliefs are held. This involves seeing religion not only in rational and philosophical terms, as a body of (false) ideas, but also as a social and psychological phenomenon with specific material causes as a form of *ideology*.

There are two aspects to this approach. It involves an account of the content of religious beliefs, and an explanation of their form. I shall discuss these in turn. As regards content, Marx does not simply reject religious ideas as pure error and illusion. In this, he follows the lead given by other philosophers at the time, particularly Feuerbach. Feuerbach starts from the fundamental thought of what Marx calls 'irreligious criticism', that 'man makes religion, religion does not make man' (Marx 1975b: 244). Feuerbach likens religious beliefs to dreams, but not simply to dismiss them as illusory. On the contrary, Feuerbach argues that they express genuine human wishes and aspirations, but in a projected and alienated form.

Religion is the dream of the human mind. But even in dreams we do not find ourselves in emptiness or in heaven, but on earth, in the realm of reality ... Hence I do nothing more to religion ... than to open its eyes, or rather turn its gaze from the internal to the external, i.e. I change the object as it is in the imagination into the object as it is in reality. (Feuerbach 1957: xxxix)

What is the 'real object' of religion? What is the true content expressed in it, though in an illusory form? According to Feuerbach, the idea of God expresses human hopes and aspirations in a projected and inverted form. 'Man ... projects his being into objectivity, and then again makes himself an object to this projected image of himself thus converted into a subject' (Feuerbach 1957: 29–30). The roles of man and God are inverted.[2] The qualities that we attribute to God love, wisdom, compassion, justice are in fact human qualities, projected and objectified. As Marx puts it, what Feuerbach shows is that 'the earthly family is ... the secret of the holy family' (Marx 1975a: 422).

There is an illuminating analogy here with the approach that Freud later adopts in his analysis of dreams and other neurotic symptoms (cf. Althusser 1971a). Before Freud, most psychologists and philosophers had dismissed dreams as purely imaginary and false mental creations. In this respect their attitude was like that of Enlightenment materialists towards religion. This is indeed the appearance that dreams present, their 'manifest content'. But Freud does not stop with this. By investigating the role that dreams play in human life he shows that they can be interpreted as the disguised and distorted expressions of real feelings and thoughts of the dreamer. He comes to see them as symptoms which reveal a true 'latent content' (Freud 1974, Part II). The true objects of a dream are the real, though often repressed, feelings and thoughts which are disguised but expressed within it.[3]

In a similar way, according to Feuerbach, religious beliefs and feelings, although they have a mistaken and illusory form, have a real and valid content. Thus, Feuerbach insists,

> I by no means say: God is nothing, the Trinity is nothing, the Word of God is nothing, etc. I only show that they are not *that* which the illusions of theology make them ... The reproaches that according to my book religion is an absurdity, a nullity, a pure illusion, would be well founded only if, according to it, that into which I resolve religion ... namely *man's anthropology*, were an absurdity, a nullity, a pure illusion. (Feuerbach 1957: xxxviii)

These ideas provide Marx's starting point. Like Feuerbach, he begins from the premise that religion is a human creation, and he regards the 'manifest', the rational and philosophical content of religious ideas as illusory and false. This is part of what he means when he says that religion is 'the opium of the people'. And yet in the very passage in which this phrase occurs, Marx equally insists that religious ideas should not be dismissed as mere errors. Following Feuerbach he treats religious beliefs as 'symptoms'. They embody a real and valid content, but this is expressed in a disguised and distorted form by being projected into a transcendent beyond. 'Religious suffering is at one and the same time the *expression* of real suffering and a protest against real suffering. Religion is the sigh of the oppressed creature, the heart of a heartless world and the soul of soulless conditions. It is the *opium* of the people.' (Marx 1975b: 244)

To understand religious beliefs, therefore, it is not satisfactory simply to criticise them in traditional philosophical fashion as mistaken and false; the suffering and hope which they express must also be brought to light. If religion is a distorted protest against a 'soulless' situation and a 'heartless' world, these conditions themselves need to be revealed and addressed. Marx's aim in this is not only theoretical but also practical. 'Criticism has plucked the imaginary flowers on the chain not in order that man shall continue to bear that chain without fantasy or consolation but so that he shall throw off the chain and pluck the living flower' (Marx 1975b: 244).

In this way, the unmasking of religious alienation and mystification leads to a criticism of the conditions which give rise to it. 'The abolition of religion as the *illusory* happiness of the people is the demand for their *real* happiness. To call on them to give up their illusions about their condition is to *call on them to give up a condition that requires illusions'* (Marx 1975b: 244). The criticism of religion thus leads directly to social criticism.

In brief outline, this is the first, Feuerbachian, aspect of Marx's account of religion. He develops it early in his life,[4] and it remains a part of Marx's outlook thereafter. There is no reason to believe that he later abandons it, or that it should be rejected as, for example, Althusser argues (Althusser 1969). On the contrary, it can be used to shed important light on the role that religion plays in the world today, as I shall argue in due course. However, Marx soon became aware of the limitations of this approach and he goes on to extend and deepen it. For although it points to the hidden content of religious and other ideological illusions, it does not explain why people perceive their situation in distorted and alienated ways.

Feuerbach does not explicitly address this question. He treats the distortions of religious consciousness simply as subjective intellectual errors. As with the Enlightenment materialists, the implication is that these can be overcome by rational argument alone. Marx's critique of this approach is presented in brilliantly clear and concise terms in the fourth 'Thesis on Feuerbach'.

> Feuerbach starts out from the fact of religious self-alienation, of the duplication of the world into a religious imaginary world and a real secular one. His work consists in the dissolution of the religious world into its secular basis. He overlooks the fact that after completing this work the chief thing still remains to be done. For the fact that the secular basis detaches itself from itself and establishes itself as an independent realm in the clouds can only be explained by the cleavages and self-contradictions within this secular basis. (Marx 1975a: 422)

This is the approach that Marx follows from this time on. It involves not only interpreting and criticising religious beliefs philosophically, but also comprehending them in causal terms as the products of material conditions. Religious ideas are not purely intellectual phenomena located only in a 'space of reasons'. They are social products. They are objectively rooted, they develop and change only with social and economic conditions. The religious outlook can be overcome, therefore, only when the material and social causes which give rise to it are superseded.

It should be noted that, according to the materialist view, the general point here applies to all beliefs not just to religious ones, in that all beliefs are material and social phenomena. Rational argument also involves causal processes according to this view, and these may well be sufficient to change beliefs. Religious ideas, however, are not susceptible to change by rational argument alone, they involve projections and distortions which have other – social and material – causes (Sayers 1989).

Unfortunately Marx does not go on to provide a detailed account of the social and material roots of religion. After his early interest in the topic his focus shifts to the secular realm of economics. His fullest and most illuminating discussion of ideological illusion is in that context, in the account of the 'fetishism of commodities' in Volume I of *Capital*, in which religion figures only in a secondary and subordinate way.

By the 'fetishism of commodities', Marx refers to the fact that, in a market society, economic value seems to be an objective property of things, and the economic laws which are associated with it appear to have an independent character and to assert themselves 'like an over-riding law of Nature' (Marx 1967: 75). According to Marx, however, these are false appearances. In order for a thing to have an economic value it must enter into particular social and economic relations in a particular way. Value is the property of a thing, therefore, only in so far as it is embedded in the social relations of commodity production and the market. Value is a social phenomenon, a social relation.

The social character of economic value was discovered by the classical political economists of the eighteenth century; but this was not in itself sufficient to dispel the appearance of objectivity which value presents.[5] For the seeming independence of economic categories is not a merely subjective illusion, it is an objective feature of the situation, 'the *objective appearance* of the social characteristics of labour' (Marx 1967: 82

my emphasis). The roots of such ideological illusions, according to Marx, are objective and social. Such illusions cannot therefore be dispelled by intellectual criticism alone; they pass away only with social and economic change.[6]

According to Marx, a similar situation holds with religious beliefs. They too persist even in the face of prolonged philosophical criticism and secular influence. This cannot be comprehended if religious beliefs are seen only as subjective intellectual phenomena. They should not be treated only as philosophically mistaken views, they must also be seen as ideological creations, rooted in and reflecting specific social conditions, not only in their content but also in their form.[7]

How are such ideological beliefs related to objective conditions? What accounts for their enduring character? A number of writers have tried to explain this. According to Cohen, ideological illusions 'survive theoretical exposé because theory does not cure the conditions which produce them ... They are not, in the first instance, errors of thought, but distortions in the world, which theory is impotent to rectify' (Cohen 1978: 340). Ideology is the result of a reality which is itself in some sense 'distorted'.

A similar theory is put forward by Larrain who picks up on Marx's early Feuerbachian language (Larrain 1979). In a key passage, upon which Larrain relies for his account, Marx writes,

[r]eligion is ... the self-consciousness and self-esteem of man who has either not yet won through to himself, or has already lost himself again. But, *man* is no abstract being squatting outside the world. Man is *the world of man* – state, society. This state and this society produce religion, which is an inverted consciousness of the world, because they are an inverted world. (Marx 1975b: 244)

In ideology, Larrain argues, reality is subjectively perceived in an 'inverted' way because the objective situation which gives rise to it is itself 'inverted' (Larrain 1979: 57).

In this way, for both Cohen and Larrain, ideology is a *true* consciousness of what is, in some sense, a 'false' and 'inverted' or 'distorted' world. Suggestive as these ideas may at first appear they are ultimately of little real value in explaining the specific character of ideological illusion. It is true that 'inversion' in the Feuerbachian sense may be said to be involved in religious thought, in that God is treated as cause and creator, whereas mankind and the material world appears as effect. However, it is not helpful to maintain that this is a 'true' perception of an 'inverted reality'. What can it mean to say that reality is 'inverted' other than that our ideas of it are? In so far as this means anything it merely restates in a metaphorical way that religion has an 'objective' character, which is what was to be explained in the first place.

A more fully worked out and illuminating account of the objective character of ideology is developed by Althusser. He argues that it is contained not only in beliefs, it is also inscribed in social relations and institutions, in material practices (Althusser 1971b). Althusser's detailed analysis is concerned particularly with the ideology of the 'subject', about which he says much that is important and illuminating. Ultimately, however, in his account the idea of the 'subject' turns out to be a mere construct of objective 'ideological apparatuses'. Thus for Althusser, as with Cohen and Larrain, the illusions and distortions of ideology are seen as objective *as opposed to* subjective creations.

This sort of account is in effect the diametric opposite of the Enlightenment materialist view that ideology is mere subjective illusion. Neither extreme is satisfactory. Neither can satisfactorily account for the character of ideological illusion. The source of such illusion is not located exclusively either in purely subjective consciousness or in the objective world considered on its own. Subjectivity and the objective world are more closely inter-related than either of these views suggest. Our consciousness of the world in the form of religion, economics or whatever is never only a subjective creation, nor is it simply a direct and passive reflection of external and independent objective conditions. These two aspects the subjective and the objective, consciousness and world are more intimately connected and closely implicated with each other than either of these views suggest.

This is a fundamental theme of classical German philosophy from Kant onwards.[8] Both Hegel and Marx are working within this tradition and it is vital to see their work in this context. For Kant, self and world have the universal and unchanging forms given to them by the operation of pure reason and the 'categories'. Hegel's distinctive and revolutionary contribution is to argue that self and world pass through a series of historically evolving shapes which involve both different forms of self-consciousness and different kinds of social practice.[9]

Hegel sees religion as a social and historical phenomenon and analyses it in these terms. According to Hegel 'the first form of religion is immediate religion, nature religion [*Naturreligion*]' (Hegel 1988: 205).[10] Hegel cites religious beliefs that had recently been reported when he was writing (1827) by explorers from African and Eskimo tribal groups, and from China and India (Hegel 1988: 229–235). The religions he is talking about are sometimes thought to involve the worship of natural entities such as the sun, animals, mountains and rivers, etc. Hobbes for example makes great fun of the variety of religious beliefs in these terms.

There is almost nothing that has a name, that has not been esteemed amongst the Gentiles,[11] in one place or another, a God, or Divell ... The unformed matter of the World, was a God, by the name of *Chaos*. The Heaven, the Ocean, the Planets, the Fire, the Earth, the Winds, were so many Gods. Men, Women, a Bird, a Crocodile, a Calf, a Dogge, a Snake, an Onion, a Leeke, Deified. Besides that, they filled almost all places, with spirits called daemons: the plains, with *Pan*, and ... Satyres; the Woods, with Fawnes, and Nymphs; the Sea, with Tritons ... every River, and Fountayn, with a Ghost of his name ... and in the night time, all places with ... Ghosts of men deceased, and a whole kingdome of Fayries and Bugbears. (Hobbes 1985: 173–174)

According to Hegel, however, this involves a fundamental misunderstanding. The religion of nature does not involve the worship of natural things as such. The object of worship in this, as in all forms of religion, is spiritual not purely natural. It is 'a religion in which the noblest element for human beings is what is spiritual, but the spiritual [recognised] first in its immediate and natural mode' (Hegel 1988: 219). Even in its least developed form, which Hegel terms the 'religion of magic', man shows that he is a self-conscious being (a being-for-self) who has 'cut himself free' from what is purely natural (Hegel 1988: 229). The important point about this in the present context is that subject and object, worshipper and the object worshipped, correspond to and reflect each other.

Nature religion is the earliest form of religion. It is associated with the stage when the self is only just emerging as something distinct from its natural environment and its natural bonds with others, such as those of family or herd. At this stage, according to Hegel, nature is seen as the objectification of the self's dawning subjective sense of something 'higher, essential and universal', but also as 'cause and power' (Hegel 1975: 315). 'There is a fear present here, a consciousness of negation ... a fear of contingency, of the forces of nature, which display themselves as mighty powers over against humanity' (Hegel 1988: 225).

Again, however, Hegel's account is quite different from that of Hobbes cited at the beginning (1988: 224). Religion is not a blind fearful illusion. On the contrary, according to Hegel, it gives subjective expression to the particular form of relation of individuals to the natural world, to each other, and to themselves. Thus a particular form of religious consciousness is bound up with a particular level of social and historical development.

> The principle by which God is defined for human beings is also the principle for how humanity defines itself inwardly, or for humanity in its own spirit. An inferior god or a nature god has inferior, natural and unfree human beings as its correlates; the pure concept of God or the spiritual God has as its correlate spirit that is free and spiritual, that actually knows God. (Hegel 1988: 203)

Marx's account of religion is directly descended from these views. Marx criticises Hegel's idealism, but he does not repudiate the fundamental insight into the unity of subject and object which Hegel's philosophy involves nor its historical account of the development of consciousness and its object (Sayers 1985: 43–45). On the topic of religion, in particular, he holds that 'the religious world is but the reflex of the real world' (Marx 1967: 79).[12] Its content and development go hand in hand with real economic and social conditions.

In the earliest forms of society, according to Marx, economic activity is at a 'low' stage and 'the social relations within the sphere of material life, between man and man, and between man and Nature, are correspondingly narrow'. Marx's account of the religion of such societies is similar to Hegel's. The economic 'narrowness' of such societies 'is reflected in the ancient worship of Nature, and in the other elements of the popular religions' (Marx 1967: 79).

Here, as with Hegel, this should not be interpreted in the terms suggested by traditional philosophical positions. In particular, we must avoid assuming either that ideology is a purely subjective form of narrowness and ignorance, or that it is a direct and immediate reflection of external social conditions. As I have been arguing, neither of these views adequately captures Marx's position. Both treat subjectivity as something metaphysically separate and distinct from the objective world. For Marx, by contrast, consciousness *is* conscious existence, it is inseparably bound up with our relations to nature and to one another. 'Consciousness can never be anything else than conscious existence, and the existence of men is their actual life-process' (Marx and Engels 1970: 47).

In *The German Ideology*, Marx describes the consciousness involved in nature religion as follows.

Nature ... first appears to men as a completely alien, all-powerful and unassailable force ... by which they are overawed[13] ... This natural religion [*Naturreligion*] or this particular relation of men to nature is determined by the form of society and vice versa. Here, as everywhere, the identity of nature and man appears in such a way that the restricted relation of men to nature determines their restricted relation to one another, and their restricted relation to one another determines men's restricted relation to nature. (Marx and Engels 1970: 51)

What Marx means is illustrated by an account he gives of traditional Indian village society and religion, as follows.

These idyllic village-communities, inoffensive though they may appear, had always been the solid foundation of Oriental despotism ... they restrained the human mind within the smallest possible compass, making it the unresisting tool of superstition, enslaving it beneath traditional rules, depriving it of all grandeur and historical energies ... We must not forget that these little communities were contaminated by distinctions of caste and by slavery, that they subjugated man to external circumstances instead of elevating man [to be] the sovereign of circumstances, that they transformed a self-developing social state into never changing natural destiny, and thus brought about a brutalizing worship of nature, exhibiting its degradation in the fact that man, the sovereign of nature, fell down on his knees in adoration of Kanuman, the monkey, and Sabbala, the cow. (Marx 1958: 350)

With economic and social development, human consciousness develops and changes. In a more complex society, involving private property and the free market, 'Christianity with its cultus of abstract man, more especially in its bourgeois developments, Protestantism, Deism, &c., is the most fitting form of religion' (Marx 1967: 79).

Thus religious ideas are social and historical products. They alter not simply as a result of intellectual and philosophical criticism, but only with social change. Marx, in contrast to Hegel, sees these social changes primarily in material and economic terms, and he believes that their ultimate result will be the disappearance of religion altogether. 'The religious reflex of the real world can ... only ... finally vanish, when the practical relations of every-day life offer to man none but perfectly intelligible and reasonable relations with regard to his fellowmen and to Nature' (Marx 1967: 79).

How can these ideas help to illuminate the role of religion in the world today?[14] To anyone of my generation this seems both extraordinary and puzzling. In the 1950s and 1960s, when I was growing up, it seemed inconceivable that religious ideas of an explicitly irrational and fundamentalist character could ever come to hold such sway in the modern world. At that time the main divisions in international affairs were those of the Cold War, between capitalism and liberal democracy on the one side and Soviet-style Communism and various forms of socialism on the other. Religious politics was confined to a tiny handful of zealots and extremists. This seemed marginal and irrelevant, a dwindling vestige of a medieval mind-set which had somehow survived on into the modern world.

Even in areas like the Middle East and Northern Ireland then, as now, divided along religious lines, politics had a predominantly secular form. Progressive aspirations, for national independence, for political power and control of economic resources, took broadly socialist forms for the most part. This was the case, for example, in Egypt. When Nasser nationalised the Suez Canal in 1956, he did not invoke Allah, he spoke the language of secular nationalism. (This did not inhibit the British and the French, with the help of Israel, from invading and trying to overthrow him.)

In Iran, likewise, it was the secular politics of national independence that led the Mossadeq government, after it was elected in 1951, to try to assert control of the Iranian operations of the Anglo-Iranian Oil Company. That government was swiftly overthrown by a coup engineered by the United States and Britain, who then installed the Shah. The Shah's regime continued on a mainly secular, Western-style path of development, but in a way that was more compliant to Western oil and other business interests.

All that changed with the Iranian Revolution of 1979 which overthrew the Shah and instituted the Islamic regime of Ayatollah Khomeini. That event sent shock waves through the Middle East and beyond, the results of which are still being felt today. To begin to comprehend these events it is important to understand the way in which capitalism has impinged on societies in the region. Until very recently the Middle East was made up of traditional, predominantly agrarian or even nomadic peoples, involved in pre-capitalist, quasi-feudal social systems, which had remained largely unchanged for centuries. Quite suddenly their isolated existence and traditional ways have been broken in upon. They have been subjected to the forces of the world market. They have been pitched into the modern world. They have been invaded by an irresistible flood of mass produced goods of every kind, cars, electronic and other consumer goods, jeans, trainers, T-shirts, even hamburgers, Coca-Cola and other alien forms of food and drink. This has undermined the livelihoods of local producers and destroyed existing social structures and economic relations. At the same time, these communities are being bombarded with images, sounds and ideas from the West which clash with traditional beliefs and subvert established values.

This process has been occurring all around the world for over two hundred years. Its effects are explosive. Typically, there are two contrasting kinds of response in the societies affected. Some members of those societies believe that they must 'modernise' in the face of these forces. They argue they must ultimately embrace Western ideas and values if they are to survive and prosper in the modern world. We may call these the 'modernizers'. Others, however, see in Western influences only a threat to established ways of life and values. They oppose and resist them in the name of the traditional culture. In response to the Western threat they cling on to traditional ways and values which are often embodied in religious beliefs, practices and institutions. This is the 'traditionalist' response. Similar divisions have occurred in many other parts of the world in the face of the onslaught of global capitalism.[15]

In view of the argument I have been developing it is not surprising that there should be these two sorts of responses. The impact of global capitalism on these communities has been so rapid and intense that people in them are in effect living simultaneously in two quite different and incommensurable social worlds, traditional and modern, which have suddenly and violently been thrown together. The contrasting responses to this situation that I have been describing are products of these different and conflicting sets of social relations. The modernisers maintain that their societies should embrace the new social order created by the global market, or at least they believe that they have no realistic alternative but to do so. The traditionalists, on the other hand, want to protect and preserve their established ways, and they believe that they must resist and exclude the forces of capitalism in order to do so.

In previous years, as I have said, most progressive forces for national liberation were of a 'modernising' kind. They put their hopes in some sort of socialism. With the demise of the Soviet Union, and the eclipse of every sort of socialist movement which occurred at the same time throughout the world, those hopes have dimmed, for the present at least. Many people in developing societies have lost faith that the path of economic modernisation could ever lead their societies in the direction of independent development and freedom. Those with radical aspirations for national autonomy and progress have looked elsewhere, and increasingly to traditional and religious ideas. Many, particularly in the Middle East, but elsewhere too, have looked to a resurgent Islam.

In this way, religious ideas have given expression to people's distress and come to embody their hopes for liberation and their aspirations for a better life. These ideas involve illusion and error, I have been arguing, but they are not simply a result of ignorance or intellectual confusion. As with the religion of nature described earlier, they are produced by objective social conditions. In particular, the kind of modern religious politics that I have been discussing has its roots in the impact which global economic forces have had in what used to be a local and familiar world. It is a result of the way in which these forces have suddenly come to affect people's lives – in ways which they do not understand, which they are powerlessness to influence, and in the face of which they feel frustration and despair.

I will conclude by citing some anecdotal evidence to illustrate the points I have been making. When I first taught at the University of Kent in the 1970s, there were many Iranian students on the campus. I ran a postgraduate course on Political Theory which regularly attracted a number of them. They were often very good students, strongly engaged in their studies, intensely concerned about the future of their country and committed to doing something about it. For the most part they were fervent nationalists whose sympathies inclined towards socialism or Marxism.

After the Iranian Revolution of 1979 which brought the Ayatollahs to power, a new breed of student began to appear. A number of Islamic fundamentalists began to sign up for the course. It seemed strange that these students should opt for a course on Western political thought, since its approach conflicted with so many of their beliefs. When one talked to these students, however, it soon became clear that many of them had political outlooks not so very different from those of the earlier generations of socialists and Marxists. They had similar aspirations for the independence and self-determination of their country. When one put it to them that these were secular political aims and asked them why they were committed to realising them through Islam, a frequent reply was that Western political ideologies had failed and provided no solutions for the problems of their society. Neither capitalism nor communism were satisfactory, they said, but Islam showed the way towards a better world and offered hope for the future.

Clearly, Marxism does not share that view. To repeat, it regards religious beliefs, of whatever kind, as erroneous and illusory. Moreover, the fundamentalist variety often involves attitudes which seem barbaric and inhuman by Western liberal standards.[16] However, it is not sufficient simply to reject and dismiss these beliefs in these terms, as fallacious and immoral. Religious ideas, as I have been arguing, can give powerful expression to people's sufferings, and embody their hopes for liberation and aspirations for a better life. The illusory form in which they are expressed is rooted in the social and economic conditions which give rise to them.

What role can philosophers and other intellectuals play in this situation? As I have been arguing, philosophical and purely theoretical criticism alone is not sufficient to dissolve ideological conceptions; their roots are material, they lie at the social and economic level. Nevertheless, it is important to insist that theoretical criticism plays an important role in bringing about social and economic change. It is an essential part of the process of creating new social conditions. There is and remains a role for traditional philosophical criticism, and the account that I have been giving should not be taken to deny this.[17]

Equally, however, an adequate theoretical response to ideology must go beyond traditional philosophical forms. As well as criticising ideological views as irrational and false, these must also be interpreted and understood as 'symptoms'. For hidden within their false form there often lie valid aspirations which are a response to real social conditions. These conditions must be acknowledged and addressed if there is to be peace and understanding in the world. That is the lesson of Marxism.[18]

Notes

1. See Sayers (1989) for an earlier discussion of this topic.
2. Following the authors I am citing and for stylistic reasons I use 'man' in its generic sense to include also women.
3. See Sayers (1985, chapter 5) for a fuller account of Freud from this perspective.
4. In 1843–1844, when he was 25–26 years old.
5. 'This fact appears to the producers, notwithstanding the discovery [of the social nature of value], to be just as real and final, as the fact, that, after the discovery by science of the component gases of air, the atmosphere itself remained unaltered' (Marx 1967: 74).

6. 'The life-process of society, which is based on the process of material production, does not strip off its mystical veil until it is treated as production by freely associated men, and is consciously regulated by them in accordance with a settled plan' (Marx 1967: 80).

7. Religious beliefs also have psychological causes. Marx does not discuss these, nor shall I in this paper, except to acknowledge that they exist and need to be considered in any full account of religion.

8. This theme has recently been taken up by writers in the analytic tradition as well, for example McDowell (1994).

9. Hegel traces this process in general terms in his account of the development of 'spirit' in the *Phenomenology of Spirit*, and in greater detail in his accounts of the development of art, religion and philosophy in his *Lectures* on these topics.

10. See especially Hegel (1988, Part II.A), Hegel (1977: 416–424), see also Hegel (1975: 303–361).

11. That is heathens or pagans (*OED*).

12. This sentence does not appear in the German text of 1867. It was added to the French edition of 1872–1875, for which Marx made numerous revisions (Marx 1969: 90). The English translation of 1886, supervised by Engels, incorporates these changes, see Engels, 'Preface to the English Edition 1886', in Marx (1967). 'Reflex' is the translation of the French '*reflet*' (reflection).

13. 'like beasts', Marx adds, 'it is thus a purely animal consciousness of nature (natural religion [*Naturreligion*]) just because nature is as yet hardly modified historically' (Marx and Engels, 1970: 51). Marx's language here is careless. For Marx, as for Hegel, even the earliest kind of religion is a distinctively human phenomenon. Religion is a form of reflective consciousness of the world and of oneself, it involves being-for-self of which animals are not capable. Marx acknowledges this earlier in the same passage. 'Where there exists a relationship, it exists for me: the animal does not enter into "*relations*" with anything, it does not enter into any relation at all. For the animal, its relation to others does not exist as a relation. Consciousness is, therefore, from the very beginning a social product, and remains so as long as men exist at all' (Marx and Engels 1970: 51).

14. In what follows I focus on radical Islam. Arguably, the same principles can be used to explain the striking role that fundamental religion has come to play in US politics, but an analysis of that phenomenon must be developed out of the specific features of contemporary American social conditions, which is beyond my competence. An account which bears out the view that fundamental religion expresses real anxieties and aspirations among people in the American 'heartlands' is developed in Frank (2004).

15. In nineteenth-century Russia these groups were called the 'Westernizers' and the 'Slavophiles' (Walicki 1979).

16. Shared by Marxism and, indeed, all forms of socialism.

17. This point is well understood by Lenin. Like Marx he believes that religion is a social product, hence that 'religious prejudices [cannot] be dispelled by purely propaganda methods' (Lenin 1969b: 10). Nevertheless, he does not deny the value of intellectual argument. 'Does this mean that educational

books against religion are harmful or unnecessary? No, nothing of the kind. It means that Social-Democracy's atheist propaganda must be *subordinated* to its basic task – the development of the class struggle of the exploited *masses* against the exploiters' (Lenin 1969a: 22).

18. Earlier versions of this paper were given at the Cambridge University Humanist Association, Philosophy Department, Mount Holyoke College, South Hadley MA, and Radical Philosophy Association National Conference, Washington DC. I am grateful to participants at these meetings for comments and criticisms. I am also grateful for financial support for this research from Mount Holyoke College.

Bibliography

Althusser, L. (1969) *For Marx*, London: Allen Lane.

Althusser, L. (1971a) 'Freud and Lacan', in L. Althusser, *Lenin and Philosophy and Other Essays*, London: New Left Books, 189–219.

Althusser, L. (1971b) 'Ideology and Ideological State Apparatuses', in L. Althusser, *Lenin and Philosophy and Other Essays*, London: New Left Books, 127–186.

Cohen, G. A. (1978) *Karl Marx's Theory of History: A Defence*, Oxford: Clarendon Press.

Feuerbach, L. (1957) *The Essence of Christianity*, G. Eliot (trans.), New York: Harper & Row.

Frank, T. (2004) *What's the Matter with Kansas? How Conservatives Won the Heart of America*, New York: Metropolitan Books.

Freud, S. (1974) *Introductory Lectures on Psychoanalysis*, Harmondsworth: Penguin.

Hegel, G. W. F. (1975) *Aesthetics*, T. M. Knox (trans.), Oxford: Clarendon Press.

Hegel, G. W. F. (1977) *Phenomenology of Spirit*, A. V. Miller (trans.), Oxford: Clarendon Press.

Hegel, G. W. F. (1988) *Lectures on the Philosophy of Religion, One-Volume Edition. The Lectures of 1827*, R. F. Brown, P. C. Hodgson and J. M. Stewart (trans.), Berkeley: CA: University of California Press.

Hobbes, T. (1985) *Leviathan*, Harmondsworth: Penguin.

Larrain, J. (1979) *The Concept of Ideology*, London: Hutchinson.

Lenin, V. I. (1969a) 'The Attitude of the Worker's Party to Religion', in *On Religion* Moscow: Progress Publishers, 18–28.

Lenin, V. I. (1969b) 'Socialism and Religion', in *On Religion*, Moscow: Progress Publishers, 7–11.

Marx, K. (1958) 'The British Rule in India', in Karl Marx and Frederick Engels, *Selected Works*, 1, Moscow: Foreign Languages Publishing House, 345–351.

Marx, K. (1967) *Capital*, Vol. 1, S. Moore and E. Aveling (trans.), New York: International Publishers.

Marx, K. (1969) *Le Capital, I*, J. Roy (trans.), Paris: Éditions Sociales.

Marx, K. (1975a) 'Concerning Feuerbach [Theses on Feuerbach]', in Karl Marx, *Early Writings*, Harmondsworth: Penguin, 421–423.

Marx, K. (1975b) 'A Contribution to Hegel's Philosophy of Right: Introduction', in Karl Marx, *Early Writings*, Harmondsworth: Penguin, 243–257.

Marx, K. and Engels, F. (1970) *The German Ideology Part I*, New York: International Publishers.
McDowell, J. H. (1994) *Mind and World*, Cambridge, MA:, Harvard University Press.
Sayers, S. (1985) *Reality and Reason*, Oxford: Blackwell.
Sayers, S. (1989) 'Knowledge as a Social Phenomenon', *Radical Philosophy*, 52, 34–37.
Walicki, A. (1979) *A History of Russian Thought from the Enlightenment to Marxism*, Stanford, CA: Stanford University Press.

9
Intellectual Labour and Social Class

David Bates

How should one conceive of the class location of intellectual labour? For Marxists, this is not simply a problem of interest, but rather a fundamental political problem. Marx placed the notion of proletarian self-emancipation at the heart of his theory of revolution,[1] but simultaneously maintained that the capitalist labour process tends to render opaque to its subjects both its exploitative basis and the possibility of future non-exploitative alternatives. Such opacity necessitated the use of social scientific tools.[2] Yet these tools – and the intellectual labourers who use them – have typically been considered as external to the proletariat.[3] The idea of intellectual labour as external to the proletariat was of course emphasised by Lenin. Left to their own devices, the workers in *What is to be Done?* could not reach beyond the immediacy of the economic struggle, beyond 'trade union consciousness'. The agents of social science – that is intellectuals of petty bourgeois origin – would therefore be required to bring revolutionary consciousness to the workers from without. I do not wish to comment on the cogency or otherwise of Lenin's position, a position which must always be assessed in terms of Russian conditions. However, in the context of contemporary capitalism, the idea of intellectual labour – and hence academic social scientific knowledge – as external to the proletariat is undergoing a process of erosion. Contemporary intellectuals I shall argue in the course of this chapter are largely proletarian in character, and therefore subjected to many of the processes of oppression, 'degradation' and exploitation which impact on this class as a whole.

In assessing the class location of intellectual labour, there are numerous Marxist authors on which one could focus, though it must be noted that this issue has not always received the attention in the Marxist tradition which it deserves. In this chapter I begin by making some critical remarks about perhaps the most well-known Marxist writer on intellectuals – Antonio Gramsci. I then move on to explore aspects of the work of one of the most original contemporary theorists of social class – Erik Olin Wright.

Antonio Gramsci

Should we consider intellectuals as an autonomous social group, or does rather 'every social group have its particular specialised category of intellectuals?' (Gramsci 1971: 5). Gramsci's answer to this question is well known. All social classes create alongside themselves their own categories of 'organic intellectuals', intellectuals which serve to give to these classes 'homogeneity' and an 'awareness of their function' in both the social and the political spheres. And Gramsci distinguishes between those organic intellectuals who belong to the bourgeoisie, and those who belong to the proletariat. The capitalist entrepreneur brings into existence a range of functions and occupations, such as the industrial technician, the specialist in political economy, as well as the organisers of the new culture, and legal system. So too the proletariat, emerging from within the body of capitalist society, must produce their own intellectuals with the ability to carry out equivalent, indeed more extensive, functions. For Gramsci, proletarian organic intellectuals would have a crucial role in the class struggle, helping to produce and organise the form of group self-awareness which is essential in the battle for hegemony.

Gramsci of course did not only write of organic intellectuals. As organic intellectuals have emerged, they have also encountered already existing intellectual strata; these intellectuals Gramsci characterised as 'traditional'. Traditional intellectuals appear to represent the idea of historical continuity, a continuity 'uninterrupted even by the most complicated and radical changes in political and social forms' (Gramsci 1971: 6–7). As such, they perceive themselves as autonomous from class relations. But this perception is a mistaken one. Traditional intellectuals have organic origins in previous social classes; moreover they frequently come to perform ideological functions for those social classes which emerge subsequently.

Though Gramsci's writings on intellectuals have been rightly celebrated, his position is at times ambiguous. Discussing his conception of organic intellectuals, Sassoon (1987) for example, identifies at least two different ways in which he uses this term. First, in a *diachronic* fashion; organic intellectuals come in to existence at the same point in time as the social class that elaborates them. As Gramsci writes: organic intellectuals are 'created together' with those social classes 'coming into existence on the original terrain of an essential function in the world of economic production' (Gramsci 1971: 5). Second, in a *synchronic* fashion, the organic character of the intellectual is defined in accordance with her/his function and superstructural location. It is on this second use of the term organic that I want to focus here. Gramsci writes:

> The relationship between the intellectuals and the world of production is not as direct as it is with the fundamental social groups but is, in varying degrees, 'mediated' by the whole fabric of society and by the complex of superstructures, of which the intellectuals are, precisely, the 'functionaries.' (Gramsci 1971: 12)

And he continues:

> It should be possible to measure the 'organic quality' [organicità] of the various intellectual strata, their degree of connection with a fundamental social group, establishing a gradation of their functions and of the superstructures from the bottom to the top. (Gramsci 1971: 12)

'Organicity' here is not so much a matter of fact as a matter of degree. Whereas social classes have a *direct* relationship to the realm of production, this is not the case with intellectuals. The intellectual's function is, Sassoon notes, superstructural; however, some superstructural functions will have a closer relationship to the realm of production than will others.

But there is a problem with such a superstructual emphasis. For Gramsci does not seem to limit his definition of the organic intellectuals to those who carry out an ideological function; he also considers as 'organic' those 'intellectuals' who perform specialised 'technical' activities, that is activities embedded in the productive process. Discussing intellectuals of the bourgeois class, Gramsci refers to the 'industrial technician', as well as the 'specialist in political economy' and those who organise the new culture and legal system (Gramsci 1971: 5). For Gramsci, the organic intellectuals of the proletariat must be fundamentally different in character to the organic intellectuals of previous social classes. Gramsci writes that: 'In the modern world, technical education, closely bound to industrial labour even at the most primitive and unqualified level, must be the basis of the new type of intellectual' (Gramsci 1971: 9).

It might seem that Gramsci's position is rather reactionary. All that is often considered as valuable with being 'an intellectual' comes to be obliterated; the intellectual will not be created in the university but in the factory. However, it could be suggested that such a criticism is founded on an unimaginative account of productive activity, an account which considers productive activity as necessarily contaminated with the specific problems of the capitalist labour process. Indeed, it is the transformation of the capitalist labour process which allows for the new type of proletarian organic intellectual to emerge; for as the capitalist division of labour is undermined, the horizon of the 'technical' expands, thus moving beyond what Gramsci refers to as 'technique-as-work' to 'technique-as-science' (Gramsci 1971: 10).

There are some critical observations which need to be made at this juncture. Beginning with the *synchronic* account of 'organicity' – it would seem here that the relationship which intellectuals have with social classes is always a relationship of exteriority and approximation. Whilst some superstructural functions will be closer to the economic base than others, the superstructure is not itself the realm of production. And as class is determined at the level of relations of production the class position of the intellectual is seemingly not something which can be theorised using Gramsci's model. Thus, most 'organic' intellectuals are those which are closer to the realm of production; however, these intellectuals are never fully of the class which they function to represent.

But what of the technical emphasis? Surely, the intellectual function is embedded in the productive process, and therefore Gramsci's work overcomes my criticisms. The difficulty however is with Gramsci's stress on the notion of function. For function, thus conceived, is what we might refer to – using the terminology of Cohen (2000) – as a material work relation, rather than a social relation of production. The latter, which comprise relations of ownership, are what constitute class relationships. Accordingly, Gramsci fails to recognise that such 'bourgeois organic intellectuals', though indeed brought into being by the bourgeoisie, would be better considered as part of the proletariat. For, the majority of such 'technical' specialists are wage-labourers; the content of that which they produce is to a significant degree dictated by their employers.

Moving from the stress on technical function to that of ideological function, a further problem is evident with Gramsci's thought. This concerns the fact that Gramsci does not recognise that the function of ideological – rather than simply technical – production is itself embedded in specific sets of productive relations. Many contemporary ideological workers can be thought of as integral to the proletariat. This, as Wright (1979) has argued, is the case with teachers who, whilst functionally organic intellectuals of the bourgeoisie, are nevertheless structurally external to that class. Accordingly, though at the specific historical conjuncture in which Gramsci was writing, the creation of proletarian organic intellectuals was undoubtedly of importance, a more adequate account of the tendencies of capitalist production would have allowed him to recognise the way in which intellectual workers have become proletarianised, not in terms of the functions they perform, but in terms of what they are.

There are also difficulties with Gramsci's conception of the traditional intellectuals. Thus on one hand Gramsci challenges the traditional intellectuals' perception of themselves as autonomous, but on the other hand writes of a situation in which: 'The traditional intellectuals are detaching themselves from the social groupings which they have hitherto given the highest and most comprehensive form' (Gramsci 1971: 270). Indeed, for Gramsci, the traditional intellectuals are more likely to be attracted to the socialist cause with the creation of proletarian organic intellectuals. Karabel (1976) has cogently argued that Gramsci fails to provide a material account of how this process of detachment is possible. For, according to Gramsci, the act of detachment is an act of choice, and an act of 'choice' can only be such if it is an autonomous act; as such 'Gramsci, an unyielding opponent of the idea of intellectuals being independent of social classes, inadvertently manages to resurrect the concept of the free-floating intelligentsia' (Karabel 1976: 145). Karabel's criticisms are cogent ones. But, such indeterminacy is not only a difficulty with Gramsci's traditional intellectual. For, there is also an extent – as I have stated – to which the functional dimension to Gramsci's argument leads him to neglect the productive relations in which all intellectual activity is embedded. It is to an account of intellectual productive relations that I now turn. Here my key focus is the work of Erik Olin Wright.

Erik Olin Wright

In many ways, Wright's argument can be best regarded as a response not to Gramsci, but to Poulantzas (1975). For Poulantzas, intellectuals were not part of the working class, but rather part of the new petty bourgeoisie. Poulantzas gave two reasons for excluding intellectuals from the working class. First, they are unproductive workers, and only those workers who produce surplus value can be considered as proletarian.

Second, they are 'mental' labourers, and ideologically, mental labour has a dominating role over proletarian manual labour. As for the claim that they are part of the 'new petty bourgeoisie', intellectuals he maintains share many of the traits most associated with the petty bourgeoisie as a class, such as individualism and an opposition to communal principles.

Wright challenges Poulantzas's claim. At least in his early work, intellectuals occupy 'contradictory class locations', meaning that they occupy class relations which are 'objectively torn between the antagonistic classes of that society'; their identity is therefore determined by their 'location between classes' (Wright 1979: 203). Wright identifies two levels of determination of contradictory class location: the productive and the ideological. Let us explore his claims about the first level in a little more detail.

Wright identifies three contradictory class locations here – a contradictory class location between the working class and the bourgeoisie, a class location occupied by managers; a contradictory class location between the bourgeoisie and the petty bourgeoisie, a class location occupied by small employers; and a contradictory class location between the petty bourgeoisie and the working class, a class location occupied by 'semi-autonomous employees' (Wright 1979: 204). The third category for Wright is the most important for the attempt to understand the class location intellectuals. The petty bourgeois producer exercises direct control over her/his labour process; this is quite different from the capitalist labour process where the worker enjoys at the most marginal control over her/his immediate labouring activity. Many intellectuals are argued to be both like other workers in that they must sell their labour to capital or the state, but unlike these workers in that they are able to enjoy a more substantial degree of control over their labour process.

This approach represents a substantial advance on the indeterminacy one finds in Gramsci's work. Nevertheless, there remain some difficulties. One of the most important advances of Marxist social theory has been in highlighting the fundamentally dominating character of the wage–labour relation; this relation has the power to shape many – though by no means all – other relations which surround it. Thus, in attempting to explain the class location of the intellectual, it becomes important to give a hierarchical account of productive relations, an account which recognises the wage–labour relation as not simply on an analytical par with the relation of petty bourgeois autonomy, but rather the fundamental relation of domination, which acts as the condition of possibility/impossibility for any relative autonomy which may persist. Let us explore this issue in a little more detail. When the labourer sells her/his labour power to the employer, the employer gains control of the *totality* of uses to which that labour is put. It is because of this that the 'semi-autonomy' which Wright identifies, while not entirely an illusion, is also not all that it might at first appear to be. Employers can at any point intervene at the site of immediate intellectual production, so as to restructure the degree of control which intellectuals have over their labouring activity. (Of course – as Wright makes clear – they must take care not to erode the ideology of intellectual freedom in doing so, in that this ideology has immense importance for the economic system as a whole.)

A further point must also be expressed at this juncture about the relationship between the capitalist mode of production and the state labour process in which a large proportion of intellectual labour is embedded. The dominating power of capital in the present social formation gives it the capacity to intervene in the state centred intellectual labour process, in order to defend the interests of accumulation. It is this close relationship between the 'capitalist' state, and capitalist production, which means that state employed intellectuals are often subjected not only to comparable modes of discipline/subordination as private sector workers – but also to the profit motive.

Wright himself gives a great deal of attention to the so-called 'proletarianisation' of educational relations of production, that is the imposition of large administrative workloads and the increase in the use of short term contracts. However, Wright's account of proletarianisation falls prey to many of the difficulties associated with non-Marxist accounts of this issue. For, whilst it is true to say that academics have been subjected to varied attacks on their labour conditions, proletarianisation is better taken to denote the subordination of the labourer to the wage–labour relation, a subordination which for many intellectuals is already a reality. What Wright wishes to call 'proletarianisation' is therefore in fact a secondary effect of this primary subordination.[4] Accordingly, the term 'uniformatisation' is better used here. Intellectual proletarians are increasingly subjected to the very same processes of degradation, etc., against which the 'traditional' proletariat have for a long time struggled.

Moving on to the second aspect of Wright's argument – Wright maintains that a situation of 'disarticulation' exists between the intellectual's class position at the economic and the ideological levels. The 'contradictory class location' of the intellectual is therefore more complex than a contradiction at the level of social relations of production. For, if at the level of the social relations of production, the intellectual's class location is one of contradiction between the proletariat and the petty bourgeoisie, at the ideological level, the intellectual's class location is torn between the proletariat and the bourgeoisie.[5] For Wright, intellectual labourers (such as university academics and teachers) are involved directly in the elaboration and dissemination of bourgeois ideology, but lack any meaningful control over the ideological apparatuses in *totality*. Such 'disarticulation' brings with it important implications for the role of the teacher in the class struggle. Wright insists: 'To the extent that teachers have a certain level of real autonomy at the level of social relations of (educational) production, they can potentially subvert bourgeois ideology at the level of ideological relations' (Wright 1979: 208).

As my more general concern in this chapter is with intellectual relations of production, the attention which I give to the ideological level is only brief. Stated simply, Wright is mistaken to give to the ideological such a fundamental role, a mistake which is further evidenced in his claim that: 'Since classes in capitalist society cannot be defined simply in terms of economic relations, neither can contradictory locations' (Wright 1979: 204). Class is an economic relation, and as such, it can be considered as analytically separate from the realm of ideology (though the ideological cannot be understood as separate from the economic). Whilst we should in no way argue that the ideological is simply epiphenomenal, it is production – and not the ideology one upholds or elaborates – which denotes one's class location. However, in asserting that the ideological dimension is what in part makes the intellectual's class location a 'contradictory' one, Wright would seem to make the ideological of determining significance, thus placing it on a par with the realm of social relations of production.[6] (This difficulty is evident in Wright's discussion of ideological proletarianisation. Developments such as 'programmed learning' in the 1970s were, Wright maintained, transforming teachers into machine tenders; thus they were ceasing to be active elaborators of bourgeois ideology. But this would seem to tell us no more about the class location of intellectuals than the fact that, at the time Wright was writing, many intellectuals were agents trusted with such processes of ideological elaboration and dissemination.)

Wright (1997a; 1998) came to criticise this 'domination centred' approach to contradictory class locations, and argued for a renewed stress on exploitation. Though in doing so he does not discuss in any detail the class location of the intellectual, much of what he does have to say is of relevance to this problem. Wright's account of exploitation is not a strictly Marxist one, in that he moves beyond the labour theory of value. For Wright, exploitation can be considered to have occurred when an individual or group benefits as a result of an unequal distribution of significant resources in relation to another individual or group (see Meiksins 1998). The main influence here is the analytical Marxism of John Roemer (1982). However, Wright extends Roemer's account, identifying four assets which act as the basis of types of exploitation, thus produce opposing interests, and hence contradictory class locations; these assets he identifies as labour power, means of production, organisation and skills. The first two forms of exploitation – which are associated with the feudal and capitalist modes of production respectively – require no further exposition; moreover, I will not discuss the third given constraints of space.[7] Rather, I focus on skills asset exploitation.

Wright notes that for skill to function as a means of exploitation, its supply must be less than the social demand for it; moreover there must be a way in which such a shortage of supply is transformed into higher wages on the part of skills possessors. Wright identifies three ways in which it is possible for such scarcity to emerge. First, there may be a requirement for skills which are 'naturally scarce'. Second, there may be a restriction of access to the relevant skill. Third, there may be a certification system in existence which restricts skills usage by the un-certificated, even where they have such skills. Such restrictions lead to exploitation when those with skills credentials are able to receive incomes that are 'above the costs of production of the skills by virtue of the scarcity of the available skill' (Wright 1998: 21).

In using the term 'skill assets exploiters', Wright is concerned with the so-called new middle classes; he includes in this category not just managers, but also experts of various kinds. And presumably, under this term 'experts', we can include many intellectual labourers, in particular academics. But which of the above three mechanisms of restriction may be considered as relevant for the concerns of this chapter? One could of course maintain that certain intellectuals enjoy a situation of relative economic privilege because nature has favoured them with certain talents which other members of the community do not have. More interesting however are the other two mechanisms to which Wright refers.

If we take the example of the academic labour process – to enter the academic career structure requires high levels of skill. And to gain access to the processes through which one can acquire such forms of skill is far from easy. The prospective academic intellectual needs extensive financial resources. For those who are not independently wealthy, such access can only be achieved by entering differing funding competitions. And the notion of a competition itself implies a restriction, that is some people will be winners, and others losers.

So, provisionally, we might be able to show the existence of some kind of appropriate mechanism of restriction. What about the third mechanism? It is difficult to address this issue adequately; nevertheless, one could refer to the way in which, in the less privileged sectors of higher education, the PhD qualification which was once not at all necessary is becoming so. Accordingly, those without higher research qualifications may become increasingly sidelined or replaced by those who have. However, for every example of this practice, there are other examples of those who have been in institutional positions for long periods enjoying relations of domination over, and higher wages than, academics who have more certified skills credentials than they do. Any argument along this line must therefore be inconclusive.

A further point needs to be raised here. Most of the intellectual labour to which I have so far referred in this chapter occurs at the level of the state. This is where most of Wright's 'semi-autonomous' employees earn their wages. And Wright speculates: 'Politically, the fact that workers and other un-credentialed employees are underrepresented in state employment ... is probably one of the reasons that there tends to be a certain amount of anti-statist sentiment in the working class' (Wright 1997a: 207). Taken as an explanation of ideological difference, this is surely a cogent argument; however, Wright is unclear as to whether it should be taken as denoting exploitation of the private sector workers by state sector workers, though it should be noted that in his earlier writings, Wright (1978) is sceptical of such argument, wishing to stress the commonality of the fundamental interests of both sets of workers.[8]

Wright's focus on relations of exploitation in *Classes* raises some important issues pertaining to the role of intellectual labour. In particular, he identifies key questions concerning forms of differentiation within intellectual wage labour. Nevertheless, it must be asked whether the factors identified above actually produce forms of exploitation which generate contradictory class locations? Criticisms levelled against Wright's arguments (see Meiksins 1998; Stinchcombe 1998) led him to reformulate his position. For example, Meiksins (1998) has questioned the extent to which workers with skills credentials benefit at the expense of workers without them, and whether therefore such exploitation can be considered as occurring at all. Is it really the case, he asks, that employers pay credentialed workers wages in excess of the value of their 'marginal product' (and therefore that such workers can be considered as appropriating the labour of someone else)?

First, for Meiksins, Wright's argument is unduly dismissive of the view that the skills possessed by credentialed workers may lead them to be more productive, thus meaning that they are 'entitled' to higher wages (Meiksins 1998: 176). Second, Meiksins insists that Wright does not give enough attention to the argument that certain forms of credential may prevent skills flooding the labour market, a flood that would lead labour to become cheaper than its actual value.[9]

Though challenging such criticisms, Wright nevertheless came to think that 'Skill exploitation and organisation asset exploitation ... are probably best viewed as the basis for strata within classes rather than for class divisions as such' (Wright 1998: 347). Indeed, in one of his most recent works Wright seems again to have changed his theoretical emphasis. Rather than skills exploitation, Wright writes of 'privileged appropriation location[s] within exploitation relations', where workers with high levels of skills (such as experts and intellectuals) can be considered to occupy such privileged locations (Wright 1997b: 22).[10] What then remains of his notion of contradictory class locations at the level of skill? Wright (1998) draws attention to the way in which the possession of skills allows workers to acquire forms of property – stocks and shares, etc. – which enable them to become capitalist exploiters. This strikes me as at least a more convincing way to argue for the existence of contradictory class locations, relating as it does not only to property ownership but also ultimately to wage–labour purchase. Nevertheless, Wright's position does remain problematic; for Wright continues to over-stress difference at the expense of fundamental aspects of unity within the social classes he interrogates. If there is a key theme at the heart of the final section of this chapter, it is the unity of the experience of exploitation.

The class location of contemporary intellectual labour

How then are we to understand the class location of the intellectual in contemporary capitalism? Before answering this question, it is important to situate the intellectual – specifically academic – labour process historically. Intellectual modes of production have various national histories. Whilst Gramsci's focus is primarily Italy and Wright's America, what I have to say focuses on the British university context.

The British university system was ecclesiastical in origin. Universities were bodies charged with among other things the training of the priesthood. However, in the course of the nineteenth century, this system underwent a process of transformation. Some (see Dearlove 1997) have written of universities as sites of something akin to a pre-Fordist 'craft like' labour process. Others have referred to the professionalisation of

British universities in the course particularly of the late nineteenth century, especially with the emergence of the great civic universities. Whether the term 'craft' or 'profession' is the best label to refer to academic work prior to the period on which I concentrate, it is the case that the – albeit highly elitist – academic labour process from the mid-nineteenth century to well into the twentieth century was characterised by a degree of autonomy and self-regulation, both of which can be considered an anathema to more recent forms of managerialism in higher education.

Particularly the second half of the twentieth century has witnessed an expansion of higher education, an expansion which could only be achieved through massive state finance. Such expansion has challenged the 'ideal' of professionalism and 'collegiality', and therefore academic autonomy. It is now the case, in Britain at least, that the state is the biggest financier of higher education. The demands which the state – accordingly – has placed on higher education are significant. For in funding higher education, the state has in a large part responded to the (perceived) demands of private industry to produce the skilled workers of the future; for state funding to be achieved, economic relevance had to be demonstrated. The period which we are now entering is an intensified version of this. Higher education is not simply in the business of responding to the demands of 'the market'; it is increasingly embedded in that market.

But how do these factors impact on our attempt to understand the class location of contemporary intellectual labour? I argue that higher education is developing in such a way that the experience of exploitation which a great deal of academic intellectual labour has, is to a significant extent comparable with the traditional working class. Some Marxists would no doubt wish to refute this. Thus they might argue that academic labour's non-productive character situates it externally to the proletariat. And there are a number of possible ways in which they could portray this unproductive labour. First, they could cite Poulantzas (1975) or Mandel's (1978) reading of Marx, and maintain that academic labour is necessarily unproductive because it is non-material. Second, they might insist on the fact that academic labour paradigmatically, despite its subjection to market processes, remains embedded in the revenue-funded state labour process.

To take the first claim – Gough (1972) and Meiksins (1981) have maintained (citing convincing textual evidence from Marx) that Marx did not hold materiality to be a necessary condition for productivity. In a well-known passage from *Capital*, Marx compared the role of the teacher in the private school with the worker in a sausage factory. In the course of their working day, both parties labour to produce profit for the capitalist employer. Moving on to the second claim – as Marx maintains that one of the necessary conditions for labour to be considered as productive is that it exchanges with capital as capital, rather than with revenue, then intellectual labour employed by the state would seem indeed to be unproductive.

The common mistake with these arguments, however, as Wood (1997) has insisted, pertains to the way in which the productive/unproductive distinction is taken to be synonymous with a fundamental class demarcation, a view to which Marx at least did not hold. For Marx, it is the sale of labour power which constitutes class locations as proletarian (see Rowthorn 1980; Meiksins 1981; Wood 1996). Indeed it is, as I insisted earlier, subjection to the wage–labour relation which opens up academic labour to potential processes of exploitation.

Returning now to the issue of commodification – though not denoting the proletariat as such, the extraction of surplus value is the purpose of capitalist production. And as processes of commodification and marketisation intensify, it is this particular type of exploitation to which larger numbers of intellectual labourers come to be subjected. In making this point, it is important to identify three inter-related forms of commodification. First, 'quasi capitalist' commodification, a process associated with the introduction of state led market and 'rationalisation' measures into higher education. Here it is not so much surplus value production that becomes important, but the type of artificial value which Harvie (2000) has termed 'research value'. Second, it is ever more the case that university courses can be considered as commodities for sale in the educational market place; here the demands of the 'consumer' come to the fore. But one could object that these are at the most mediated forms of capitalism. However, this leads to the third point. Capitalism in a purer sense of that term is ever more part of the contemporary university (see Slaughter and Leslie 1997). This is attested to by the fact that many universities now seek with increasing vigour to attract private capital, with the aim of improving their facilities; and private capital in turn considers universities as low cost sites for research and development. But how does this relate to my claim that many intellectuals can now be thought of as capitalistically exploited?

In relation to the first type of commodification, though exploitation in a broader sense may occur, the necessary conditions for surplus value production have not been met – the worker's wage is paid simply out of revenue generated taxation. The picture becomes a little more complicated with my second claim. Both Marx and Engels allowed for the possibility of what we might term 'state capitalist' production, at least when the state carries out production with the intention of gaining a profit. Workers so employed could then be viewed as producing surplus value.[11] Nevertheless, this view is likely to continue to be a controversial one. With the third claim, we see that productive labour in the capitalist sense of that term is now a feature of the academic mode of production. As private sector finance enters the university, the wages of academics come to be paid in a process of exchange with capital as capital; their labour can then be deployed in a productive fashion. It is important however not to stress this point in a one sided fashion. It will rarely be the case that the sole source of the academic's income will be the private sector; for the academic labour process is clearly a mixed economy funded from the public and private purse. It is likely that the intellectual will therefore be subjected to a range of complex exploitation relations, relations which may be in some sense 'contradictory', but in a different sense to Wright's use of that term.

We must take care in stressing this increasingly uniform experience of exploitation not to neglect the way in which intellectual labour is internally differentiated. Writing in 1979, Wright acknowledged the highly differentiated character of the American system of higher education. At one end of the spectrum were the community colleges, and at the other end the Ivy League universities such as Harvard and Yale, with the intellectuals employed in the former enjoying less favourable conditions of labour. Though British higher education has a quite different history to that of America, nevertheless there exist substantial divisions between Oxbridge and the ex-polytechnics and former colleges of higher education. In the Oxbridge colleges the old ideal of collegiality still has some force at least ideologically, whereas in the ex-polytechnics managerialism is more perspicuous, though managerialism is becoming more dominant in the former.[12] But within both the elite and non-elite sectors hierarchies of labour are apparent. In the elite sector, there are research stars with the ability to secure extensive funding in part on the basis of their reputations, and can therefore demand relatively favourable conditions of labour. There are then junior academics with more extensive – particularly undergraduate – teaching loads, but who nevertheless have permanent contracts. Next, we have academics on short-term contracts as well as postgraduate students employed particularly for tutorial work with the purpose of cutting labour costs and of freeing research times for their more senior colleagues. And below all of these levels are the reserve armies of needy postgraduates and unemployed scholars, who act as a constant reminder particularly to the lower echelons of intellectual wage labour that they can be replaced at a moment's notice.

Some political conclusions

At the beginning of this chapter, I referred to the tension at the heart of the Marxist project between the demands of proletarian self-emancipation and the recognition that such self-emancipation would not be possible without the tools of social scientific knowledge, tools wielded by agents who were typically considered to be external to the proletariat – that is intellectuals. A central claim of this paper has been that the idea of intellectual labour as external to the working class is increasingly a misconception. Accordingly, a key barrier to the possibility of proletarian self-emancipation would seem to have been removed by the development of the capitalist labour process.

Nevertheless, I end in a somewhat pessimistic mode. As the proletarianisation of academic labour removes one barrier to the possibility of proletarian self-emancipation, it puts another in its place. For the academic proletariat come to be subjected to the alienating and fetishising processes which have for so long shackled the working class as a whole. Intellectual workers come to relate to one another as commodities for sale in the market place, and consequently to their products as entities which appear to have an existence external to the labouring activity bestowed in them. At the political level, one can see this in the fact that there seems to be a failure amongst academics to understand the connections between the intellectual labour process in which they are embedded and proletarian labour more generally, a response in which the need for common collective political action is recognised. Indeed, the responses amongst academics to their conditions of labour largely seem to have occurred at the micro-political level. While some academics – as Prichard and Willmott (1997) note – strive to create spaces in which there is at least the possibility of non-commodified scholarly activity, other academics – as Worthington maintains – respond to these realities negatively; thus they seek in an atomistic fashion to sustain their position within (or indeed to climb) the academic hierarchy at the expense of their colleagues.

Notes

1. See Marx and Engels (2000a).
2. Cohen (2000) refers to the notion of 'subversive science'. For a discussion of this issue, see Chapter 7 in Part II of this book.

3. Benton (1981) refers to this as the 'paradox of emancipation'.
4. Other authors writing more recently have made a similar mistaken emphasis. Wilson (1991), for example, focuses on reduction in pay and conditions as a definitional aspect of proleterianisation, rather than a symptom. See also Dearlove (1997).
5. Wright identifies three main class locations at this level. First, a bourgeois class location, a location which enjoys control 'over the process of ideological production as a whole' (Wright 1979: 207). Second, a contradictory class location, comprising 'those positions which are involved in the elaboration and dissemination of bourgeois ideology, but not in the overall control of the apparatuses of bourgeois ideology' (Wright 1979: 207). Finally, a working class location. This comprises positions which both lack control over the ideological apparatuses as a whole, and are prevented from disseminating ideology within these apparatuses.
6. Of course for Marx it is precisely relations of production which constitute class relations. See Marx (2000b).
7. This is not to imply that this issue is not relevant; it is. For a discussion of the difficulties associated with Wright's view of organisation asset exploitation, see Meiksins (1998).
8. Wright later developed a concept of 'mediated relations' which again stresses such commonality of interest (see Wright 1998).
9. For his initial response to these criticisms, see Wright (1998: 191–199).
10. In his recent work, Wright discusses class along two main axes – first in relation to authority within production (the sphere where contradictory class locations can be considered to obtain) and in terms of the possession of skills and expertise (i.e. of privileged positions within exploitation relations). Though lacking the symmetry of his earlier view Wright considers this formulation to be 'conceptually sounder' (Wright 1997b: 20). For a discussion of Wright's argument, see Carling (2005).
11. In *Notes on Adolph Wagner*, Marx wrote that 'Where the state is a capitalist producer, as with the exploitation of mines, forests etc., its product is a "commodity", and therefore possesses the specific character of any other commodity' (Marx 1996: 243).
12. In some ways, commodification might be considered as more intensive in the more the established universities, in that they are more attractive targets for private funding, particularly from major multi-national corporations.

References

Benton, T. (1981) 'Objective Interests and the Sociology of Power', *Sociology*, 15 (2), 161–184.
Braverman, H. (1974) *Labour and Monopoly Capital*, New York: Monthly Review Press.
Cachedi, G. (1998) 'Classes and Class Analysis', in E. O. Wright et al. (eds), *The Debate on Classes*, Second Edition, London: Verso, 105–126.
Carling, A. (2005) 'The Wright Stuff: Erik Olin Wright and the Rehabilitation of Social Class', *Imprints: A Journal of Egalitarian theory and Practice*, 8 (2), 171–186.
Cohen, G. A. (2000) *Karl Marx's Theory of History: A Defence*, Second Edition, Oxford: Oxford University Press.
Dearlove, J. (1997) 'The Academic Labour Process: from Collegiality and Professionalism to Managerialism and Proletarianisation?', *Higher Education Review* 30/1, 56–75.

Engels, F. (1947) *Anti-Dühring*, Moscow: Progress Publishers.

Gough, I. (1972) 'Marx's Theory of Productive and Unproductive Labour', *New Left Review*, 76, 47–73.

Gramsci, A. (1971) *Selections from Prison Notebooks*, Q. Hoare and G. N. Smith (ed. and trans.), London: Lawrence and Wishart.

Halsey, A. H. (1992) *The Decline of Donnish Dominion*, Oxford: Clarendon Press.

Harvie, D. (2000) 'Alienation, Class and Enclosure in U.K. Universities', *Capital and Class*, 71, Summer, 103–132.

Karabel, J. (1976) 'Revolutionary Contradictions: Antonio Gramsci and the Problem of Intellectuals', *Politics and Society*, 123–172.

Lenin, V. I. (1946) *What is to be Done?* Moscow: Progress Publishers.

Mandel, E. (1978) *Late Capitalism*, London: New Left Books.

Marx, K. (1963) *Theories of Surplus Value*, Part 1, London: Lawrence and Wishart.

Marx, K. (1976) *Capital*, Vol. 1, Harmondsworth: Penguin.

Marx, K. (1996) 'Notes on Adolph Wagner', in T. Carver (ed.), *Marx: Later Political Writings*, Cambridge: Cambridge University Press, 227–257.

Marx, K. and Engels, F. (2000a) 'Circular Letter', in D. McLellan (ed.), *Karl Marx: Selected Writings*, Oxford: Oxford University Press, 620–622.

Marx, K. (2000b) 'Preface to a *Critique of Political Economy*', in D. McLellan (ed.), *Karl Marx: Selected Writings*, Oxford: Oxford University Press, 388–391.

Meiksins, P. F. (1998) 'A Critique of Wright's Theory of Contradictory Class Locations', in E. O. Wright *et al.* (eds), *The Debate on Classes*, Second Edition, London: Verso, 173–183.

Poulantzas, N. (1975) *Political Power and Social Classes*, London: Verso.

Prichard, C. and Willmott, H. (1997) 'Just How Managed is the McUniversity?', *Organisation Studies*, 18 (2), 287–361.

Roemer, J. (1982) *A General Theory of Exploitation and Class*, Cambridge, MA: Harvard University Press.

Rowthorn, B. (1980) *Capitalism, Conflict and Inflation: Essays in Political Economy*, London: Lawrence and Wishart.

Sassoon, A. S. (1987) *Gramsci's Politics*, Second Edition, London and Melborne: Hutchinson.

Slaughter, S. and Leslie, L. L. (1997) *Academic Capitalism: Politics and the Entrepreneurial University*, Baltimore, MD and London: John Hopkins University Press.

Stinchcombe, A. (1998) 'Education, Exploitation and Class Structure', in E. O. Wright *et al.* (eds), *The Debate on Classes*, Second Edition, London: Verso, 168–172.

Wilson, T. (1991) 'The Proletarianisation of Academic Labour', *Industrial Relations Journal*, 250–262.

Wood, E. M. (1998) *The Retreat From Class*, Revised Edition, London: Verso.

Wright, E. O. (1978) *Classes, Crisis and the State*, London: New Left Books.

Wright, E. O. (1979) 'Intellectuals and the Class Structure of Capitalist Society' in P. Walker (ed.), *Between Labour and Capital*, Hassocks: Harvester Press, 191–211.

Wright, E. O. (1997a) *Classes*, Second Edition, London: Verso.

Wright, E. O. (1997b) *Class Counts*, Cambridge: Cambridge University Press.

Wright, E. O. *et al.* (1998) *The Debate on Classes*, Second Edition, London: Verso.

10
Critical Intellectuals and the Academic Labour Process[1]

Frank Worthington

This chapter deals with some of the issues raised in other chapters in this book within the context of labour process theory (LPT) in organisation and management studies. For over three decades, particularly in the United Kingdom (Smith and Thompson 2001), LPT has become a growth area in management school teaching and research (Jaros 2001). The stated aim of those working in the labour process tradition in management education is to challenge the mainstream management view that the practice of management is a purely technical-rational actively designed to meet organisational complex goals. LPT contests this assumption by showing how the conditions under which labour is bought and sold in capitalist society are fundamentally exploitative (Knights and Willmott 1990).

This approach to management education locates what students are taught about work organisation and management practice firmly within a political-economic context. Its aim is to provide students with a wider radical understanding of how the current nature and organisation of work and management control methods play a central role in reproducing forms of oppression, exploitation and degradation that sustain political, economic and social inequality in work and society. Its overall aim is to provoke a greater level of political (Thompson 1990; Smith and Thompson 1999) and ethical (Wray-Bliss 2005) commitment to forms of resistance that will lead to more emancipatory forms of work and organisations that serve collective rather than minority interests (Alvesson and Willmott 1998).

However, given the primary purpose of the role they are required to perform to ensure that capitalist work organisations remain competitive, to what extent current and future managers and employees in organisations generally are likely to be inspired by, or willing to embrace, radical approaches to management education is open to question. As Alvesson and Willmott (1999) point out, following Macintyre (1981), given the dominant assumptions that underpin and legitimise treating labour as the object of capitalist managerial decision-making, as a resource to be exploited to generate profit, most managers in organisations are unlikely to entertain the notion that the roles they perform carry any ethical or moral responsibility for individual employee or societal well-being. This is also true of employees in organisations at all levels. As a wealth of labour process research shows, both workers and their managers are often indifferent towards their plight as waged labour and remain primarily concerned only with their immediate economic interests, individual or professional self-advancement and, in the case of managers, personal and professional aggrandisement.

Not only do workers or their managers rarely struggle against their exploitation (Burawoy 1979; Willis 1977), other than by merely distancing themselves from management control (Collinson 1994), through various overt or covert strategies of resistance (Jermier, Knights and Nord 1994) or misbehaviour (Ackroyd and Thompson 1999), they actively consent to the very conditions that reproduce their exploitation (Burawoy 1979). Covert as opposed to overt collective forms of employee resistance to capitalist exploitation, however, are both politically ineffective and essentially self-defeating (Collinson 1994). As Collinson (1994) argues, distancing strategies of resistance and misbehaviour merely disrupts management control, allowing subjects to temporarily evade the demands of authority, prevailing power structure (Clegg 1989), or, more recently, the rise of power/knowledge regimes of control, surveillance and regulation in today's organisation (Sewell and Wilkinson, 1992), in the sense that they fail to actually contest the root cause of oppression.

There is a danger here of portraying the working class as 'cultural dopes', duped by a system – supported by dominant political-economic, ideological and managerial control mechanisms that obscure the reality of capitalist social relations – against which they may occasionally protest but to which they can see no alternative. As Clegg (1989) notes, research provides evidence of workers who are seemingly ignorant of the nature of capitalist political and ideological control, yet others who are seemingly more politically astute. A lack of awareness of the conditions of exploitation under capitalism does not prevent resistance; it simply prevents radical collective political resistance to capitalism. Injustice and ill-treatment by the system clearly does provoke sporadic protest, but not collective resistance that fundamentally contest the sources of oppression.

Ackroyd and Thompson explain how, particularly in recent decades, following the rise of new subtle managerial forms of surveillance, control and accountability in organisations, misbehaviour is now *the* dominant mode of resistance to exploitation (Ackroyd and Thompson 1999).

Resistance in the new workplace

From the late 1970s we have seen the rise of new organisational, managerial and peer-review based employee control methods and performance measure designed to improve organisational effectiveness (Child 2005). Mainstream management theorists claim that these innovations in organisational structures, control and performance strategies, are designed to release employees from traditional top-down hierarchical and bureaucratic management control methods as a way of harnessing their creative potential and ingenuity to achieve complex organizational goals (Child 2005). In LPT, however, these innovations are in effect a subtle panoptic system of surveillance (Foucault 1977) that has led to the intensification of labour's subjugation to managerial power and control from which there is no escape (Sewell and Wilkinson 1992).

This contention has been widely debated in LPT, and will not be rehearsed here. Instead, the chapter focuses on the importation of the ideology of quality (Tuckman 1995) into higher education in the United Kingdom, its impact on academic labour, and how and why critical academics have failed to resist this mode of control. What I show is how resistance to quality by academics is not only mainly covert but also how its success rests upon what I refer to as *peer exploitation*. Specifically, I show how peer exploitation is enacted through various covert tactical micro-political manoeuvring by individuals that enables them to absent themselves from the burden of the institutional and personal pressures of quality assurance at the expense of others who are left to shoulder the responsibility. I also show how this form of resistance reproduces hierarchical and gender inequalities in university academic departments, which I contend raises serious questions about the conditions of possibility of realising the emancipatory intent of LPT. The empirical content of the chapter is drawn from over 70 interviewees with (mainly critical) academics in 22 academic departments in 15 UK, 3 Australian and 2 New Zealand Universities.

Academics and quality audits

Various literature from the different branches of the social and management sciences have examined the importation of quality into HE critically. What this literature shows is that considerable opposition to quality. University vice chancellors, managers, trade unions and academics alike have all expressed concerns about the negative impact of teaching and research audits on the academy. Not only in terms of its financial cost and drain on time and resource, but also in terms of its implications for traditional academic working practices and values (Willmott 1995; Martinez and McKenzie 1999; Harley 2001). Yet, this literature says virtually nothing about academics' resistance to these changes. Drawing on research findings presented below, what I show is that although quality does have a considerable self-disciplinary power-effect over the academic labour process, resistance does occur. What is noteworthy about the resistance, however, is that not only is it ineffective it is also *unethical* in that it includes practices that result in *peer exploitation*.

As noted above, a dominant form of resistance to new management surveillance techniques in organisations is 'distancing'. For Collinson (1994), 'resistance through distance' is merely a way in which subjects try to escape or avoid the demands of authority, prevailing power structure and power/knowledge regimes of control, surveillance and regulation in organisations. Collinson argues that this form of resistance is both ineffective and self-defeating because it fails to contest that to which subjects are actually opposed. As we see in the academy, 'distancing' does not actually challenge quality auditing in any real sense, it merely provides subjects with 'space' from the full extent of its power-effect and, more notably, relies to a large extent on 'peer exploitation'. In some cases *peer exploitation* is an unintended consequence of 'distancing' but in others it is clearly a conscious strategy, which both plays on and reproduces prevailing hierarchical and gender inequalities in the academy.

Quality resistance and peer exploitation

The primary role of quality assurance in higher education is to create a culture of continuous organisational and professional *self-development* and *self-regulation* within universities that provide better value-for-money teaching and research that is compatible with the needs and expectations of both individual consumers and business organisations. To resist quality, as Morley (2003: 70) argues, is to be totally at odds with these aims and ideals. Those who resist these values, in other words, suggesting, for example, that the primary 'purpose of education is [or should be] to develop critical thought, find themselves labelled not as radicals but as conservatives' whose views are likely to be seen as a misguided attempt to preserve outdated intellectual values. Those who resist quality, in other words, are likely to be perceived as suffering from 'golden ageism', or, worse, as undesirables who are either unwilling or incapable of making the necessary changes and readjustments to university teaching and working practices deemed necessary to achieve improvement. For labour process theorists what this rhetoric hides is the growing commodification of education. As Willmott (1995) contends, the introduction of private sector concerns with productivity, output and tighter financial accountability and results-based funding in the academy, coupled with new forms of accountability and close surveillance, has led to both the erosion of traditional academic 'frontiers of control' and work intensification.

Morley claims that quality is therefore a form of governmentality; a regime of power/knowledge driven by managerial values and normative working practices, performance evaluations, classifications and '*judgments*' about academic work (Foucault 1977). The pressures of achieving a score of 'excellent' in the Teaching Quality Exercise and Periodic Reviews, in other words, produce a normative power-effect on the subjectivities of academics. Because scores are published in league tables and linked to funding, and because a poor score can have potentially serious financial and symbolic consequences for themselves and for their institutions, academics feel they have no choice but to comply with the ideological aims, values and assumptions of quality auditing. For Morley, it is this that has allowed the Teaching Quality Exercise to expand its domain of discursive control over the academic labour process.

As Morley explains, universities have become compelled to become *learning organisations* in terms of teaching and learning practices, student support, research and staff development. Quality is said to achieve this by encouraging a culture of continuous institutional and individual self-evaluation and self-reflection within the academy to maintain high standards of service. However, as its critics argue, rather than empowering them to achieve this aim, in reality quality compels academics to internalise responsibility for 'policing themselves and others in the service of quality assurance' (Morley 2002: 47). This has led to academics becoming demoralised and confused about their traditional professional values and the meaning and purpose of education in modern society, resulting in stress, anxiety and alienation. As De Groot puts it, quality has precipitated a 'growing sense of separation between work and personal identity experienced by many academics, resulting from the loss of control and influence over many aspects of teaching, learning and research' (De Groot 1997: 134, cited in Morley 2003: 76). To be clear, academics do not totally object to being held to account for their performance; what they resent is the way in which accountability has been systematically extended to areas of the academy where it has previously not existed. Quality auditing has displaced traditional self-regulatory forms of professional accountability and trust relationships, with a culture of institutionalised *distrust* (Power 1997).

Ostensibly collegiate activities, such as the Subject Programme Review (SPR) and Periodic Review (PR), and resistance to them, have to be understood therefore within this culture of distrust. These review processes are said to be designed to provide evaluation, information and feedback on practices and standards of performance in a language, which assumes that institutions, departments and individuals should be *continuously improving* their learning and teaching and student support. This automatically presupposes that improvements in practices and performance are there to be made, that certain deficiencies must already exist within the system that need to be corrected.

The power-effect of this on the subjectivity of many of the interviewees from the research finding presented here was evident. For example, in their 'self-assessment' documentation for SPR, and during the process itself, many felt compelled to actually find for themselves and then 'confess' to at least some *deficiencies* in departmental practices, so as *not to look too good in the eyes of the assessors*, who, they believed, would have difficulty with, or be suspicious of, a department claiming to be 'excellent' in all areas of teaching and assessment and student support. This need to 'confess' to (at least some) 'deficiencies' in teaching and learning practices calmed fears of being perceived by the assessors as trying to hide something. This need to offer up what subjects perceived quality inspectors *expected* to find is a common reaction to quality (Morley 2003). This reflects the feelings of insecurity and fear that is produced by the knowledge that the outcome of SPR is never certain. It also reveals the asymmetrical nature of the power relations between assessors and the assessed. To score badly, as Morley shows, is perceived by academics as both degrading and humiliating as it is a direct insult to their professional integrity and self-identity. Inefficiencies exposed by quality audits do not remain in-house matters. On the contrary, the whole purpose of SPR is to place its assessment, classification and ranking of each university's teaching quality standards and performance within the public domain, in league tables, to allow funding bodies and paying customers of education to make informed choices about the quality of different institutions and the market-value of their products.

The prospect of being open to both institutional and public scrutiny puts each university department and their members of staff under considerable pressure. First, in terms of the implications of SPR for the standing and reputation of a university and each of its various department and subject areas, and second in terms of its impact on the subjectivity and identity of academic staff in terms of their individual reputation within the academic community. Many academics thus feel their professional reputation is being put on trial. This sense of being watched makes them *watchful* of their practices and performances and extremely conscious of the possibility of letting their department and *themselves* down in some way. These pressures have considerable negative psychological side effects on those most closely involved in SPR. In turn this causes intense feelings of insecurity, fear, anxiety, isolation, self-*recrimination*, guilt and bad conscience about the apparent shortcomings of the old system. This reveals the extent to which the self-disciplinary power-effect of the quality auditing culture colonises academics' subjectivities and identities, and why SPR, supposedly based on self-evaluation – on what departments and subject areas say they do, as opposed to what the assessor's may claim they should be doing – produces conformity and compliance. As one of our own research subjects put it:

It stands to reason that once you start to say that you need to measure what people do, you're saying that there's something wrong. What you're then saying is that something needs to be done to improve things. Nobody has a problem with that. But with quality it's not just about looking at what's wrong and doing something about it, its about holding someone to account, its about *naming and shaming*. People automatically then think that what's wrong could have something to do with *them* as individuals. I would imagine we all do the job in pretty much the same way. But when it comes to *quality* you can never really be sure that what your institution does and what you do yourself is actually up to scratch in quality terms.

The vast majority of Morley's respondents shared this view, perceiving SPR to be both threatening and *dis*empowering. The relentless pursuit of evidence of the strengths and weaknesses in practices, competencies and performance by the SPR auditors, whose own position and practices remain unquestioned, creates a climate of *unspoken* mutual suspicion and mistrust which subjects resent, but which they cannot afford openly to contest for fear of being accused of hiding something. This effectively guarantees not only compliance but also creates a situation whereby subjects feel compelled to impersonate the assessors, 'to present themselves in a language that quality assessors will understand and value' (Morley 2003: 70).

Resistance to subject programme review

Morley's analysis of the lived-experience of SPR touches on, but does not explore, where and how resistance to teaching quality audits occurs. Her analysis of how and why academics comply with the requirements of the quality auditing in HE, however, although she does show how small *local* forms of resistances do occur, does not examine in detail how resistance is enacted. This neglect is due in part to her totalising reading of the self-disciplinary power-effect of SPR, which she sees as being inescapable, and the fact that she is mainly concerned with the 'psychic economy' of quality; its psychological and emotional costs. This leads Morley to neglect an important element of the psychological and emotional consequences of SPR. Because she does not recognise that there is room to resist incorporation into these processes, she also fails to note that such resistance depends upon particular relationships amongst colleagues. As the research findings presented in this chapter shows, many of those given responsibility for their department's preparation for SPR were frustrated not only by the amount of time and effort involved in gathering and organising the various quality assessment documentation but also by the attitude and behaviour of many of their colleagues.

As number of interviewees pointed out, many of their colleagues provided them with little or no real support above and beyond producing their own programme and module documentation, which was often inadequate and rarely delivered on time. Some failed even to do this, leaving others to produce or complete missing documentation. To justify their lack of involvement and cooperation, almost all those who resisted quality in this way resented the time and effort that they were expected to devote to quality, which they claimed could be put to much better use doing research, and gave no consideration of the effect of their recalcitrance on others. Some also resisted by claiming that they failed to understand what was expected of them in terms of the content of module resource boxes and module documentation, or what would be expected of them during the SPR itself. Others resisted by declaring that they were fundamentally opposed to the aims and objectives of quality, and thus called for (but made no effort to organise) resistance.

Peer exploitation: *Devolvers and shirkers*

It is possible to identify four different roles adopted by those resisting the quality audit process, all of which involve some form of peer exploitation: (1) *The Devolver;* (2) *The Shirker;* (3) *The Ditherer* (4) *The Deceiver.* In all of the departments visited SPR was officially led by departmental heads and senior academic staff, but in most cases delegated to junior members of staff, mainly female. Not all of those interviewed resented being given this responsibility, but almost all reported that they felt poorly supported and often let down by their Head of Department (HoD) and many colleagues, who 'just left them to it.' As almost all of the interviewees pointed out, certain colleagues in their departments took every available opportunity to absent themselves from SPR activities in spite of the added pressure this put on their colleagues. As one interviewee put it:

> What was most annoying was that everyone was informed of the importance of SPR, and the consequences for the department if it got a 'bad score', but didn't seem to care. They couldn't afford *not to care* really. They knew what was at stake. So when I say they didn't care whether or not things got done, what I'm actually saying is that they didn't care as long as [preparation for SPR] didn't affect them.

All of the interviewees in all of the departments visited reported that they had at some point encountered recalcitrance of one form or another by certain colleagues who, although they recognised and in some cases openly acknowledged the impact of their behaviour on other colleagues, in most cases nevertheless remained totally unconcerned or unembarrassed by the consequences of their lack of support and cooperation. As one interviewee, a female professor who managed to maintain her distance from any real involvement in SPR, following her department achieving a score of 23 in the SPR, admitted after the exercise itself: 'I don't know what all the fuss was about, and I don't see why we had to put so much effort into it. It's not important, even though we did get there in the end. The 23 will keep the university happy I suppose, but it doesn't do anything for your CV.'

Along with the Head of Department, this professor was reported as having had little involvement in SPR, 'from start to finish', by *devolving* responsibility for its preparation to junior members of staff. As her colleagues reported, she remained:

> Totally disengaged from SPR from start to finish. For her to now say that she didn't see what all the fuss was about is insulting. She did

absolutely nothing to help. Not once did she deliver any of the documentation she was asked to produce. As far of the rest of us are concerned, she shouldn't have had to be *asked* in the first place, as second in department she should have been doing the asking.

Staff in this department and other departments who faced the same problem reported how senior members of staff similarly exploited their position to *shirk* responsibility for the planning and preparation for SPR. What was most infuriating, as one put it, was that 'they presented the impression to the university that they were coordinating the planning and preparation' but in reality did *virtually* nothing. Many interviewees also reported that what they found most insulting was that after having been totally disengaged from the planning and preparation process, leading up to the inspection itself, it was senior members of the department who greeted the assessors.

Female lecturers in four departments visited reported that they were treated as 'domestic labour' within their departments. Most of the female academics interviewed also reported that it was mainly male colleagues who were the most recalcitrant towards SPR. Many dismissed this as a 'macho thing', which they saw as just one of a number of tactics used (by men) to distance themselves as much as possible from SPR to protect their research time and career interests. As one of a number of interviewees pointed out:

> [Those] who were most against what we needed to do for TQA argued that we should be doing no more than the absolute minimum needed to achieve a decent score. When we argued that you can't actually predict in advance what score you're likely to get because it's impossible to be sure how the assessors will see things, they took absolutely no notice. They just argued back that the [TQA] process was 'bollocks' and that it wrecks research time. [...] I'm not sure it was their intention at first, but I think some learned from this early on that if we couldn't be sure that they would prepare their part, because we couldn't trust them to do it, we would do it for them.

This kind of tactical resistance to SPR was also evident elsewhere. However, the level of frustration and tension it caused varied. In large departments it seemed more acceptable and a less contentious issue which can be explained in part perhaps by the fact that in most large departments visited it was mainly administrative staff that managed the planning and preparation for SPR, with academic staff simply overseeing the process. As a result, resistance by *devolving and shirking* was less of an issue than in smaller departments. Larger departments also have the luxury of 'hiding away' *renegades*, as they were referred to in one department, who were seen as being potentially detrimental to the department; those in other words who 'might not play the game in front of the assessors'. Indeed, in three large management schools in leading universities we were told that certain academic members of staff 'were kept well out of the way of the quality assessors' for fear that not only would they not cooperate but it was believed they may actually attempt to antagonise the assessors'. Three such renegades were interviewed, all of whom, far from being displeased with being perceived in this way, found it somewhat amusing that their HoD deemed it necessary to 'hide them away'. Because all academic staff in smaller departments are more directly involved in SPR, and because acts of resistance are consequently much more visible, *devolving and shirking* caused considerably more tension and greater resentment and frustration.

The research also shows that tactical *dithering and deceit* are also commonly used to resist responsibility for quality and involvement in SPR. Resistance through *dithering* and *deceit* are similar to what Ackroyd and Thompson (1999) refer to as 'learned incompetence', or what may more accurately be referred to as 'calculated recalcitrance', whereby subjects learn how to *deceive* others into believing that what is required of them is beyond their understanding and capabilities. Academics in five departments in three universities visited pointed out that they had encountered *ditherers*, who claimed to find it particularly difficult to understand what was expected of them, in terms of how they should present their programme and module handbooks, what needed to be included in module resource boxes and why they had to write module documentation in a particular way. Some were in fact seen as being incapable of writing quality documentation to the required standard, but most it was believed were in fact 'playing the fool' as a subtle way off-loading their share of responsibility onto others. As one senior lecturer in a sociology department explained:

> We were all asked to write up the different TQA documentation. Once it was done we'd review it at meetings. Some of what was produced was pretty dreadful at first, and some of it was pathetic [...], either badly written, or it didn't have the level of detail that was needed. When we pointed this out to [those responsible], and tried to explain that we couldn't afford not to get [the documentation] right they just sat there looking all flustered and apologetic, saying that they didn't really know what they were supposed to be doing. I think one person

actually didn't know what he was doing, but one or two people, *who shall remain nameless*, knew *exactly* what we needed, and *could* do it, but wouldn't because they could see how much time it would take up. They got away with it because they have five star research output.

Similarly, as one of our interviewees in a politics department pointed out:

When we were given the date of the assessment we had just over a year to prepare. We were told at a meeting by [the HoD] that quality had to be given total priority over everything else, including research. We were also told, in no uncertain terms, by the HoD that research had to be shelved until after the [SPR] inspection. This didn't exactly go down well but we accepted it. But we then had two members of staff who just totally ignored this. One of them very quickly arranged leave to do research overseas. The other carried on working as normal and actually produced about five publications over the 15 months when the rest of us were tied up with [SPR], and on the back of that actually got a senior lectureship straight after the inspection at [a different university].

This interviewee went on to explain how this colleague also totally ignored all emails requesting her to write SPR documentation, and also failed to collect and organise the various course and module material she was allocated to produce. When confronted about this at meeting she simply claimed that she 'just didn't understand it all'.

In three other departments we were informed of rather more insidious instances of peer exploitation, in one case by a longstanding leading labour process theorists, who was reported as having been not only uncooperative but also somewhat malevolent towards those responsible for, or who willingly cooperated in, the planning and preparation for SPR. When interviewed, two of these three individuals confessed that they had in fact initially volunteered themselves to take primary responsibility for SPR, with the expectation that a 'score of excellent' would put them in good standing with their university a pay increment and promotion. Later realising that this was unlikely to happen, not only did these individuals retract their offer to take the lead role but they also embarked on an aggressive 'anti-quality campaign' within their departments, condemning TQA as a form of 'managerial manipulation', and those who cooperated in it as 'fools who ought to know better than to play into management's hands', as one put it. When pressed about the hypocrisy of his actions, this academic parried the accusation by stating:

> Quality is management's problem not mine. I do what I have to do before the inspectors arrive, but I'm not spending every minute of every day thinking about it. I leave that to the idiots in the department who've taken it on. If they're daft enough to worry about it, when it's the university management who as far as I'm concerned are paid to worry about it, then that's their problem. If they want me to do that they can pay me for it.

Resistance and the critical community

Quality assurance processes have created a situation in which university teachers today are compelled to fashion their teaching in accordance with pre-given quantifiable teaching objectives and learning outcomes that correspond with managerial notions of 'best practice' that meet individual student needs and expectations and those of industry. New research funding criteria, research performance indicators and league tables have similarly created a situation whereby academics remain constantly aware of the importance of publishing the 'magic four' articles in the top listed journals in their field, for the RAE. As a result academics are more concerned with output, rather than with making a 'significant contribution to knowledge'. Given these consequences, how can we explain why academics have accepted the importation of quality audit into HE without a fight?

There are at least four ways to explain academics' apparent passivity. First, academics see their work as vocational. As Hugh Willmott points out, although academics sell their labour to provide income for themselves and their dependents, 'the notion that they work for a wage is directly at odds with their self image as professionals, for whom payment for their work is, or has [traditionally] been regarded more as a necessary condition for providing a (vocational) service to society than a means of providing them with an income' (Willmott 1995: 995). As a result they tend not to analyse their work from a critical standpoint, let alone from a labour process perspective (Miller 1991). According to Willmott they are also unlikely to view changes in the nature and organisation of their work within the context of any wider socio-political- economic forces from which such changes arise. Second, and more important, in spite of the rise of cohesive methods of accountability, academics are still able to legitimately work independently from close management control. Until this aspect of academic work is entirely eroded they are therefore unlikely to contest openly the introduction of new quality control practices, or to interpret them as coercive control and surveillance. As the research findings presented above shows, in spite of the power-effect of quality on the profession most academics still continue to perceive their teaching practices and research performance as being governed primarily by traditional self-regulatory practices set by the profession itself through peer review and standards of scholarship within a given field. Third, in spite of high union density within the profession, few academics are active trade unionists. Fourth, those who *are* attentive to the political implications of quality in higher education seem to 'do their resisting' only through academic writing.

But resistance to any mode of control, panoptic or otherwise, is always possible (Kunda 1990; Casey 1996; Ezzamel and Willmott 1998; McKinley and Taylor 1998; Ezzamel, Willmott and Worthington 2001). Indeed, as our research demonstrates, how academics perform when under the normative 'gaze' of the quality auditing inspectors and what they actually do in practice are often two very different things entirely. Quality auditing has undoubtedly made a significant impact on the academy, and academics are acutely aware of the consequences of receiving a poor quality score in teaching and research, but it is not the all-pervasive panoptic force that Foucauldian readings of quality suggest. Nor does it reach all subjects in the same way. Many interviewees reported that they have had no real involvement in quality assurance, other than having to provide the requisite course and module teaching and learning documentation for those who, as one academic put it, *do the quality stuff*, and when under the disciplinary 'gaze' of the quality inspectors.

Those who 'do the quality stuff', however, tell a rather different story. For them quality assurance can be a highly stressful, thankless and time-consuming task, and also potentially detrimental to both career and personal well-being. Many of those given responsibility for, or most closely involved in, departmental preparations for SPR felt that they received little or no recognition or reward for their efforts within their departments, inadequate support from their institutions, and little or no real support or cooperation from many of their colleagues. Many reported how this caused them not only considerable frustration but also in some cases bouts of depression, anxiety, feelings of isolation and an overall sense of having been betrayed. This raises questions concerning institutional obligation, legal and moral, to the health and safety of its employees.

There is a tendency in (some) labour process literature to celebrate covert forms of resistance to management control, including quality control methodologies, as 'heroic' defiance against the degradation of work (Braverman 1974). Whether or not these covert forms of resistance can be seen as defiant, they do depend upon unequal labour, where some colleagues – usually senior members of the 'academic team' – extract and use the labour of others – usually junior and female for their own ends. Existing hierarchies within the academy are utilised so that junior members of staff, facing the normative pressures of the quality process, and the situational power of senior colleagues, feel compelled to follow through with their responsibilities: where opting out no longer appears to be a choice. This brings into question the so-called critical academic community's commitment to the politico-ethical values that it claims to hold dear. An internal analysis of labour dynamics might help to make explicit the implicit conditions for an individual being able to resist teaching assurance and concentrate on his, or her, research and perhaps thereby provide the grounds for different kinds of resistance.

  Nigel Piercy, writing about the distorting and irrational effects of the research assessment exercise on business schools, claims that there is only one reason for these negative effects: 'we have been craven in allowing others to dictate the terms under which our research is to be measured and evaluated. In this sense it is our own fault' (Piercy 2000: 28). This is also true for teaching quality assurances processes. However, this chapter has suggested one reason why the academic community has found it so difficult to voice its opposition to these processes. While quality assurance processes have a damaging psychological and emotional effect on those brought within it, they are *not* totalising. The belief that they are disguises the fact that resistance is possible and diverts attention from the reality of internal labour dynamics. Where individual members of the academic community depend upon, and exploit, the gendered labour of others the community itself fragments, which leaves everyone subject to the Taylorist work practices of a newly global education market.

Conclusion

Given the amount of attention that the critical academic community has invested in research into the implication of the ideology of quality (Tuckman 1995) in other industries, and how and to what extent workers in these industries are able to resist these implications, the conditions of possibility of resistance to quality in the academy itself seems to be a rather neglected area of research. Indeed, critical academics so readily go out into the so-called real world of work and bring back tales of consent and resistance to their subjugation (Sewell and Wilkinson 1992; McKinley and Taylor 1996; Ezzamel, Willmott and Worthington 2001) to such modes of discursive power and control, and yet seem to pay virtually no attention to these phenomena in their own work environment.

This is somewhat odd given what the critical academic community deems to be at stake for the academy, in terms of the implications of quality auditing for traditional academic working conditions and professional values. At the same time it raises rather interesting questions. As many have argued, the quality auditing culture challenges not only academics' traditional self-regulatory professional codes of practice, but also their professional autonomy (Miller 1991; Power 2001; Child 2005) and to a certain degree their professional integrity (Morley, 2003). So why do so many academics so readily accept the importation of quality audit into higher education without a fight? Moreover, why do they see writing as a form of resistance as being in any way meaningful let alone effective? Given that the industry is unionised, this is certainly not the only possible channel of resistance open to them. Academic publications may well raise political awareness of the implications of quality auditing for their profession, but by and large academic papers are produced primarily for the consumption of other academics whose most likely inclination will be to respond first and foremost, as intellectuals, to their conceptual and theoretical content rather than to be provoked to engage in concrete political action against what they demonstrate is at stake – in this case, for the academy itself. This of course is certainly not entirely true of the critical academic community as a whole, but it is undoubtedly a dominant tendency. As Wray-Bliss (2005) argues, many of those working within the labour process tradition seem to embrace its emancipatory ethical and political intent in their teaching and writing, but do not *embody* what this demands of them in real terms in the field and especially in their own workplace.

In the process of conducting the fieldwork for this chapter these issues were in fact raised with the research subjects, all of whom acknowledged that yes, we teach and do research into the subjugating power-effect of managerial control methods, including quality assurance, for workers and managers in other industries, yet at the same time readily submit to the very same normative modes of power, control and surveillance in our own profession. When pressed to account for this, almost all of the respondents gave more or less the same answer. When it comes to quality, we have no choice! This statement has profound implications for the critical academic community. From Marx (1976) through Braverman

(1974) to Burawoy (1979, 1985) and beyond labour process theorists and, more lately critical management theorists have wrestled with the question as to why the working class seems to consent to its own exploitation. Much has been written about this. Much has also be been written in response to Foucauldian readings of this phenomenon. In particular, the claim that managerial power/knowledge surveillance methods, such as total quality control techniques, are so all pervasive in today's organisations they are effectively immune to worker resistance. This has been an extremely contentious issue. Barker (1993), Delbridge (1992), Zuboff (1988) and, in particular, Sewell and Wilkinson (1992), to mention but a few, have been heavily criticised within the literature for claiming that contemporary managerial surveillance and quality control techniques have succeeded in totally eliminating any form of meaningful resistance to them. And yet, ironically, as the findings of the research presented above illustrate, even some of their strongest critics some of whom were interviewed seem to *confirm* their contention that resistance to quality is futile. For Howie (2002: 144), this is because academics are in a position whereby they 'have the freedom to reason critically in letters and papers [about the normative implications of quality assurance in higher education] but not when acting in role: when at the pulpit we must sing from the same [quality] management songbook'. The 'truth effect' of the various teaching quality 'performance trials', she argues, makes any other form of resistance impossible. Thus, for Howie, irrespective of their critical insights into the ideology of managerial quality control regimes, like workers in other industries, academics are seemingly caught up in a contradictory situation whereby they are compelled to consent to practices to which they are fundamentally opposed.

Howie makes an important point, but she is wrong; resistance is always possible. Those who engaged in 'distancing' practices recognise this, yet self rather than collective professional interest fuels their resistance. They also recognise, and fully acknowledge that 'distancing' is essentially self-defeating, and that it has serious consequences for those who are thus left to 'do the quality stuff'. The concept of 'peer exploitation' in the academy therefore clearly raises serious questions about the (so-called) critical academic community's solidarity, its (apparent) commitment to its espoused political-economic goals and values, and, moreover, the conditions of possibility of any real emancipatory social and organisational change in work and society, given the evidently wilful unethical resistance practices of some of its members.

Note

1. The empirical content of this paper was first published with Julia Hodgson in the journal *Critical Quarterly* 27 (1–2), Spring/Summer 2005. The author and editor would like to express their gratitude to Blackwell Publishers for allowing it to be republished here.

References

Ackroyd, S. and Thompson, P. (1999) *Organisational Misbehaviour*, London: Sage.

Alvesson, M and Willmott, H. (1999) *Making Sense of Management: A Critical Introduction*, London: Sage.

Barker, J. (1999) *The Discipline of Teamwork*, London: Sage.

Braverman, H. (1974) *Labour and Monopoly Capital*, New York: Monthly Review Press.

Burawoy M. (1979) *Manufacturing Consent: Changes in the Labor Process under Monopoly Capitalism*, London: The University of Chicago Press.

Burawoy M. (1985) *The Politics of Production*, London, Verso.

Casey, C. (1996) *Self, Industrialization and Society*, London: Sage.

Child, J. (2005) *Organization*, London: Sage.

Clegg, S. R. (1989) *Frameworks of Power*, London: Sage.

Collinson, D. (1994) 'Strategies of Resistance: Power, Knowledge and Subjectivity in the Workplace', in J. Jermier, D. Knights and W. Nord (eds), *Resistance and Power in Organizations*, London: Routledge, 25–68.

Collinson, D. (1992) *Managing the Shopfloor: Subjectivity Masculinity and Workplace Culture*, Berlin: Walter de Gruyter.

De Groot, J. (1997) 'After the Ivory Tower: Gender, Commodification and the "Academic" ', *Feminist Review*, 55 (Spring): 130–142.

Delbridge, R. and Turnbull, P. (1992) 'Human Resource Maximization – "The Management of Labour under a JIT System" ', in P. Blyton, and P. Turnbull (eds), *Reassessing Human Resource Management*, London: Sage, 56–73.

Edwards, P. K. (1986) *Conflict at Work*, Oxford, Blackwell.

Ezzamel, M. and Willmott, H. C. (1998) 'Accounting for Team Work: Some Limits of Group-Based Systems of Organizational Control', *Administrative Science Quarterly*, 43, June, 358–396.

Ezzamel, M., Willmott, H. and Worthington, F. (2001) 'Power, Control and Resistance in the Factory that Time Forgot', *Journal of Management Studies*, December, 1053–1079.

Foucault, M. (1977) *Discipline and Punish*, London: Penguin.

Harley, S. (2001) 'Accountants Divided: Research Selectivity and Academic Accounting Labour in the UK', Working Paper, De Montfort University Business School.

Howie, G. (2002) 'A Reflection of Quality: Instrumental Reason, Quality Audits and Knowledge Economy', *Critical Quarterly*, 44(4), 140–148.

Jermier, J. Knights, D. and Nord, W. (1994) (eds), *Resistance and Power in Organizations*, London and New York: Routledge.

Jaros, S. (2002) 'Labour Process Theory: A Commentary on the Debate', *International Studies in Management and Organisation*, 30 (4), 25–29.

Knights, D. and Willmott, H. (1999) *Management Lives: Power, Identify and Work Organization*, London: Sage.

Kunda, G. (1990) *Manufacturing Culture*, Philadelphia, PA: Temple University Press.

Macintyre, A. E. (1981) After Virtue, London: Duckworth.

Martinez, L. and MacKenzie, R. (1999) 'Quality Management: A New Form of Control?', in S. Corby and S. G. White (eds), *Employee Relations in the Public Services*, London and New York: Routledge, 188–219.

Marx, K. 1867 (1976) *Capital*, Vol. 1, Harmondsworth: Penguin.

McKinlay, A and Taylor, P. (1998) 'Foucault and the Politics of Production', in A. McKinlay and K. Starkey (eds), *Foucault, Management and Organization Theory*, London, Sage, 1–37.

McKinlay, A and Starkey, K (1998) 'Managing Foucault, Foucault, Management and Organization Theory', in A. McKinlay and K. Starkey (eds), *Foucault, Management and Organization Theory*, London: Sage, 224–258.

Miller, H. (1991) 'Academics and their Labour Process', in C. Smith, D. Knights and H. Willmott (eds), *White-Collar Work: The Non-Manual Labour Process*, London: Macmillan, 108–139.

Morley, L. (2003) *Quality and Power in Higher Education*, Buckingham: Open University Press.

Piercy, N. (2000) 'Why it is Fundamentally Stupid for a Business School to Try to Improve its Research Assessment Exercise Score?', *European Journal of Marketing*, 34 (1), 2–32.

Power, M. (2001) *The Auditing Society: Rituals of Verification*, Oxford: Oxford University Press.

Puxty, A. Sikka, P. and Willmott, H. (1994) 'Systems of Surveillance and the Silencing of UK Academic Accounting Labour', *British Accounting Review*, 26, 137–171.

Sewell, G. and Wilkinson, B. (1992) 'Someone to Watch Over Me: Surveillance, Discipline and the Just-in-Time Labour Process', *Sociology*, 26(2), 271–298.

Smith, C. and Thompson, P. (1999) 'Reevaluating the Labour Process', in M. Wardell, L. Steiger and P. Meiksins (eds), *Rethinking the Labour Process*, Albany, NY: State University of New York Press, 205–233.

Thompson, P. (1990) 'Crawling from the Wreckage: The Labour Process and the Politics of Production', in D. Knights and H. Willmott (eds), *Labour Process Theory*, London: Macmillan, 95–124.

Thompson, P. and McHugh, D. (1995) *A Critical Introduction to Work Organizations*, London: Macmillan Business.

Tuckman, A. (1995) 'Ideology, Quality and TQM', in A. Wilkinson, and H. Willmott (eds), *Making Quality Critical*, London and New York: Routledge, 96–118.

Willis, P. (1977) *Learning to Labour*, Farnborough: Saxon House.

Willmott, H. (1995) 'Managing the Academics: Commodification and Control in The Development of University Education in the UK', *Human Relations*, 48 (9), 993–1027.

Wray-Bliss, E. (2005) 'Abstract Ethics, Embodied Ethics: The Strange Marriage of Foucault and Positivism in Labour Process Theory', in C. Grey and H. Willmott (eds), *Critical Management Studies*, Oxford: Oxford University Press, 83–417.

Zuboff (1988) *In The Age of the Smart Machine*, Oxford: Heineman.

11
Mediated Intellectuals: Negotiating Social Relations in Media

Lee Salter

Social life is mediated in numerous ways. Ideas, social interaction and practical activity are all mediated in part by communication or media technologies. Whilst it would be folly to suggest that media technologies mediate most people's entire experience of political and intellectual life, it is the case that the presence of these technologies in people's lives is such that they cannot be ignored. To a degree the capacity of media technologies to facilitate critical political and intellectual engagements is limited by the context of their production and use. However, in this chapter I argue that a paradigm shift, the 'cultural' or 'linguistic turn' filtered through to media and cultural studies, often has the effect of sidelining the question of production. Consequently, the role of the intellectual changes from a producer of media messages to at best an interpreter, and at worst nothing at all. The ideas behind the postmodern elements of the cultural turn were, in part, a response to the perceived reification of ideology as a concept and to a supposed understanding of media communications as 'hypodermic'. This is to say that postmodern media and cultural studies stylised the Marxist understanding of media as one in which capitalists transmitted their one-sided messages to a passive audience, which then accepted them. In contrast to this, the postmodernists 'empower' audiences by arguing that they actively produce meanings in a process of negotiation, often rejecting or transforming intended meanings. The problem, however, is that the so-called active audience is never as important as the active producer, and both are constrained by relations of production. I then move to consider Gramsci's understanding of the intellectual, pointing out that the critical intellectual ought to be practically active and aim to change methods of production. In the next section, I investigate the degree to which different forms of broadcasting enable critical intellectuals to participate in media production. In the final part I question how new media technologies may allow an increase in critical intellectual activity in media production, whilst altering the relation of such intellectuals to their publics.

Media studies, consumption and production

Some strands of Marxist theory (and recent practice) tend to regard the academic study of media as something of a deviation. Certainly there is some justification for such concerns over forms of media studies that abstract media from the historical context of development and use, from their overall structuring within a capitalist system of production, and its associated forms of economic and political power. Without understanding the context of media practices, institutions and technologies, we cannot begin to understand current functioning and future potential of media technologies.

However, in many areas of media and cultural studies, Marxism has been the dominant paradigm for half a century at least. The work of the Frankfurt School, Leicester's Centre for Mass Communication Research, Birmingham's Centre for Contemporary Cultural Studies and of the Glasgow Media Group have all been heavily influenced by Marxist thought, in one vein or another. Before these academic schools, communist investigations of media (for example, Eisenstein on Film, Vertov on documentary, Trotsky on Radio, and Brecht on theatre and radio) saw media technologies as tools whose uses could and should be understood in relation to revolutionary activity, albeit under the restraints of the capitalist state (see, for example, Brecht 1979/1980; Trotsky 1993). The aim of these investigations was to think about how to place media *production* in the hands of workers. Individual scholars in the United Kingdom, such as Graham Murdoch, Colin Sparks, Peter Golding, Michael Chanan, James Curran, Mike Wayne and many others have understood media technologies, organisations and workers as integral parts of capitalist economy, and have argued that without understanding media in terms of forces and relations of production, one cannot begin to understand the role and potential of media technologies as such.

Many such schools and scholars have argued that media production and its embeddedness in more general economic relations must be supplemented by understanding the process of symbolic reproduction, that is, to understand media in the context of production, consumption and exchange at the same time. However, in the 1980s, a number of left media and cultural studies scholars began to pull apart this holistic approach, and started to focus almost exclusively on the circulation and interpretation of symbols.[1] The central concern of such post-Marxist or postmodern approaches to media studies is to analyse the ways in which different messages circulate, are accepted, challenged or rejected. However, the development of these currents in media and cultural studies, which focus on 'consumption', 'pleasures', reception/audience studies, identity politics and 'domestication' of media, led to the now normal abstraction from the question of production. This cultural turn celebrates what are perceived to be instances of difference and subversion of meaning that somehow resist something/everything. The general conclusions seem to be 'look, they didn't take X at face value' and 'not everyone does/thinks/needs everything in the same way' and so on. On this approach, domination takes place through discourse, discourse can be resisted in interpretation, and therefore domination can be resisted. That discourses can be mis- or reinterpreted (or indeed that the functioning of discourses depends upon a form of 'agreement' on the part of participants) may be interesting, but is limited in its significance. There are some interesting things to be said about how signs, meanings and artefacts are appropriated and changed by recipients, but for these to be of any value they must be linked up to the question of the access to the mechanisms of production and distribution of those signs, meanings and artefacts in the first place. Without understanding the relations between production, consumption and exchange, understanding is fragmented and potential for resistance is undermined.

The disregard of production and the concomitant emphasis on consumption and the 'strategies of interpretation' of audiences limits the explanatory capacity of such analyses. Media and cultural studies that do not understand the full process of production may thus believe that strategies of interpretation provide sufficient bases for resistance to the forms of domination that accompany capitalism. However, consideration of *production* leads one to realise that the point is to *change* production not to just *interpret* it. In understanding general relations of production we can see how media give rise to hegemonic representations, what the implications of these are, and also what alternatives might be proposed.

In the first instance, capitalist media organisations produce commodities. These commodities often tend to reflect the broad circumstances under which they are produced and consumed. This is to say that technologies are commodities, content is made up of commodities, workers are commodities, audiences are commodities to be sold to advertisers, but also media organisations themselves are usually tradable commodities. This commodity relation is not, however, complete. Many Marxists (e.g. Wayne 2003: 17–18) argue that intellectual workers, which include those working in 'the media', are relatively autonomous, or perhaps less constrained by capital than other workers. However, this relative autonomy is qualified and contextual. For example, if we interrogate the status of 'autonomous' (even if only relative), we have to consider what one is autonomous from. At base media workers *are workers*, that is, they are usually employed by a company that owns many of the tools they must use in order to carry out the work assigned to them and controls the general organisation of production, general (legally structured) parameters of consumption and exchange of their products. This employment sets the worker in relation to other workers of differing levels of seniority and so on. Eventually we come to see the media worker as situated in an institutional complex which itself is part of an industrial complex of production, consumption and exchange, from the manufacture and installation of light bulbs (and the electricity required to power them), cameras, ink and paper, to the presentation of newspapers or DVDs in shop displays (so, for example, Negt and Kluge (1993) argue that even public service television is embedded within a capitalist system of production). Control over production equates to control over what is excluded and included.

The possibility of 'resistance' through the 'production' of meaning in reception (see, for instance, Fiske 1987) is perhaps the *least* one can expect, and becomes a great deal more problematic when applied in more obviously oppressive political systems, such as Nazi Germany or Stalinist Russia. It is more than a little insulting to suggest that people under such systems merely needed to reinterpret the propaganda in order to change things. A good deal of the motivation of such postmodern arguments stems from deformations of Antonio Gramsci's and Raymond Williams' arguments about popular culture and capitalism. For example, there are a number of studies that abstract 'cultural artefacts' from the conditions of their production, serving to extinguish the distinction between a commodity (such as a CD of a manufactured pop band) and a traditional folk song; that is, they mistake commodities for what Gramsci and Williams meant by popular culture – culture produced by and in the interests of the people. Indeed, Gramsci and Williams both understood that intellectuals must be deeply involved with class struggle in organised political movements (which few postmodernists recognise). To this end, both joined and became activists in their respective communist parties and in the labour movement. They also understood, against many postmodern uses of their work, that symbolic production is intimately tied to material production; so much so that one cannot simply change one without the other. So, Hall's (1996: 268) argument that organic intellectuals 'must work on two fronts at one and the same time', that they are to 'know more than the traditional intellectuals do', and are to realise a 'responsibility of transmitting those ideas' should be supplemented with a third front – a more direct physical struggle over the organisation of material production. Indeed, Gramsci is quite explicit about this latter part of the intellectual's role, and it is this part of the role that we should understand as missing from post-Marxist and postmodern media studies.

Gramsci's intellectual and capitalist media

A more serious attempt to challenge hegemonic media representations would include paying attention to their production, consumption and exchange, which would involve the engagement of practically active intellectuals of the sort proposed by Gramsci. Whilst Gramsci noted that 'all men are intellectuals', to understand his concept of the intellectual, we must remember that he adds that 'not all men have in society the function of intellectuals' (Gramsci 1971: 9) and these 'functions' of intellectuals are numerous and contradictory. On the one hand, the traditional intellectual claims to be independent of the 'dominant social group', yet serves to sustain the social order. On the other, the organic intellectual, who grows out of new classes[2] and from the new relations in which he/she is situated, challenges the existing hegemony. The distinction between traditional and organic intellectuals is not, however, a simple distinction. Gramsci makes it quite clear of the latter that

> every social group, coming into existence on the original terrain of an essential function in the world of economic production, creates together with itself, organically, one or more strata of intellectuals which give it homogeneity and an awareness of its own function not only in the economic but also in the social and political fields. (Gramsci 1971: 5)

This is to say that organic intellectuals help shape emerging classes and social groups, and develop their self-awareness. The interests of organic intellectuals correspond to those of the class or social group in which they are embedded. Thus there are organic intellectuals who are embedded in sections of the capitalist class and others embedded in the subjugated classes and groups. It is for this reason that Gramsci argues that the 'most widespread error' is to look to distinguish intellectuals on the basis of the 'intrinsic nature of intellectual activities, rather than in the ensemble of the system of relations in which these activities (and therefore the intellectual groups who personify them) have their place within the general complex of social relations' (Gramsci 1971: 8). On this account the traditional intellectual acts as a conservative, representing and perpetuating (*sic*) continuity. The organic intellectual of the capitalist class organises society so as to 'create the conditions most favourable to the expansion of their own class', working, once established, to perfect and preserve such conditions (Gramsci 1971: 5–6). On the other hand, the proletarian (or 'critical' if we are to understand social groups within a class) intellectual seeks to change such conditions in two respects. First, and perhaps what is least often recognised, especially among cultural theorists, the critical intellectual has a (direct) material role, engaging 'muscular-nervous effort', in 'active participation in practical life' (Gramsci 1971: 9). Second, the critical intellectual is concerned with intellectual and physical production to establish a proletarian hegemony through organisational and directive functions. As Hoare and Smith (Gramsci 1971: 4) put it: 'The organic intellectuals of the working class are defined on the one hand by their role in production and in the organisation of work and on the other by their "directive" political role, focused on the Party.'

What is perhaps most important to remember is that Gramsci did not believe that the building of what some (e.g., Sassoon 2000) have called 'alternative hegemony' could take place beyond the economic struggle, that is, only in the superstructure. This is to say that, Gramsci's concept of an Historic Bloc, in which base and superstructure are dialectically unified, serves to counter what he called 'economism', in which base and superstructure are separated, often with the intention of reducing the superstructure to a mere shadow of a dominant and quasi-autonomous economic base. For Gramscians, then, intellectuals must be involved in a holistic struggle.

Understanding media as embedded in a system of production helps illustrate the limits to involving critical intellectuals in mass media. Such involvement is difficult when, as Garnham notes, there is 'a symbolic system within which both the power to create symbols and access to the channels of their circulation is hierarchically structured and intimately integrated into a system of economic production and exchange, which is itself hierarchically structured' (Garnham 1992: 373). What Garnham points to is the central problem of media. Though it is reasonable to suggest that media workers and media intellectuals have a degree of relative autonomy, as we have seen, the industry in which they work is bound to a system of capitalist industrial production.

Thus we are faced with the problem of how critical intellectuals can produce media space; as Negt and Kluge (1993: 143) suggest, 'the one-sidedness of the products of the media can only be defeated by counter-products' within 'counterpublic spheres'. This space, particularly in the form of counter – or critical – public spheres, is necessary, not just in media but also in the workplace, communities, educational institutions and so on, in both times of stability and crisis, to give voice to the oppressed, articulate problems, circulate ideas, discuss strategy and so on. It is this space that critical intellectuals must produce and engage. Such spaces – mediated or otherwise – have been part of every great rebellion, created through newssheets, pirate radio, demonstrations, occupations, lockouts and the seizure of communication systems. In more stable times, such (media) spaces tend to be found in public service broadcasting, some newspapers and radical (or alternative)[3] media projects. In the following section, I will consider the role of critical intellectuals in public service and radical media projects.

Intellectuals under two models of media use

I propose that two models of media use may provide the sort of public space in which critical intellectuals may function. These two models are themselves suggested by critical intellectuals in defence of public space; both models are attempts to wrest media away from the state and the economic system.

Nicholas Garnham's problematic is noted above – media communication is integrated into a capitalist system of production. His position must also be understood through its concern for democracy as self-determination, against the imperatives of the state and the economic system. Until the economic system is changed, public service media provides a space in which critical intellectuals can address a general public. The concept of a general public is important on Garnham's (2000) analysis because it is from the general public that a general interest can be produced. Because of the mismatch between publics and economic power, there must be constructed 'systems of democratic accountability integrated with media systems of matching scale that occupy the same social space over that which economic and political decisions will impact' (Garnham 2000: 91).

Garnham points out that the postmodernists in media and cultural studies are right to be wary of the role of the intellectual in perpetuating the use of elitist high culture 'and its repressive uses in a class society' (Garnham 2000: 97). However, whilst their 'dethroning of the expert' can be 'a healthily democratizing process' (Garnham 2000: 106), they are led to abandon the grounds upon which critique can take place. The result is an abandonment of generality, a focus on difference for the sake of difference (or for commodification, corporate marketers and advertisers) and therefore the loss of any ground for critical judgement, policy intervention or critical pedagogy (Garnham 2000: 98). For postmodern media and cultural theorists, the intellectual has been replaced by (at best) a 'populist communitarianism' in which talk shows 'militate against rational, critical discussion', which is condemned as 'out of touch, ivory-tower, academic' and so on, and in which 'only the personal is political' (Garnham 2000: 106). Against this, Garnham argues for a number of roles for what he calls 'critical intellectuals'.

In accord with Said's (1994) conception, Garnham argues that critical intellectuals, who are active in the public sphere, should aim to dispute images, official narratives, and jusifications of power by providing unmaskings and alternative visions. The intellectual's role is to overcome or see through ideological filters, which 'the public' is presumed not to (be able to) do. Thus, the critical intellectual must undertake a 'strategy of intervention in the media' as well as 'critical media pedagogy' (Garnham 2000: 102). In the former case, Garnham recommends extending what Jay Rosen (1995) has referred to as public journalism. His concern is less with the connection of the journalist-as-intellectual with the public, but her or his mediation of 'experts'. In this sense, whilst he retains the objective of making 'everyone an intellectual', most people do not possess the ability to transcend dominant ideological symbolic systems and understand generalisable interests (Garnham 2000: 100–101). To this end, the intellectual must be involved in the 'creation and circulation of public meanings to publics they in part create through their chosen modes of address' as legitimate representatives of knowledge and the public (Garnham, 2000: 108). The other role that Garnham sees for the intellectual, against those he refers to as 'the *boulevardiers* of contemporary culture', is to lead judgement of truth, beauty and other aspects of media critique (Garnham 2000: 107). To this end, media intellectuals should educate the public and at the same time be involved in the negotiation of media policy and judging media performance at every level.

For Garnham, the expansion of the mediascape and increasingly media-savvy citizens does nothing to diminish the importance of the intellectual. On the contrary, as indicated above, the importance of the scale of intellectual activity increases as the degree and reach of mediation increases. The problem, however, is that as mediation increases in degree and reach, the concomitant increasing commodification of media representations further displaces *critical* intellectuals, owing to the fact that they do not contribute to the commodification process (or in the case of public service broadcasting to the legitimation of the state). A further problem for Garnham's approach is that he underemphasises the question of the intellectual involving her or his self in 'muscular-nervous effort' in the organisation of production. Whilst Garnham has made calls for reform to media ownership structures, alongside more general economic structures, his lack of attention to the forms and processes of radical media means that for him specifically *organic* intellectuals – as opposed to those who seek to develop the consciousness of a group or class from the 'outside' – play a limited role in the alteration of media practice as such.

Perhaps, a more radical approach to facilitating critical intellectuals can be found in alternative or radical media projects. Though it should be noted that radical media should be considered a compliment to rather than substitute for public service, they exemplify a significantly different way of organising production. Such radical media projects have been historically important in the workers' and other liberation movements. James Curran and Jean Seaton (1991) illustrate how the nineteenth-century radical press struggled against the establishment and capitalist press, and Chris Atton (2001) has shown how radical or alternative media projects attend not only to content, but to alternative relations of production, subverting the normal organisation of production and division of labour. In the same vein, Downing's (2001) studies of Italian radical media projects found that traditional distinctions between technicians and reporters were eliminated, editorial and policy decisions were taken by all participants in the project, contributions to discussions and decisions were equally weighted (editorial collectives replaced editorial hierarchies), and to the extent that participants in the projects were paid, wages were paid not according to seniority (for this was erased) but at a flat rate. When the radio projects faced financial problems, wages were paid according to need (depending on, for example, number of dependents, etc.). Such relations of production can also be regarded in various Marxist publications, such as *Socialist Worker* (along with the Socialist Workers' Party's other publications) and the *Morning Star*.

Douglas Kellner shows how the 'three fronts' outlined above might be put into practice. In his (1990) work on *Television and the Crisis of Democracy* he not only analyses the emerging 'conservative hegemony' in American broadcast media of the 1980s, but also suggests methods of establishing a counter hegemony with the use of public access cable television. This latter enables intellectuals to take over the *production* process in television, to give voice to other intellectuals, including 'movement intellectuals' who represent the interests of the oppressed and the forgotten, pointing to disjunctures between their experiences and hegemonic ideology, but also proposing alternatives. Kellner's experiences as a 'media intellectual' are not uncommon in the United States, that is, it is not uncommon for United States intellectuals on the left (and right) to be involved in media production, creating television and radio channels through which they organise and mediate critical discussion and draw attention to (and facilitate production by) critical movements in the United States, Latin America and across the globe, from trade unions and workers' movements to peace and homosexual groups.

The poverty of postmodern media studies is made clear by such exercises, which struggle to control or facilitate the production of representations, led by critical intellectuals. Such exercises also signify the unrealised potential of television technologies in most of Western Europe; few European states allow public access broadcasting. Of course the US experience is not one of media companies simply ceding space to oppositional groups, but, certainly since the US State revoked the legal requirement for the former to make space available in the 1980s, involves the latter struggling for such space. This struggle can be seen not only in cable television but also in the production and distribution of critical documentary films, many of which face serious problems of distribution. The experience that Kellner describes can certainly be understood in accord with the notion of critical organic intellectuals, who undertake practical activities that do change the immediate relations of production and aim to challenge broader social relations.

New Technologies, production and the intellectuals

The two accounts outlined above relate largely to broadcast media; that is, media technologies, such as print, television and radio, in which closed messages are monologically transmitted to receivers. Such uses are not inherent to the 'essence' of these technologies, but rather reflect their historical conditions of development. Any account of the historical development of media technologies must factor in the impact of political and economic regulation of those media, and how this regulation influences possible alternative uses (i.e., used to *produce*). Some restrictions are greater than others, so that radical uses of printed media tend to be more common than radical uses of television. This is partly because of the way the 'institutions and social policies which get established in a formative, innovative stage ... have extraordinary persistence into later periods if only because they accumulate techniques, experience, capital or what come to seem prescriptive rights' (Williams 1974: 147).

If media have been shaped or formed to accommodate certain uses or forms of production, consumption and exchange, do new or emerging media, especially those, like the Internet, that only very minimally prescribe uses,[4] escape these relations and might then be used to create dialogic critical spaces?

It is not unusual for neo-Marxists to claim that the Internet is a new force of production (see, for example, Castells 1996, 2000, 2003; Hardt and Negri 2000) that gives birth to new contradictions between labour and capital (Hardt and Negri 2000). However, whilst there is a lot to be said for this set of technologies, many of the estimations as to what they can do, or more accurately, what can be done with them, are based on two misunderstandings. In the first instance, the structure of the technology is misunderstood. For example, Hardt and Negri argue, the Internet is a 'prime example' of a 'democratic network'. However, it is not the case that there is 'no central point of control', that it is 'hard to control', that it has a 'nonhierarchical and noncentred network structure', nor for that matter that it is 'democratic' (Hardt and Negri 2000: 299). To be sure, against the dominant understanding, the Internet is neither an *inherently* horizontal, non-hierarchical (Jordan 1999) decentralised (Holmes 1997) network, nor is it beyond the ownership and control of the state and the economy (Jones 1997).[5] It is often forgotten that the Internet exists within already existing socio-economic formations, ordered by the state that brought it into being and that continues to exert a dominant influence on its continued development. Notwithstanding this cautionary note, the Internet and World Wide Web are *relatively* distributed (as opposed to decentralised), interactive, cheap, flexible and multi-directional. These characteristics, whilst not constituting an *essential* mode of functioning, do afford users with communicative capacities that surpass previous media. Crucially, they lead us to question the function of intellectuals where the medium is not structured in such a way as to privilege certain actors, where access to production is relatively open, flows of communication are multi-directional, where critical public spheres can be produced relatively easily from 'below' and where audiences are not necessarily geographically concentrated.

There are two aspects to the Internet and Web that I would like to investigate in relation to the role of intellectual activity; the openness of the system as a whole, and the openness of particular sites.

Specific technical[6] decisions in the 1970s and 1980s resulted in an Internet which was to be open to a massive number of (scalable) connections. This is to say that there is no formal *technical* limit to the number or the type of networks that could adopt the Internet's TCP/IP[7] protocol and therefore become part of the Internet as a whole. This contrasts with the controlled environment of broadcast media and, to a lesser extent, print. This openness initially enabled critical networks, such as LaborNet (*sic*), GreenNet and PeaceNet, to interconnect and be available to anyone connected to the Internet so that workers' and peace movements could thus be connected and accessible across national boarders. One of the most notable early consequences of this was the use of the networks by the Zapatistas, in particular Subcomandante Marcos, made possible by the Association for Progressive Communications (APC) network. The significance of this network for the Zapatistas was made apparent in a report by the US military think tank, the RAND Corporation (see Rondfelt *et al.* 1998). They note that the APC was the most important support organisation for the Zapatistas in the 1990s insofar as it, organised in a 'networked' fashion, was able to help affiliates support the Zapatista informational (or propaganda) struggle. The utilisation of computer networks enabled members of the Zapatista support network to consult each other and to co-ordinate campaigns inside and outside Mexico, especially by putting pressure on governments and other institutions such as banks by mounting fax-writing and e-mail campaigns and disseminating news and other information (especially the writings of Marcos and other 'movement intellectuals'). If we compare the Internet with Kellner's description of cable television we find that there is increased openness of production and distribution on the former. With the Web, networks connected to the Internet became more easily navigable, resulting in greater interactivity, and, potentially, in a greater exposure of content to a greater 'public'. Thus, Web sites such as ZNet (www.zmag.org) have become central nodes for the writings of critical intellectuals, by hosting and linking a vast network of Web sites, and coordinating actions and training in alternative media use. Further to this conglomeration of critical intellectuals, individual intellectuals have taken the initiative in creating their own Web sites and WebLogs (blogs) that aim to make their work available to a far greater audience than had previously been the case.

The general openness of the Internet, however, may also weaken the dominance of particular intellectuals and particular movements as the range of representations disaggregates, fragments and weakens the sense of collectivity, solidarity, compromise and tolerance, which enable collective action. Such openness may result in a pick-and-mix mentality amongst people deciding which particular topics and struggles they are concerned with without being able to grasp the whole. The importance of this is noted in relation to Gramsci's intellectuals, who were organised around a solidaristic party, collectively organising for a specific agenda. The openness of the Internet may act to reduce monopolies of direct communicative and informational power (and propaganda), though this should not be considered a simple and straightforward good.

In addition to this openness of the Internet, the interactivity made possible by the Web may be utilised to set up a rather different communicative relation between intellectuals and their publics. Configured accordingly, Web sites may be formed to facilitate a 'horizontal' communicative space that again weakens the sometimes-domineering role of the critical intellectual. Independent Media Centres (IMC – www. indymedia.org), are a paradigm example of this sort of configuration, refusing to accept a hierarchical relation within or between audiences, contributors of content, editors and technicians. IMCs are very much egalitarian public space in which anyone can participate or develop the technologies and policies to which use is subject without any form of registration, membership or identification. Perhaps Garnham's invocation of Gramsci's 'everyone is an intellectual' is approximated on the IMC. Certainly there are no privileged actors, every utterance can be contested, and importantly, 'muscular-nervous effort' and *active participation* in practical life is encouraged within and without the IMC. Again, though, perhaps this form pales in comparison with the organised party with its focussed critical intellectuals, coherence, foresight and a sense of purpose, which are lacking in fragmented movements that have no centre and little cohesive sense of direction, no matter how much they resist what is. However, the Marxist left (particularly outside the United States) has been painfully slow in taking advantage of the opportunities afforded by Internet and Web technologies, especially in terms of how critical intellectuals can reach and engage new publics and propagate international class-consciousness.

Conclusions

Postmodern media studies are limited in terms of what they can tell us about their object of study. Its bracketing out of the problems of production and the relations that constrain it leave the intellectual (if the intellectual is accepted) in subservient relation to the system of production. It is only when we consider the arrangement of media production, consumption and exchange that we can understand how media can be configured so as to allow people to produce spaces and content. Whilst public service broadcasting can arrange people into a public, its current closeness to the state limits its capacity to allow critical intellectuals to engage in anything other than a marginal manner. Alternative media projects, on the other hand, provide truly critical spaces, with little interference from state or economic interests, but pay for that with their marginalisation within the mediascape.

The Internet has made access to the means of media production in this area much easier. Though the scope of the Internet means that the effectiveness of the filters and gatekeepers that plague older media is reduced, at the same time, some forms of mediation that have been conducive to the participation of critical intellectuals have been altered. This should, however, be regarded as an opportunity for the left, and for Marxists in particular. Unfortunately, the suspicion with which new media has been treated by the left, and the Marxist left in particular, outside the United States, has meant that they missed an opportunity to use these media for their interests. The unexplored potential of media must be considered more carefully so that movements and their critical intellectuals take advantage of the ambiguous potential of developing media technologies. Further, the role of the intellectual must be examined in relation to changes in the media environment lest Marxists lose out in an important aspect of their politics.

Notes

I would like to thank David Bates for his patience, humility, and careful editing!

1. One of the key texts in this move was Hall's (1980) 'Encoding/Decoding'. This was an excellent attempt to consider the full cycle of a media product through production (encoding), exchange and consumption (decoding). The purpose was to point to the decoding of texts as part of the process of the production

of meaning. Thereafter, scholars argued that since decoding depended on the cultural situation of the subject, media messages were not such firm and influential things, for their meaning was established not just by the encoder, but also by the decoder.

2. Translations of Gramsci refer to 'social groups' rather than classes, though it is clear that the latter are regarded as the fundamental group. Nevertheless, the sophistication of Gramsci's model leads him to discuss other social groups, such as black people in the United States, and their struggles.

3. The appropriate name for such media projects is a point of contention, with 'radical' and 'alternative' being the most common adjectives. I will use 'radical'.

4. The TCP/IP protocol – which is the defining feature of the Internet – acts as a thin meta language that enables networks of any sort to communicate, without prescribing the form that communication takes.

5. The reasons for this have to do with the historical (and contemporary) control over the development of the Internet by the (mainly US) state but also the way that the physical and what I refer to as 'constitutive' structures of the Internet (and the Web) are organised. In the case of the Internet, 'gateways' were set up to run part of the Internet protocol and mediate between networks. This meant not only that there is a structural hierarchy, but that the Internet is centred around multiple nodes. In terms of the Web, there is a clear hierarchical relation between servers and clients.

6. To reiterate, it is not the intention here to separate 'technical' from other domains. The use of the word 'technical' embodies political, economic and social interests.

7. Transfer Control Protocol/Internet Protocol.

References

Adorno, T. and Horkheimer, M. (1997) *Dialectic of Enlightenment*, London: Verso.

Atton, C. (2001) *Alternative Media*, London: Sage.

Brecht, B. (1979/80) 'Radio as a Means of Communication', in *Screen*, 20 (3/4), 24–28.

Castells, M. (1996) *The Network Society*, London: Blackwell.

Castells, M. (2000) *End of Millennium*, London: Blackwell.

Castells, M. (2003) *The Power of Identity*, Second Edition, London: Blackwell.

Curran, J. and Seaton, J. (eds) (1991) *Power Without Responsibility: The Press and Broadcasting in Britain*, Fourth Edition, London: Routledge.

Downing, J. (2001) *Radical Media, Rebellious Communication and Social Movements*, London: Sage.

Fiske, J. (1987) *Television Culture*, London: Methuen.

Garnham, N. (1992) 'The Media and the Public Sphere', in C. Calhoun (ed.), *Habermas and the Public Sphere*, Cambridge, MA: The MIT Press, 359–376.

Garnham, N. (2000) *Emancipation, the Media, and Modernity: Arguments about the Media and Social Theory*, Oxford: Oxford University Press, 359–376.

Gramsci, A. (1971) *Selections from the Prison Notebooks*, Q. Hoare and G. N. Smith (ed. and trans.), London: Lawrence and Wishart.

Habermas, J. (1987) *The Theory of Communicative Action*, Vol. 1, London: Polity.

Hall, S. (1980) 'Encoding/Decoding', in S. Hall (ed.), *Culture, Media, Language: Working Papers in Cultural Studies 1972–1979*, London: Hutchinson/Centre for Contemporary Cultural Studies, University of Birmingham.

Hall, S. (1996) 'Cultural Studies and its Theoretical Legacies,' in D. Morley and K. H. Chen (eds), *Stuart Hall: Critical Dialogues in Cultural Studies*, London: Routledge, 262–275.

Hardt, M. and Negri, A. (2000) *Empire*, Harvard, MA: Harvard University Press.

Holmes, D. (1997) *Virtual Politics: Identity and Community in Cyberspace*, London: Sage.

Jones, S. (1997) *Virtual Culture: Identity and Communication in Cyberspace*, London: Sage.

Jordan, T. (1999) *Cyberpower: The Culture and Politics of Cyberspace and the Internet*, London: Routledge.

Kellner, D. (1990) *Television and the Crisis of Democracy*, Boulder, CO: Westview Press.

Mattelart, A. and Siegelaub, S. (1983) *Communication and Class Struggle*, London: International General.

Murdoch, G. (1982) 'Large corporations and the control of the communications industries', in M. Gurrevitch, T. Bennett, J. Curran, and J. Woollacott (eds), *Culture, Society and the Media*, London: Routledge, 118–150.

Negt, O. and Kluge, A. (1993) *Public Sphere and Experience*, P. Labanyi, J. Daniel, and A. Oksiloff (trans), Minnesota, MN: University of Minnesota Press.

Ronfeldt, D., Arquilla, J., Foller, G. and Fuller, M. (1998) *The Zapatista 'Social Netwar' in Mexico*, Santa Monica, CA: The RAND Corportation.

Rosen, J. (1999) *What Are Journalists For?*, New Haven, CT: Yale University Press.

Said, E. (1994) *Representations of the Intellectual: The 1993 Reith Lectures*, London: Vintage.

Sassoon, A. S. (2000) *Gramsci and Contemporary Politics: Beyond Pessimism of the Intellect*, London: Routledge.

Trotsky, L. (1993) 'Radio, Science, Technology and Society', in *Semiotext(e)*, 6 (1), 241–252.

Volosinov, V. (1973) *Marxism and the Philosophy of Language*, L. Matejka and I. Titunik (trans) London: Harvard University Press.

Wayne, M. (2003) *Marxism and Media Studies*, London: Pluto Press.

Williams, R. (1974) *Television: Technology and Cultural Form*, London: Fontana.

12
Enduring Echoes: Feminism, Marxism and the Reflexive Intellectual

Jayne Raisborough and Dawn S. Jones

The intellectual traditions of Feminism and Marxism have, for some time, faced the challenges posed by post-structuralism. This chapter explores the ways in which proponents of each have mirrored the other in the nature of their responses, reflecting what has been for each an immense challenge to the ways in which the intellectual is conceptualised, yielding several timely and pertinent questions: How, do Feminist debates around the role of the intellectual echo those within Marxist theory about the status, role and function of 'intellectuals'? To what extent can debates within feminist theory address ongoing tensions and contradictions of classical, contemporary and post-Marxist theorising about the function and place of the intellectual in social and political struggle?

These questions bring us to the relationship between the role of the theorist as intellectual voice for a theoretical tradition and the role of the intellectual as subject of analysis. In Marxist conceptualisations of the intellectual the focus is directly on what Marxism implies about the nature of agency and struggle for the proletariat subject. Similarly, we find within some varieties of materialist Feminist thought, a concern to outline the role played by the feminist as a socially active intellectual. However, if the Feminist/Marxist theorist posits a distinctive role and identity for a particular group of social actors ('intelligentsia') in directing the thoughts and actions of others, this in itself suggests for the theorist a role that is politically driven, with a particular ontological 'take' on the role of social action and the potential for political and social change. This means that theorising about the roles of the intellectual involves a reflexive process, which necessarily draws critical attention to our own embedded practice and identities. It is important we feel, that we recognise these connections in thinking through the relationship between *who* is doing the theorising and who it is that is being theorised *about*.

The chapter is organised into three sections. Part 1 explores the tensions and contradictions within feminist theory, focusing specifically on themes of agency, representation and self-reflexivity. The debates surrounding materialism and post-structuralism inform similar difficulties found within Marxism when attempting to 'place' the intellectual in terms of his/her autonomy, authority and self-identity. Part 2 picks up these themes and explores the extent to which Marxist theory can learn something from the very self-reflexive nature of feminist theorising in trying to understand the dilemmas involved in both speaking of and for, social groups. Part 3 suggests that the dilemma facing Marxism and Feminism can be overcome through the ongoing process of self-reflection and reflexivity. We conclude with the claim that the questioning intellectual can strengthen each theoretical tradition, producing a more meaningful account of what it is that the intellectual is theorising *about*.

The feminist intellectual: who can speak, and where can it lead?

Second Wave Feminism, emerging from the 1960s, created a space of articulation characterised by certainty and political urgency, which joined women into a universal sisterhood (Daly 1978). From here the oppressed (women) and their oppressors were identified and the systematic processes of their damaging relationship made visible through conceptualisations of the workings of patriarchy (Rich 1979). From this space, feminist intellectuals worked to empower women by raising their consciousness to recognise and then revolt against the oppressive power relations that formed the normative backdrop of their lives (Smith 1977). Yet, the security and authority of feminist claims to 'know' oppression were undermined by hegemonic normalising forces. The authority from which and with which, Second Wave Feminism spoke was that of white, middle class, heterosexual, able-bodied women who generated a politics born of their own normative locations to the exclusion of women located elsewhere (Spelman 1988; Scraton 1994). The voices of marginalised women gathered momentum and their critiques led to the explosion of feminism into numerous spaces, each haunted by the enduring echoes of the seemingly inextricable exclusions that accompany universal claims to 'know' (Ahmed *et al.* 2000).

The legacy for contemporary feminism and feminist intellectuals is one that may be characterised in terms of trauma (see Bell 1999). The roar of different and diversely located voices radically challenged models of gender that assumed linear, universal oppression between two gender 'classes', and ruptured the politics of resistance and equality that had logically extended from them. The consequence of these challenges ensured that feminism lived through and experienced the complexity of the multiple intersections and re-formations of power relations. As a result, feminism is now projected into modulating spaces of uncertainty characterised by self-conscious epistemic doubtful awareness, from which it proceeds with extreme caution (Ramazanoglu and Holland 2000).

There is however a caveat; Jackson (1999) warns against the general trend to over-simplify early feminist work. It has, she argues, become too easy to write off early feminism for its foundationalism and its ignorance of the heterogeneity of women. Such mis-readings create illusionary comparisons that flatter contemporary feminist theory and deny feminism's rich theoretical legacy. It is important to note then, that the space of certainty was a politically and theoretically expedient one. Second Wave Feminism was aware of the differences between women and the ways in which race and class carved differing realities for different women (McNeil 1996). While this awareness was emotionally felt, it struggled to be theorised within social science frameworks that emphasised structural analysis, and was uncomfortably repressed in the need to form a conventional 'one-voice' politics to bring about social transformation for all women (Scraton 1994; Beasley 1999). Suppressing difference was not then, a politics borne from ignorance but was a timely political strategy with many observable, albeit sketchy successes (Ahmed *et al.* 2000; Gregson *et al.* 1997).

Consciousness raising and the cultural turn

A concern with consciousness resounds through a wealth of feminist writing (Stanley and Wise 1993), with consciousness raising being a major political strategy in the 1960s. Consciousness raising forms part of the 'scopic economy' defined by Ahmed *et al.* (2000: 16) as a means of rendering visible a reality that has been previously and deviously hidden to political effect. There is much here that is implicitly Marxist; first, in the assumption of an objective reality that can be 'seen'; second, in the hope that liberation derives from the possession of true sight, and, third, in the promise of future social organisation that can also be known and 'seen' (Stanley and Wise 1993; Jackson 1999; Ahmed *et al.* 2000). It is within the scopic economy that the intellectual possesses the revolutionary capital of feminist theory and philosophy. It is she who possesses 'true' sight and can lead others through the haze of their individualistic explanations for 'their lot' (explanations that form their false consciousness) to the recognition that 'their lot' is systematically and universally produced through oppressive power relations. Through consciousness raising, women could escape the psychological oppression of self-blame and instead look with askance to those systems of power that worked so effectively to render them culpable for the oppressive practices of others (Smith 1977). Integral to the scopic economy then was the somewhat problematic distinction between 'unreal realities' and 'real realities' (Stanley and Wise 1993: 130), the classification of which formed the very stuff of feminist intellectuals. However, the seemingly confident, politically motivated and *set* distinction between 'unreal' and 'realities' realties did not survive the political upheavals arising from the roar of different voices within Second Wave Feminism, or the 'cultural turn' prompted by feminism's engagement with post-structuralism.

The cultural turn from 'things' (such as low pay, rape and domestic labour) to 'words' (symbols, representation, discourse), while uneven and contested (Scraton 1994; Jackson 1999), challenged the very certainties of the scopic economy and its rather unwieldy conceptualisations of power. There were three fatal blows launched by French deconstruction (Barrett 1992). First, Foucauldian theories called into question the dominance of materialist perspectives through their insistence that discourse forms the objects of which they speak. Second, the notion of causality was challenged and so too the universalistic explanations and politics of a known oppression (Butler 1990). This was a bitter blow for a feminism, which has at different times sought to expose and oppose the relations of women's oppression (Maynard 1994). Third, language was rethought from a means of expression and translation of reality, to the very means by which realities were constructed (Barrett 1992). The consequence is a critical focus on the processes of meaning-making and the denial of both a fixed, static 'known' and that of a coherent and stable subject on which politics is traditionally based (Butler 1990). From a Foucauldian perspective the issue was less what 'is said', to what 'could be said' within the shifting shapes and forms of language (Barrett 1992). The truth, once the stock-trade of the feminist intellectual, is thus problematised. The deconstructive implosion troubled spaces from which the feminist politics was mobilised and also questioned the justifications and effects produced by its claims to authority (Ahmed *et al.* 2000).

As such feminism is thrown into a period of self-reflection and caution, but one of intense epistemological awareness and cultural sensitivity, evidenced in a self-evaluative project concerned with the processes through which gendered realities are 'known' and through which one takes up and speaks from a position of 'being' a feminist (Bell 1999; Marchbank and Letherby 2001). It is this project which for some lifts the feminist intellectual from grassroots consciousness raising, to the elite spaces of academic production far-removed from the lived realities of many women (Hollows 2000; Marchbank and Letherby 2001). That this should trouble feminism to the extent it does stems from the inherently political nature of feminism. Feminism is, as Elam (1994) puts it, 'resoundingly political', as its endeavours are animated by the political desire to transform social relations for women and other oppressed groups (Elam 1994; Ahmed *et al.* 2000). The political impulse beats from the feminist 'fact' that women's lives are still materially shaped and experienced in terms of inequalities and discrimination (Deem 1999; Lorber 2000), a materiality which struggles to be conceptualised as the cultural turn eclipses the social (Jackson 1999). McNay (2000) points to enduring aspects of gendered power relations that persist through changing social and economic landscapes. Other work highlights how 'old' engendered processes are repackaged and reformulated to appear palatable to women, or enter the cultural realm poorly disguised as irony or humour (Forbes 1996). The enduring relations of gender suggests the political need to stress 'woman' as a shared experiential and material category (Maynard 1994).

The political impulses of feminism set up specific tensions that erupt from the political necessity of speaking of women's lives and oppression, and the 'problem' that feminism 'cannot simply tell the truth' (Ramanzanoglu and Holland 2000: 208). These tensions are clearly produced through the combination of three factors; a fear of re-producing exclusionary politics and theories, a lesson painfully learnt through feminism's own history; post-structuralism's suspicion towards claims of stable authoritative knowledge which carry assumptions of a coherent and fixed subject that can be known; and finally, the awareness that women's lives are shaped by enduring material realities that persist despite the epistemic debates raging within intellectual circles (Jackson 1999). The feminist intellectual is thus thrust into shifting spaces of uncertainty and reflection, questioning what can be said and with what effect, yet charged with the political imperative to bring about transformation in the name of social justice. What then can be produced from these tensions?

For us the tension between possibilities of knowing and ways of acting opens up a useful theoretical and political space to think through the subtleties of power relations. Before we discuss how the feminist intellectual can 'be' within these tensions, it is important to first rescue deconstruction from mis-readings as 'apolitical' and identify it as a useful tool for feminist political action.

Life after deconstruction?

The deconstructionist critique of foundationalist politics is often used as evidence of its own apolitical nature (Elam 1994). There has been much suspicion of the timing of deconstruction, which seemed to coincide with the sudden power-gains of identity-based political movements – such as the Women's Liberation Movement. Harstock (1997) for one is particularly sceptical of a critique against the possibilities of 'woman' just at a time when real material and social gains were being made in the name of 'woman' for women. Yet, the important theoretical contribution of deconstruction is missed if it is read in such ways that suggest the end or redundancy of feminist politics.

For Butler (1992) and Elam (1994), albeit with a different emphasis, deconstruction is itself a political tool. For Butler, deconstruction is a means of rethinking and re-imagining the assumptions and shapes of politics (1990). That a rethinking is needed is not only theoretically prompted by post-structuralism but by the emotional and political legacy of feminism's attempt to establish a politics that could identify and then destroy an oppression of all women. That such a politics could be not only exclusionary but also be the very vehicle through which women in hegemonic locations could oppress others through processes of racism, homophobia/heterosexism, and class *inter alia*, shocked feminism to its core values. Butler (1992) argues that deconstruction offers an important check with its critical and necessarily invasive probing of the assumptions that both constitute and feed epistemic supports to authoritative claims to know, and in so doing, probes the very investments and desires that feminist intellectuals have in their claim to 'be feminist'. Deconstruction in this sense not only opens up a wider critical space, thinking beyond the limitations of 'subject' that have been previously authorised (Butler 1992), but a suspicion of how and why one may speak and with what effects, as a feminist. The tensions between deconstruction and transformatory politics as identified by Ramazanoglu and Holland (2000) are therefore *useful* tensions that emerge from a need to 'think' and the need to 'act', between the quietly reflecting on what can be said and what needs to be said with loud urgency, between the need to position oneself within ways of knowing yet opening them up to contestation. In short, the tensions produce a shifting ground from which the feminist intellectual may only achieve temporary and transient moments of 'authority' for which she is held accountable.

A new consciousness raising? A constant work in progress

In their critique of consciousness raising, Stanley and Wise (1993) question the concise, choreographed stages assumed within a linear trajectory towards 'truth' and revolutionary consciousness. The temporal development through false consciousness to partial vision to achievement of a revolutionary consciousness suggests a final end-stage point of 'feminist' with which Stanley and Wise are deeply uncomfortable. For them, 'being' feminist is not a point of arrival and a cause of celebration. Rather, 'doing' feminist consciousness raising is an ongoing process, performance and range of actions, in which one struggles to realise and form one's political commitments within a constant ebb and flow of different degrees of consciousness. Here the emphasis is not about the difficulties of maintaining a true vision that may be temporarily clouded by the fogs of false consciousness, but rather that consciousness is a process of interpretation of differently situated experiences (Stanley and Wise 1993: 125). Here there is a departure from the scopic economy to 'see' a universal truth, to the realisation that different experiences of women differently situated at differing stages of their life-course, and exposed to differing interpretive frameworks, produce many feminist consciousnesses.

What then of the feminist intellectual? Consciousness as interpretation coupled with a deconstructive suspicion of any emotional, social and psyche investments through which we favour particular interpretations, necessarily forces critical attention to the interpretive journeys of intellectual knowledge. The feminist intellectual denied the certainty of true vision works now with, and between, the differing realities of women's lives. She strives to seek new ways of speaking, seeing and listening through, across and with the shimmering and enduring differences and material realities. That this may involve confronting our own investments, desires and ambitions is necessary (Ahmed *et al.* 2000) if we are to be aware of the affective and material dimensions of multiple and shifting relations of privilege and oppression in which we are all implicated. She seeks to be 'made and re-made' (hooks 2000) in her interpretations/consciousness. A politics based on consciousness in progress is itself temporary, but not toothless. The calls within feminism for a politics based not on identity but on alliances and networks around specific events or issues is evidence of vibrant new models of being feminist and of doing feminist politics (Ahmed *et al.* 2000; Butler 1990).

The Marxist intellectual: rethinking the political?

Just as feminism has in many ways had to deal with the 'loss' of certainty, authority and political intent, so too has Marxism had to deal with intellectual challenges that threaten the very underpinnings of the Marxist intellectual tradition. As with Feminism, we must be careful, however, of representing the process as a shift from certainty to uncertainty for, to be sure, Marxism has historically developed out of a process of critique and debate, often from within its own ranks (Deutscher and Deutscher 1984; Przeworski 1997). Nevertheless, as can be witnessed from debates across the academic field – from the pages of *New Left Review* to *International Socialism* – never more than now can Marxism be said to be facing its demons, to the extent that even those who once avowed undying allegiance to the cause are packing up and relocating to a somewhat more comfortable academic plinth (e.g., Barrett 1991). As with feminism, the 'attack' comes from many quarters, but in the confines of this chapter it is the 'threat' posed by post-Marxism and post-structuralism – or the 'cultural turn' – that is principally considered. How have such challenges encroached on the authority of the Marxist intellectual as one who can speak from a place of ontological certainty on behalf of the working class? Has the rise of the politics of difference, of 'movementism' (Smith 1994) displaced working-class agency to such an extent that the very momentum of the Socialist movement disappears in a cloud of semantics?

In writing of 'Socialism' here alongside Marxism, we hint at another threat to the Marxist intellectual – that, as with the Feminist tradition, Marxism is somewhat more than an academic tradition, but carries with it an intrinsically moralistic and symbolic element. As Erik Olin Wright argues in *Class Counts* (1997), Marxist intellectualism is not simply reflective of purely theoretical commitments, but has a 'symbolic component' that lifts it out of the realms of academia into avowedly anti-capitalist praxis. If, as Smith (1997: 16) argues, there has been a shift from the politics of production to 'declassed citizenship', how can the Marxist intellectual survive what is in essence a threat to its very identity, its 'species being'?

In the following section, we look at the process of 'consciousness rais-ing' in Marxist thought, reflecting on what it suggests about the status of the Marxist intellectual and how the shift from a focus on historical materialism to the fluid nature of social relations effects not only what can be said *by* the Marxist theorist, but challenges too the very epistemo-logical basis of the place from which Marxists have historically spoken.

Consciousness-raising and the role of the intelligentsia

As with the feminist tradition, the process of the academic intellectual writing about the role of the intellectual, both traditional and 'organic' to use Gramsci's terminology reflects a certain subject position. That both Marxism and Feminism are underpinned by a relationship to knowledge and truth that permits the theorist to speak on behalf of another group in order for that group to be able to gain 'true' sight (Ahmed *et al.*'s 'scopic economy'). Gramsci's writing on the role of the intellectual as a crucial element in the mobilisation of working class agency provides a useful example, revealing how in writing *about* the role of the intellectual as a thinking, organising social actor, certain claims can be made too about the *authority* of the Marxist tradition to speak in the ways in which it does. For instance, as Burke (1999) argues, the creation of the organic intellectual from the working class implies at the same time a role for the traditional intellectual (once 'recruited') in 'assisting' the transformation of class consciousness within the emerg-ing 'intellectual' working class (Burke 1999: 6). Thus the Marxist intel-lectual here is shifting from the purely theoretical to 'grass-roots' social action, reinforcing the ethically premised nature of the Marxist meta-narrative. To quote from Gramsci himself: 'the mode of being of the new intellectual can no longer consist in eloquence ... but in active partici-pation in practical life, as constructor, organiser, "permanent persuader" and not just a simple orator ...' (Gramsci 1971: 10).

The creation of a socialist consciousness through ideological struggle mirrors the attempts within Marxist theory to map out and 'prescribe' for the intellectual the path that must be taken if the 'objective' basis of the proletariat's material conditions are to be effectively realised. Smith stresses the centrality of class struggle to the process of consciousness raising:

> [W]orkers' objective relationship to the productive process leads them to struggle, and to struggle collectively, as the only way to win. While workers may engage in struggle spontaneously, without prior

organisation or class consciousness, class struggle helps to re-educate workers … although other groups in society suffer oppression, only the working class possesses this objective power. (Smith 1994: 24)

Here there is evidence of the centrality of historical vision (historical materialism) for the Marxist intellectual. This lends an ontologically-generated sense of certainty about the centrality of working class agency to the process of the 'becoming' of the revolution, and of class-identity as in some ways having a 'superior' (objective) relation to the power structure than other forms of identity. It is the *threat* to this sense of certainty, this 'authority to speak' on behalf of another, that will be considered in the next section when addressing the threat of the 'cultural turn' in sociology to the Marxist intellectual.

The cultural turn and the threat of post-Marxism

As with the Feminist legacy, Marxism as a theoretical tradition has faced a serious challenge to its epistemological grounding – so much so that the prefix 'post-' does for some represent a strong sense of loss and trauma (Sheehan 1994). However, whereas reactions within the feminist intelligentsia may have provoked a reflexive, thought-provoking self-consciousness, and recognition of the necessity to respond in some ways to the claims of post-structuralist and postmodern feminisms, the reaction on the Left has been somewhat less accommodating. As Chamsy (2000) states, the shift within social theory towards post-structuralism/postmodernism can be seen as representative of a 'break' with Marxism – and Feminism's – secure, claims to 'know' people's true interests. That post-structuralism, particularly that of Foucault, be seen as representative of a shift towards, at very best, a 'post' type of Marxism, echoing fears felt by politically motivated Feminist intellectuals, is however mistaken.

In examining the challenge to the philosophical and theoretical basis of Marxism posed by post-Marxism, it might be thought that the prefix 'post-' necessitates a total reworking of the role of the Marxist intellec-tual. However, it should be noted that we do not accept that the recent theoretical shifts imply a 'closure' of the epistemological basis of classi-cal Marxism and Feminism. Rather, that they in fact open up a reflexive space for the intellectual, creating a timely opportunity for the clarification and indeed embellishment of the Marxist and Feminist meta-narratives. (See Callinicos's (1989) discussion of the 'Marxisant' Frederick Jameson.)

Nonetheless, while we will be suggesting that the 'cores' of each tradition may be strengthened, and not dissolved, by the manifest tensions and 'crises' of the new, there is – as with feminism – a serious case to answer.

The politics of the specific and the rise of contingency

The tradition most readily associated with the post-structuralist 'turn' against the Marxist orthodoxy, is that of post-Marxist writers Ernesto Laclau and Chantal Mouffe (1985). As with challenges to the Feminist orthodoxy, the threat is best understood in terms of the claimed 'subjectivity' of exploitation and oppression, with new forms of subjectivity 'cutting across' the categories of social and economic structure. Class, then, is no longer privileged, or even included at all, as something which workers simply have to identify 'with' in the work of the post-Marxist – making the integral process of class consciousness 'raising' redundant as a key part of the Marxist intellectual agenda. All certainty is lost with the substitution of the 'complexity of the social' for the dull compulsion of the economic (Mouffe 1993), and the 'arbitrary nature of any social relation' for the materially given relation to capitalist productive forces (Laclau and Mouffe 1985). The Marxist intellectual is thus faced with the prospect of a de-politicised, de-classed 'subject', who exists (contingently) within the 'democratic imaginary' through which relations of subordination when they occur (for there is nothing 'inherent' or objective about class antagonism) develop contingently and are in no way premised on a materialist reading of history. And so the very epistemological foundations of the Marxist political project are not only abandoned, but are ontologically disabled in a shift from a focus on classes to de-classed, contingently formed and shifting groups that are not, in any sense 'attached', materially grounded and structurally enabled political projects. 'Identity politics' – a politics of 'local, contingent acts without any pre-existing criteria' (Ebert 1995) based around discursive construction and not materialism – is all that is left, leaving Sheehan (1994), to cry in response, 'Has the red flag fallen?'

And yet we believe that both Marxist and Feminist traditions can be re-invigorated by this – albeit uncomfortable – 'recasting' of the Marxist and Feminist political projects, and in ways that actually strengthen, rather than detract from, the ethically driven task of the intellectual.

Thinking within the academy?: Rethinking our responses

Ebert (1995) argues that the role left for intellectuals might be said to resemble that of a middle class, self-absorbed group that has more in common with each other than the very groups is attempts to speak of. Indeed, Smith (1994) writes of the legacy of post-Marxism and post-Feminism as that of enabling, through the rise of subjectivity and the personalisation of identity, one to see intellectuals *as* political classes (the subject of revolution is ourselves! Barry (1979)). Indeed, there are grounds for claiming that the essential desire by the Marxist and Feminist intellectual to speak in increasingly relevant terms for those they seek to represent (and the 'cultural turn' might be seen as part of this attempt) has ironically resulted in a further distancing of the academic from those that she is politically driven to write about. For instance, 'academic feminism' has become a pejorative expression for an elitist feminism that has little resonance with women's everyday lives (Marchbank and Letherby 2001), with the distinction between 'academic feminism' and 'everyday' women threatening to re-assert a distinction between 'real' and 'unreal' realities. Taking on board the critiques provided by 'movementism' or not, it can be claimed that (post-) Marxist and (post-) Feminist intellectuals are doing little more than representing the unreality of the 'ivory tower'. We have sympathy for this position and join our voices with writers such as hooks (2000) who plea for an intellectual endeavour that is understandable, accessible and speaks with and through many lived realities. Yet we are uncomfortable with the assumption that intellectuals are only politically and personally situated within academic spaces that are dislocated from material realities elsewhere. Leaving aside the engendered, class-ridden nature of the academy with which feminist intellectuals still battle, the Marxist and Feminist intellectual – like other subject positions/identities – is fragmented through its inhabitation of a portfolio of spaces, relations and realities. There is not one set of experiences that inform the consciousness of this intellectual but many, each exposing the Feminist and Marxist intellectual to differing experiences and interpretive frameworks. The subject positions or identities of 'Feminist' or 'Marxist' are not only 'done' in academic spaces but experienced by the intellectual in many different forms and degrees across the differing contexts that make up her life, and which feed into her shifting consciousness. It is those shifting intersections of embodied life across many contexts, and the subtle and shocking materialisations and manifestations of power that emerge there, that politically motivate the intellectual to seek the connections and disconnections between the differing realities of those we seek to learn about, and to seek political alliances and networks formed for specific social transformations.

In summary, then, we see emerging an intellectual who occupies the space of one who is part of, and not separate to, the subject groups of which she attempts to write. This necessitates a degree of fluidity and reflexivity, of taking stock of material contexts and symbolic roles in which we find ourselves situated. Recognising that we as individuals are grounded should inspire but not foreclose continual self-examination.

In the concluding section we put into practice this need for openness and accountability, recognising the effects of our own shifting relationships to knowledge, while at the same time holding true to our essential moral and political imperatives.

Enduring Echoes: who can hear them and where do we go from here?

If we are, as reflexive intellectuals, to negate the possibility of 'holding' the truth about a subject group, a fixed truth that pre-exists any investigation, analysis and questioning, we may claim too that assumptions of a stable and authoritative space of articulation are troubled by the post-structuralist critique. In consequence, and if we accept as intellectuals, this subject position (ironically prescribed for us by the legacy of 'contingency') there will then exist a tension between the political imperative *to know and to act*, and the inability of Marxism and Feminism to speak the 'truth'. We share the hopefulness of Ramanzanoglu and Holland (2000) for the possibilities that can emerge from these tensions.

Indeed, within the traditions of Marxism and Feminism, there has, relatively recently, been a shift towards the acceptance that 'the cultural turn' does indeed suggest ways forward that might strengthen the possibilities for political transformation while at the same time 'opening up' the space in which such transformations are 'intellectualised'. Wright (2001) speaks of his ongoing commitment to the problematic of class, but accepts the necessity of reflexive self-critique for the Marxist intellectual tradition:

> The broad Marxist tradition of social thought remains a vital setting for advancing our understanding of the contradictions in existing societies and the possibilities for egalitarian social change, *but I do not*

> *believe it provides us with a comprehensive doctrine that automatically gives us the right answers to every question.* (Wright 2001: 3 (our emphasis))

While coming from a different intellectual space, a shift – if of a rather more 'epistemic' nature – comes from the well-known neo-socialist feminist Michele Barrett, who has announced in *The Politics of Truth*, 'I am nailing my colours to the mast of a more general post-Marxism' (cited in Ebert 1995).

And the self-questioning, reflexive intellectual is present too amongst those to whom indeterminacy was once the 'new' determination. The recent work of feminist writers such as Judith Butler and Elizabeth Grosz demonstrates a re-engagement with the 'non/extra-discursive', building on a recognition of the 'conservative and constraining' nature of an adherence to such contingency and indeterminacy. To quote from Ebert on this, there is a growing recognition within post-feminism of the fact that

> [t]he indeterminacy that it [post-feminism] posits as a mark of resistance and freedom is, in actuality, a legitimation of the class politics of an 'upper- middle class' EuroAmerican feminism that is obsessed with the freedom of the entrepreneurial subject and as such privileges the 'inventiveness' of the sovereign subject. (Ebert 1995: 8)

We argue that such tensions open up useful theoretical and political spaces. Rather than delegitimising the work that intellectuals of both traditions have done, and are doing, such continual reflection, and modification can only enrich and progress the intellectual endeavour. Marxism then, has little to fear from the shift from production to consumption, of the recognition that a seemingly 'fixed' category such as the working class (like 'gender') may in fact contain individuals that – while possessing a similar objective relationship to the means of production – have in fact very different subjective identities and are in different 'places' on the journey to class/gender consciousness. We suggest then, that there exists a 'space of contingency' – albeit within structured, materially shaped limits – in which actors daily 'live out' their relationship to patriarchy/capitalism, sometimes reflecting a degree of consciousness through counter hegemonic actions, sometimes not. It is here that the legacy of post-structuralism can perhaps clarify, even explain for intellectuals the nature of agency and social (in)action that typifies the lives of many today, while at the same time by no means 'diluting' the necessity of pushing forward with political projects for emancipation.

Echoing this space or 'gap' that exists between structured relations and day-to-day 'performance', is how we as intellectuals experience the tensions and contradictions between our own structured identities (whether these be material or discursive) and the ways in which, in our daily lives, we continually repackage and reinvent the ways in which we 'live out' and experience these realities and relationships. And that while these places may be inhabited only fleetingly and self-consciously, or indeed through consciously oriented social action (perhaps through event-led political mobilisations), we claim the necessity for intellectuals within feminist and Marxist frameworks to acknowledge how these spaces create room(s) to think through their own multiple positions.

So to conclude, we make the following claims. Feminist/Marxist epistemic grounds should be as contested as other claims to knowledge (Ahmed *et al.* 2000), but this does not suggest that one cannot make a claim to knowledge (Elam 1994). We may, and should, work from a position of epistemic insecurity but there is, as Ramazanoglu and Holland state, a 'political expediency' that demands we proceed in 'investigating and accounting for people's social existence' (2000: 207) even as we may, periodically, be troubled to justify that process. We recognise that reflexive thinking should not prevent political engagement. Indeed, it can only strengthen it. Confronting the imperfection of our ability to speak should not, then, render us silent, for politically we cannot afford the luxury of silence as those material realities that early Second Wave Feminism and classical Marxism raged against still shape the lives of the oppressed. The possibility of Feminist, and Marxist intellectualism, is then in maintaining transformatory goals. As part of this process we need, too, to recognise that we are as much a part of the object of our analysis as those we are attempting to 'intellectualise' about. Consciousness raising is, consequently, not seeing a truth that one may be objectively positioned against, but rather seeing the imbrications and intersections of power-plays that exist through a constant awareness that we – as intellectuals, workers, women, men – are always implicated within. The task then remains more pressing than ever. For it is only when we embrace the necessity of continual reflexive questioning, and of recognising that the 'contingent' does not by definition render the ethically driven project of radically transforming relations of exploitation invalid (and may indeed strengthen such projects) that we can offer meaningful and relevant accounts of the tensions, contradictions and realities, of contemporary life.

References

Ahmed, S., Kilby, L., Lury, C., McNeil, M. and Skeggs, B. (eds) (2000) *Transformmations: Thinking Through Feminism*, London: Routledge.

Barratt, M. (1991) *The Politics of Truth: From Marx to Foucault*, Cambridge: Polity Press.

Barratt, M. (1992) 'Words and Things: Materialism and Method in Contemporary Feminist Analysis', in M. Barrett and A. Phillips (eds), *Destabilising Theory: Contemporary Feminist Debates*, Polity, 201–218

Barry, K. (1979) *Female Sexual Slavery*, New York: New York University Press.

Beasley, C. (1999) *What is Feminism?*, London: Sage.

Bell, V. (1999) *The Feminist Imagination: Genealogies in Feminist Theory*, London: Sage.

Burke, B. (1999) 'Antonio Gramsci and Informal Education', http://www.infed.org/thinkers/et-gram.htm

Butler, J. (1990) *Gender Trouble: Feminism and the Subversion of Identity*, London: Routledge.

Butler, J. and Scott, J. W. (eds) (1992) *Feminists Theorize the Political*, London: Routledge,

Chamsy, el-Ojeili (2000) *A Post-modern Socialism?* PhD Thesis, Massey University, 2000.

Callinicos, A. (1989) *Against Postmodernism*, Cambridge: Polity.

Daly, M. (1978) *Gyn?Ecology: The Metaethics of Radical Feminism*, Boston, MA: Beacon Press.

Deem, R. (1999) 'How do We Get Out of the Ghetto? Strategies for research of gender and leisure for the twenty-first century', *Leisure Studies*, 18, 161–177.

Deutscher, I. and Deutscher, T. (eds) (1984) *Marxism, Wars & Revolutions: Essays from Four Decades*, London: Verso.

Ebert, T. (1995) '(Untimely) Critiques for a Red Feminism', in M. Zavarzadeh, T. Ebert and D. Morton (eds), *Post-Ality, Marxism and Postmodernism*, Washington DC: Maisonneuvre Press, 113–149.

Elam, D. (1994) *Feminism and Deconstruction*, London: Routledge.

Forbes. J. S. (1996) 'Disciplining women in contemporary discourses of sexuality', *Journal of Gender Studies*, 5 (2), 177–189.

Gregson, N., Kothari, U. Cream, J., Dwyer, C., Holloway, S., Maddreu, A. and Rose, G. (1997) 'Gender in Feminist Geography', in Women and Geography Study Group (eds), *Feminism Geographies*, Harlow: Longman, 26–46.

Hartsock, N. C. M. (1997) *The Feminist Standpoint Revisited and Other Essays*, New York: Basic Books.

Hollows, J. (2000) *Feminism, Femininity and Popular Culture*, Manchester: Manchester University Press.

hooks, b. (2000) *Feminism is for Everybody: Passionate Politics*, London: Pluto Books.

Jackson, S. (1999) 'Feminist Sociology and Sociological Feminism: Recovering the Social in Feminist Thought', *Sociological Research Online*. 4/3 http://www.socresonline.org.uk/socresonline/4/3/jackson.html

Laclau, E. and Mouffe, C. (1985) *Hegemony and Socialist Strategy: Towards a Radical Democratic Politics*, London: Verso.

Lorber, J. (2000) 'Using Gender to Undo Gender: A Feminist Degendering Movement', *Feminist Theory*, 1 (1), 79–95.

Marchbank, J. and Letherby, G. (2001) 'Not Missing but Marginalized: Alternative voices in feminist theory', *Feminist Theory* 2(1), 104–107.

McNay, L. (2000) *Gender and Agency: Reconfiguring the Subject in Feminist and Social Theory*, Cambridge: Polity.

McNeil, S. (1996) 'Identity Politics', in L. Horne and E. Miller (eds), *All the Rage: Reasserting Radical Lesbian Feminism*, London: The Women's Press, 32–46.

Maynard, M. (1994) ' "Race", Gender and the Concept of "Difference" in Feminist Thought,' in H. Afshar and M. Maynard (eds), *The Dynamics of Race and Gender: Some Feminist Interventions*, London: Taylor & Francis, 9–26.

Mouffe, C. (1993) *The Return of the Political*, London: Verso.

Ojeili, C. (2000) 'Postmodernism, the Return to Ethics, & the Crisis of Socialist Values', http://www.democracynature.org/dn/vol8/ojeili-ethics.htm

Przeworski, A. (1997) 'Democratization Revisited', *Items: Social Science Research Council*, Vol. 15, 6–11.

Ramazanoglu, C. and Holland, J. (2000) 'Still telling it like it is? Problems of Feminist Truth Claims', in S. Ahmed, L. Kilby, C. Lury, M. McNeil and B. Skeggs (eds), *Transformations: Thinking Through Feminism*, London: Routledge, 207–220.

Rich, A. (1979) *On Lies, Secrets and Silence: Selected Prose 1966–1978*, New York: W.W. Norton.

Scraton, S. (1994) 'The Changing World of Women and Leisure: Feminism, "Postfeminism" and Leisure', *Leisure Studies*, 13 (4), 249–61.

Sheehan, H. (1994) *Has the Red Flag Fallen?: The Fate of Socialism in the 1990s*, Dublin: Attic Press.

Smith, D. (1977) *Feminism and Marxism*, Vancouver: New State Books.

Smith, S. (1994) 'Mistaken Identity – Or Can Identity Politics Liberate the Oppressed?', *International Socialism Journal*, Issue 62, Spring, http://pubs.social-istreviewindex.org.uk/isj62/smith.htm

Spelman, E. (1988) *Inessential Woman: Problems of Exclusion in Feminist Thought*, London: The Women's Press.

Stanley, L. and Wise, S. (1993) *Breaking Out Again: Feminist Ontology and Epistemology*, London: Routledge.

Wright, E. O. (1997) *Class Counts: Comparative Studies in Class Analysis*, Cambridge: Cambridge University Press.

Wright, E. O. (2000) 'Working-class Power, Capitalist-class interests and Class Compromise', *American Journal of Sociology*, 104 (4), 957–1002.

Wright, E. O. (2001) *Reflections on Marxism, Class and Politics: An Interview with Chris Polychroniou*, http://www.ssc.wisc.edu/~wright/Polyc-in.PDF

Wright, E. O. (2003) *Deepening Democracy: Institutional Innovations in Empowered Participatory Governance* (with Archon Fung), London: Verso.

Index

academy, 12, 14, 15, 137, 150, 189, 190, 191, 200, 201, 202, 232
academic, 3, 7, 32, 33, 37, 90, 107, 138, 140, 141, 150n2, 169, 175, 176,177, 178, 180, 182, 188, 189, 190, 192, 194, 196, 198,199, 200, 201, 202, 206, 212, 225, 228, 229, 232
  labour, 16, 179, 180, 181, 183, 186, 189, 190, 191, 193, 195
  proletariat, 183
Ackroyd, S., 188, 196
Adorno, 12, 13, 16, 68, 119–32
  see Aesthetic Theory, 119, 127, 128, 129, 132
  see Dialectic of Enlightement (DE), 120, 125
  see also Negative Dialectics, 119, 121, 122, 123, 127, 128
Althusser, L., 11, 12, 16, 107, 108, 109, 111, 113, 114, 115, 116, 117, 138, 140, 155, 158
  For Marx, 107, 112, 113, 138
  Lenin and Philosophy, 110, 113, 115, 116
  Spinoza, 107
Analytical Marxism, 5, 6, 16, 137, 139, 140, 141, 142, 143, 146, 147, 149, 150, 151, 174, 176, 177
anti-essentialism, 13
  see Laclau and Mouffe
Arblaster, A., 3, 7
  see institutionalization of intellectual life, 3
Association for Progressive Communications (APC), 216
Avineri, S., 30, 31, 36, 39n7

Bauman, Z., 5, 8
Benjamin, W., 119, 122, 128, 132
Berman, M., 29, 37, 38
Bernstein, E., 111, 119, 130
Birchall, I.H., 92, 99, 102n10, 102n11, 103n18, 104n26

Birmingham's Centre for Contemporary Cultural Studies, 206
Blackledge, P., 9, 21, 38
Bolsheviks, 43, 57, 58, 60, 61, 62, 110
bourgeois
  hegemony, 80
  ideology, 29, 32, 47, 88, 110, 111, 112, 176, 184n5
  intellengentsia, 47
  modernist, 119, 120
  radicals, 35
  revolutionaries, 34
Braverman, H., 28, 29, 201
Brecht, B., 68, 128, 206
British Labour Party, 60
British New Left, 143
Brunetière, F., 2
Burawoy, M, 187, 202
bureaucratization, 62
Butler, J., 224, 226, 234

capitalism, 9, 12, 24, 25, 27, 30, 34, 38, 39n2, 47, 48, 52, 53, 72, 88, 100, 119, 124, 144, 146, 162, 163, 165, 169, 179, 181, 187, 207, 208, 234
capitalist
  class relations, 43, 144
  hegemony, 127
  labour process, 169, 172, 174, 183
  social relations, 9, 15, 143, 146, 187
Carver, T., 41, 85
'Circular Letter', 9, 10, 17, 38
  see Marx and Engels, 9
class
  capitalist, 43
  class location, 16, 29, 30, 169, 174,179–81, 184n5, 184n10
  contradictory, 174, 176, 177, 179, 184
  intellectual, 175, 176
  revolutionary, 21, 35, 70, 75
  ruling, 24, 30, 34, 35, 36, 74, 78, 94, 95, 148

class – *continued*
  working, 9, 11, 13, 15, 16, 22,
    23, 28, 29, 32, 36, 37, 38, 40,
    44, 46, 47, 50, 51, 52, 55, 57,
    58, 59, 63, 64, 65, 70, 78, 80,
    81, 91, 92, 99, 101, 104, 108,
    110, 112, 117, 139, 173, 174,
    178, 180, 183, 187, 202, 210,
    228, 229, 230
Clegg, S.R., 187, 189
Cohen, G.A., 9, 15, 35, 137,
    139, 141, 142, 143, 144, 145, 147,
    149, 157, 172
Cold War, 138, 162
Collinson, D., 187, 189
communism, 44, 62, 92,
    162, 165
Communist Manifesto, 34, 35, 37, 41,
    65, 68
Critical Theory, 12, 68, 119, 121, 122,
    123, 125
Croce, B., 76, 78, 79, 80, 82n5, 82n10
Culbertson, L., 11, 16n5
Cuoco, V., 70, 82n3

de Beauvoir, S., 89, 92, 95, 102n7,
    103n13
deconstruction, 121, 224, 226
Derrida, J., 5, 7, 107
division of labour, 2, 3, 6, 8, 23,
    24, 25–30, 36, 37, 37n5,
    37n6, 39n3, 48, 68, 72, 74,
    117, 172, 213
dominant ideology, 94, 95, 111
Draper, H., 32, 39n7
Dreyfus, Capitan A., 2
    Dreyfus affair, 1, 2, 3, 4, 68
Dühring, E., 33

Ebert, T., 232, 234
Elam, D., 225, 226, 235
elitism of intellectuals, 34, 37
elitist culture, 22
Elster, J., 137, 140, 147, 148, 149
Engels, F., 9, 21, 24, 25, 29, 30, 33, 34,
    35, 37, 38, 47, 68, 143, 166n12,
    166n13, 182, 183n1, 185
    The Peasant War in Germany, 35
    Anti-Dühring, 185

Enlightment, 115, 154, 155
    thinkers, 152

fascism, 63, 71, 90
feminism, 8, 14, 15, 221–26, 228–30,
    231, 233–35
    see Raisbourough and Jones
    Second Wave Feminism, 222, 223,
    224, 235
Feuerbach, L., 31, 83n12, 84n19, 153,
    154, 155
Flaubert, G., 88, 97, 98, 104n21
Flynn, T.R., 87, 93
Foucault, M., 5, 16n3, 69, 98, 131, 230
Fourth International, 63
Frankfurt School, 119, 123, 124, 143, 206

Geras, N., 13, 65
Garnham, N., 210, 211, 212–13, 217
Gender, 14, 139, 188, 189, 223, 225, 234
German Social Democratic Party, 33, 38
German socialist movement, 32, 34
Glasgow Media Group, 206
global capitalism, 163
Gramsci, A., 10, 16, 22, 68, 70, 72, 74,
    75, 76, 77, 82n2, 82n7, 83n11,
    83n12, 83n15, 83n16, 83n17,
    83n18, 84n19, 84n20, 84n21,
    84n22, 107, 121, 140, 146, 148,
    149, 170, 171, 172, 173, 174
    Prison Notebooks, 10, 69, 70,
    72, 73, 77, 78, 81n1, 82n6,
    83n12
Gouldner, A. W., 9, 21, 31, 36, 79

Habermas, J., 68, 115, 125, 126
Harding, N., 9, 31, 32, 36, 38, 65n1
Hegel, G.W.F., 26, 30, 31, 115, 121,
    158–59, 160, 166n9, 166n10,
    166n13
Hegemony, 17, 32, 60, 70, 71, 72, 74,
    76, 77, 78, 80, 81, 82, 83, 84, 127,
    148, 170, 209, 210, 214
Hindess, B., 143, 149
Hobbes, T., 115, 152, 153, 159
Hohendahl, P.U., 126, 128
Holland, J., 226, 235
Holocaust, 119, 120, 124, 126
    anti-semitism, 126

Honneth, A., 68, 124, 125, 131
Horkheimer, M., 68, 124, 125
  see Dialectic of Enlightenment (DE)
hooks, B., 228, 232

Ideological State Apparatus, 108, 110, 138
Ideology, 16, 21, 24, 29, 32, 47, 68, 77, 79, 88, 94, 95, 100, 103n14, 108, 110, 111, 117, 123, 124, 125, 137, 140, 146, 147, 149, 152, 153, 157, 158, 160, 161, 163, 175, 176, 188, 200, 202, 205, 207, 214
Independent Media Centres (IMC), 217
intellectuals, 51, 56, 68, 70, 72, 74, 75, 79, 81, 84n20, 87, 93, 95, 100, 101, 107, 108, 117, 121, 122, 137, 144, 145, 148, 170, 171, 172, 173, 174, 175, 201
  academic intellectual, 1, 10, 177, 180, 229
  burgeois intellectuals, 12, 24, 51, 98
  classic intellectuals, 94, 96, 103n16
  contemporary intellectuals, 16, 169
  critical intellectual, 11, 12, 16, 119, 120, 121, 123,125, 186, 187, 189, 191, 193, 195, 197, 205, 206, 210, 211–13, 214, 217–18
  enlightment intellectual, 4
  feminist intellectual, 14, 222, 223–27, 230, 232
  individual intellectual, 22, 50, 87, 217
  left-wing intellectual, 132
  Marxist intellectuals, 1, 4, 5, 15, 124, 140, 141, 143, 146, 228, 229, 230, 231, 232, 233, 235
  media intellectuals, 1, 16, 211, 212
  modern intellectual, 4
  movement intellectual, 214, 216
  organic intellectuals, 75, 78, 79, 81, 170, 171
  postmodern intellectuals, 1, 7
  as 'interpreter' 5
  political definition of, 2, 4, 7, 8
  proletarian organic intellectuals, 10, 170, 173
  public intellectuals, 1, 119
  radical intellectuals, 1, 45
  revolutionary intellectuals, 9, 11, 12, 21, 45, 55, 57, 86, 98

socialist intellectuals, 23, 34, 43, 44, 47, 48, 57, 64, 65n2
social-democratic intellectual, 53
sociological definition of, 2, 3, 6
traditional intellectuals, 10, 22, 27, 33, 75, 76, 77, 80, 170, 173
working class intellectuals, 32
intellectual knowledge, 97, 104n22, 227
Intellectual labour/labourers, 1, 2, 3, 15, 16, 34, 83n15, 169, 175, 176, 177, 178, 179, 180, 181, 182, 183
intellectual proletarians, 6, 175
intellectual radicalism, 21, 23, 34, 35
intellectual work/workers, 6, 7, 16n4, 31, 69, 173, 183, 208, 229
Intelligentsia, 21, 22, 23, 24, 28, 29, 32, 34, 47, 52, 53, 54, 59, 112, 173, 221, 229, 230
  members of, 21
Internet, 215, 216–19
  see TCP/IP
Iran
  Anglo-Iranian Oil Company, 162
  Islamic regime of Ayatollah Khomeini, 162
  Mossadeq government, 162
Iranian Revolution, 162, 164
Islam, 164, 165, 166n14
Italian Communist Party (PCI)

Jacobin moment, 70, 72, 78
Jameson, F., 130, 131
Jennings, J., 2, 3

Kant, I., 115, 125, 158
Kautsky, K., 10, 33, 112, 117, 143
Kellner, D., 214, 216
Kemp-Welch, A., 2, 3

labour movement, 13, 23, 58, 209
Labour Process Theory (LPT), 167n7, 186, 188
labour theory of value, 140, 176
Laclau, E., 5, 13, 14, 231
Larrain, J., 155, 157, 158
Lazerfield, P., 123
Lenin, V.I., 9, 12, 21, 44, 45, 46, 47, 49, 50, 52, 53, 56, 62, 64, 113, 114, 116

Lenin, V.I. – *continued*
see Bolshevik-Menshevik split
(1903)
What is to be Done?, 10, 47, 49, 57,
61, 62, 117, 169
see also Luxemburg, R
Lukács, G., 133

Machiocchi, M.A., 108, 109,
113
Madonia, F., 113, 114
Maoists, 93, 98
Marcus, H., 68, 122
Marx, K., 9, 12, 16, 21, 24, 25, 27, 33,
34, 63, 68, 117, 121, 148, 152,
153, 156, 157, 158, 160, 161, 181,
182, 201
The Poverty of Philosophy, 36
Grundrisse, 39n9
*A Contribution to a Critique of
Political Economy*, 36
Theories of Surplus Value, 27
The German Ideology, 24, 68,
161
Marxism, 8, 15, 82n6, 91,
107, 111, 139, 143, 145,
164, 165
crisis of, 13
materialism, 15, 21, 31, 110, 138, 139,
140, 141, 143–45, 152, 222, 229,
230
media technologies, 205, 206, 214,
215, 218
Meiksins, P.F., 178, 179, 180, 181,
184n7
Merleau-Ponty, M., 95
Middle East, 162, 164
Montag, W., 11, 108
Morley, L., 189, 190, 191, 192,
193
Mouffe, C., 5, 13, 14, 69, 231

Parti communiste francaise (PCF), 99,
101, 108, 112
passive revolution, 68, 70, 71,
73, 76, 77, 78, 80, 81, 82n2,
82n3
peer exploitation, 16n7, 188, 189,
194, 197, 202
Petty-bourgeoisie, 174

philosophy of praxis, 77, 78, 80,
82n5, 83n17
Popper, K., 111, 123
popular culture, 12, 119, 124, 130,
131, 132, 208
postmodernism, 5, 8, 131, 230
poststructuralism, 130, 131, 221, 222,
224, 226, 228, 230, 234
post-structuralist critique, 14
radicalism, 35
Practico-inert, 96, 100
see Sarte
Przeworski, A., 140, 228
Poulantzas, N., 28, 173, 174, 180
professional revolutionaries, 46, 48,
49, 50–2, 57, 58, 64
proletariat, 21, 22, 23, 28, 29, 30, 31, 43,
35, 36, 37, 38, 39n2, 43, 50, 51, 52,
53, 55, 59, 63, 65, 80, 84n21, 96,
103n17, 117, 138, 169, 170, 171,
173, 175, 176, 180, 183, 221, 229
proletarian hegemony, 70, 72, 78, 80,
81, 83n11, 84n21, 84n22, 210
proletarianisation, 22, 28, 29, 30, 175,
176
of academic labour, 183
of intellectuals, 34
process of, 34
Protestantism, 161

radicalism, 21, 23, 24, 34, 35, 38, 120,
121, 138, 139
radical democracy, 13, 83n11
Ramazanoglu, C., 226, 235
Reflexivity, 86, 101, 222, 233
Reformation, 79, 83n16
Religion, 108, 119, 152, 153, 154,
155, 156, 158–62, 164,
166n7, 166n13, 166n14, 166n16,
167n17
Renaissance, 72, 79, 83n16
Research Assessment Exercise (RAE),
200
Revolutions, 29
in China, 21
Cuba, 21
French, 51, 79, 99
Risorgimento, 70, 78, 79, 82n3,
83n16
Roemer, J., 137, 140, 177

Roman Catholic Church, 75, 79, 108,
    83n18, 84n18
Russia, 43, 45, 46, 47, 55, 56, 58, 61,
    65, 73, 166n15, 208
Russian Revolution, 10, 43, 55, 61, 62,
    63, 71, 99
Russian Social Democratic and labour
    Party (RSDLP), 44, 49– 54, 56, 60,
    61, 64

Salter, L., 15, 16
Sartre, J.P., 1, 7, 10, 16, 86, 88, 89, 90,
    93, 94, 96, 97, 99, 100, 128
    Baudelaire, 88, 89, 98
    Nausea, 89
    Search for a method, 101
    The Communists and Peace, 93,
        103n12
    Words, 90, 98
Sassoon, A.S., 170, 171
Sayers, S., 16, 165n1, 165n3
Scriven, M., 88, 89, 90, 99, 102n3,
    104n21
secular nationalism, 162
Shils, E., 8, 164n4
Smith, A., 25, 26, 27, 117, 210, 219,
    210, 228, 230
'social-democratic' consciousness, 47,
    51
socialism, 12, 13, 21, 22, 23, 25, 26,
    30, 31, 32, 36, 44, 45, 46–48, 53,
    57, 59, 64, 65, 71, 91, 100,
    102n18, 102n11, 122, 126, 146,
    162, 164, 166n16, 228
Soviet Union, 44, 63, 138, 164
Spinoza, B., 107, 109, 111, 118
Stalin, J., 44, 63, 65, 138
Subject Programme Review (SRP), 191,
    192, 193, 194, 195, 196, 197, 199

Taylor, C., 46, 50, 65n1, 199, 201
Transfer Control protocol/Internet
    protocol (TCP/IP), 216, 219n4,
    219n7
Technicians of Practical Knowledge
    see Sartre
Thompson, P., 27, 188, 196
'trade union' consciousness, 9, 47, 169
Tsarism, 45, 46, 47, 49, 56
Trotsky, L.D., 8, 9, 16, 43, 44, 50, 51,
    52–7, 59, 60, 62–5, 102n11, 139,
    206
    In Defence of the Party, 67
    Our Political Tasks, 52, 65
    The Challenge of Left Opposition, 67
    The Intelligentsia and Socialism, 67

Universities, 44, 138, 150n2, 179, 180,
    181, 182, 184n12, 188, 189, 190,
    196

Wage-labour, 174, 175, 179, 181
Wagner, A., 33, 129, 184n11
Weimar Republic, 71
Weitling, W., 32
    see German socialist movement, 33
Williams, R., 2, 208, 215
Willmott, H., 183, 187, 190,
    199, 201
Wolin, R., 127, 128
Wood, E.M., 14, 28, 181
World Wide Web, 215, 216–17, 219n5
Worthington, F., 16n7, 183, 187
Wright, E.O., 8, 9, 10, 28, 170, 173–9,
    182, 184n5, 184n7, 228, 233, 234
    see intellectual labourers
    see also labour theory of value

Zapatistas, 216